THE GROWTH OF EDUCATIONAL KNOWLEDGE

CREATING YOUR OWN
LIVING EDUCATIONAL THEORIES

THE GROWTH OF EDUCATIONAL KNOWLEDGE

CREATING YOUR OWN
LIVING EDUCATIONAL THEORIES

JACK WHITEHEAD

Hyde Publications

First edition 1993

Published by Hyde Publications
57, Exeter Road, Bournemouth, Dorset.
BH2 5AF

ISBN 1-874154-05-8

Typeset, Printed and Bound by
Bourne Press Limited, Bournemouth

CONTENTS

PART ONE: THE GROWTH OF EDUCATIONAL KNOWLEDGE AND LEARNING ABOUT POWER

CHAPTER 16

PART FOUR—INTO THE MARKET PLACE

CHAPTER 17

CHAPTER 18

Publisher's Note

This is a powerful and innovative text, in content and form.

You will see that the text is organised, through the use of graphics and typographical devices, to guide your reading.

Within Jack Whitehead's main story he includes copies of his published papers, which are distinguished by two ruled lines at the top of the page and an open book icon:

The contributions from his students are distinguished by shadow-boxing, thus:

At other points, devices such as boxing are used to highlight significant passages.

Hyde Publications

ACKNOWLEDGEMENTS

I love John Raven's acknowledgement in work undertaken for the Scottish Council for Research in Education in 1977:

'I myself believe that it would be in the interest of society to record the names of those who have done most to obstruct this work, but I am advised that to do so would not only be socially unacceptable but actually illegal'.

Identifying individuals through their names is a contentious, ethical issue in educational and social science research. As this book is a story, as far as I can make it, of real life, every name identifies a real individual.

To all my family, friends, colleagues and students I am sure that you know what has gone into the production of this text and the warmth of my feelings for the part you have played in it. Without the political integrity, commitment and understanding of Geoff Whitty, Michael Young, David Hamilton and John Griffiths the work would not have been possible. Without the conviviality, intellectual abilities, energy and communication skills of Pam Lomax and Jean McNiff the work would not have been published. Without the care of my colleagues Moira Laidlaw, David McConnell, Mary Tasker and Cyril Selmes I doubt if I would have survived some of the pressures directed against me. To all my students and friends who contributed their work to Parts Three and Four, including Erica Holley, Kevin Eames, Andy Larter, Paul Hayward, Chris Walton and Margaret Jensen - you give me hope for the future and pleasure in the present. Thank you.

I also wish to acknowledge the following for enabling me to publish together for the first time a collection of my papers:

i) The Editors of the *British Journal of In-Service Education* in relation to:

Improving Learning in Schools - An In-Service Problem. Vol.3, No.2, 1977.

In-Service Education - The Knowledge Base of Educational Theory. Vol.6, No.2, 1980.

The Use of Personal Educational Theories in In-Service Education. Vol.9, No.3, 1983.

ii) Falmer Press in relation to:

An Analysis of an Individual's Educational Development: the Basis for Personally Orientated Action Research, a chapter in *Educational Research: Principles, Policies and Practices*, Marten Shipman, (ed)., Falmer, 1985.

iii) The Editors of *The Cambridge Journal of Education* in relation to:

Creating a Living Educational Theory from Questions of the Kind, 'How do I improve my practice?', Cambridge Journal of Education, Vol.19, No.1, 1989.

iv) The Editors of the proceedings of the First and Second World Congresses on Action Learning, Action Research and Process Management in relation to:

How do I improve my professional practice as an academic and educational manager?, in Colins, C. and Chippendale, P. (eds.), *Proceedings of the First World Congress on Action Learning, Action Research and Process Management, Vol.1*, 1991, Acorn Press, Australia.

How can my philosophy of action research transform and improve my professional practice and produce a good social order? A response to Ortrun Zuber-Skerritt, in Bruce, C.S. and Russell, A., (eds.), *Transforming Tomorrow Today. Proceedings of the Second World Congress on Action Learning, Action Research and Process Management*, 1992, ALARPM Association Incorporated, Brisbane, Australia.

INTRODUCTION

I HOPE that you finish this book with a commitment not only to study your own educational development in the workplace but also with a commitment to act politically to enhance the professionalism of teachers.

Other cultures have shown great wisdom in elevating teachers to positions of high social standing. I also want to give them a privileged position in society because of their potential influence in forming the lives of the next generation. Yet I do not want to restrict my audience to teachers. I also want to show that I value industry, commerce, science and technology because they contribute to our material wealth. However, I want you to understand that I have seen what the uncontrolled search for profit can do to support corruption and to act against justice and freedom. Hence I want to suggest that education in industry and commerce can contribute to the creation and sustaining of a sense of integrity, business ethics and social justice within the society as a whole.

I also value public service and administration. I intend to show how educational action research within government can help to protect the public good by ensuring that local democracy acts as a buffer against its domination by the private market. Unfortunately the power of present legislation may be pushing the destruction of local democracy and public service forward too quickly to resist.

I am a 48 year old academic working as a Lecturer in Education in the University of Bath in the South West of England. As a student of education at the University of Newcastle in 1967 I was influenced by the work of the philosopher Richard Peters on ethics and education and by the humanistic psychology of Erich Fromm on the marketing personality. Both warned of the dangers of permitting market forces to penetrate and dominate education. They advocated action to protect democratic procedures in creating a just and free society. Peters emphasised the importance of other values such as rationality, consideration of interests, respect for persons and worthwhile activities. He also believed in the value of educational theory for the professional development of teachers and saw education as being related to the creation of a good social order. Fromm examined what happened to individuals when their personalities were formed under the dominant influence of the private market. He believed in resisting this dominance through developing a productive rather than a marketing personality. I recall the emancipatory influence of the introduction to his *Fear of Freedom* where I indentified with his point that if a person can face the truth without panic she will realise that there is no purpose to life other than that which we create for ourselves through our own loving relationships and productive work.

I can now reflect on 26 years' professional experience of education and offer you my story as evidence of a productive life in education. The first six years were spent teaching in comprehensive schools. The other twenty have been spent researching and teaching at the University of Bath. The last fourteen years have been under Conservative Governments. Their legislation has been directed at enabling the private market to penetrate **all** aspects of social policy. Their re-election in April 1993 has ensured that this process will continue. This book is based on the view that the unconstrained influence of the market must be resisted for the good of education and society. This book places education at the centre of the public good and educational theorising in the workplace at the centre of improving the quality of life in our society.

For this to be achieved I am suggesting that a new form of workplace-based, educational knowledge is required: a form of knowledge which is being created by people like ourselves in our personal educational theories as we describe and explain our own educational development in explorations of questions of the kind, 'How do I live my values more fully in my practice?'. In other words, my intention is to convince you that your educational theorising about your own learning at work offers a hope for the future in creating a good and productive society.

At the centre of my analysis is the importance of productive work in paid employment. Given that many millions of workers in Europe and the rest of the world are unemployed I want to stress the importance of paid labour for a person's sense of well-being and for creating a good and productive society. For example, in three counties around Bath - Avon, Wiltshire and Gloucestershire - thousands of workers face unemployment as cuts are made in the public services. I identify with the pain that this will bring. I still recall the searing experience of receiving a letter some seventeen years ago terminating my own employment at the University, and the strenuous collective efforts by others which went into sustaining my employment. The vital importance of such sustained collective action in protecting the rights of employees is a lesson I would like to share with you in the story of my educational development. I imagine that many of us share a need to live a productive life and the sense of well-being which often accompanies secure employment.

In your work do you find yourself asking questions of the kind, *'How do I improve what I'm doing?'* and valuing the opportunity to act in ways which you believe will improve its quality and efficiency. In other words, I think you might want your own originality and contribution to be valued by those you work with.

I think you will be interested in my responses to having my originality and contribution denied and the efforts of myself and others to have them acknowledged.

I am convinced that you might recognise your use of a common-sense yet disciplined form of action and reflection cycle as you resolve practical problems and attempt to improve the quality of your work. I think you will have expressed a concern that something needs improving when some of your values are not being lived as fully as you wish. You will have imagined ways forward, devised an action plan and acted. You will have evaluated the outcomes of your actions in terms of their quality and effectiveness. If you do not recognise this action reflection cycle in your professional life then a fundamental assumption of my work is destroyed. I submit my account and convictions to you for validation or rejection through your experience.

I also think you might have experienced working in a hierarchical organisation where another individual has used the power of a superior position rather than a rational argument to overcome the rationality of your own or a colleague's views. I doubt, however, if your organisation has instructed you that under no circumstances could you question the judgements of a person in authority. It may surprise you to learn that even within a University where you might expect academic freedom to be exercised without constraint, there are examples of pressure being exerted which could constrain an academic from expressing ideas freely. If we do not fight to protect our freedom to express our ideas within our workplaces do we not risk being dominated by authoritarian personalities? I hope you find the story of my educational development, in which I continue to insist on my right to question those in authority where there is evidence of bias, prejudice or inadequate assessment, an example of what might be achieved with persistence.

I imagine that you have been anxious at times that you might receive critical appraisals from someone in authority in your organisation. I feel sure that you would want such appraisals in all cases to be justly made. You might have made some errors at work which could lead to disciplinary action. You might also know someone else who has been disciplined. In these cases you might have felt that the action was justified because of the error. In other cases you might have seen that unjust claims were made which were nevertheless supported in the disciplinary procedures of your organisation. In these latter cases the judgements are dominated by the truth of power rather than the power of truth. In the story of my educational development in the workplace I will explain how I have responded to the disciplinary power of my employers and supported the power of truth rather than the truth of power, by ensuring that information on the case is placed in a forum which is publicly committed to the values of integrity, truth and justice.

Because I want you to value the professional development of teachers I will locate some of my analysis in classrooms. This is because of the significance of teachers' positions in society in carrying values, understanding, knowledge and skills to the next generation. I am also interested in persuading you to support the power of truth in the particular power relations which structure our political, industrial and commercial life.

The way in which politicians use power to sustain their ideas and view of the truth influences the social structure within which we all work. Such structures can support honesty and integrity as well as their opposites. For example, Robert Maxwell was permitted to flourish in the market place and to steal over £440 million from pension funds. I have a particular interest in this case because the late Lord Kearton, whilst Chancellor of the University of Bath, was allegedly influential in re-establishing Maxwell in the market place, in spite of the most damning criticisms by Government Agencies (Bowers, 1992). I imagine that, like me, you are outraged by Maxwell's corruption and want to ensure that it is not repeated by others. However, what do you do when you believe that the public has a right to know but you are subjected to political and economic pressure not to publicise your findings? In this book I will give examples which show how individuals have attempted to retain a sense of their own integrity whilst being subjected to such pressures.

By focusing on the above experiences in the story of my educational development I intend to reveal the fundamental values which I believe I have embodied in the workplace. I then want to show you the case-study evidence of how teachers are living these values in their educative relationships with their pupils and students. In this way I want to convince you of the vital importance for our social order of enhancing the professionalism of teachers and how, as a concerned citizen, you might help them. What I have in mind is providing support for teachers' continued professional development as they produce accounts of how they are answering questions of the kind, 'How do I live my values more fully with my pupils?', in the context of the values of dialogue and social justice, supported among others by Morwenna Griffiths (1993), Chris Day (1993) Caroline Gipps (1993) and Gaby Weiner (1989).

When I first use the words 'epistemology' and 'methodology' with teachers and students the terms are often greeted with amused indifference. You may not use such terms in your professional conversations. However, they are important for this text. I will be sharing my understanding of the importance of testing the validity of one's claim to know one's own educational development. This I associate with epistemology. I will also be sharing my understanding of the appropriate ways of answering questions of the kind, 'How do I improve my practice?'. This I associate with methodology.

Finally I want to go further than convincing you that the life of an educational researcher can be personally fulfilling, that it can have value for other professionals, that it can help to improve the quality of learning, that it can be entertaining, and that it can contribute to improvements in the quality of life in our communities and society. I also want to show you the growth of a new form of educational knowledge. This new form of knowledge includes a living 'I' together with the more traditional conceptual frameworks which usually constitute a form of knowledge. In this new form of educational knowledge individuals speak in their own voices in offering explanations for their own educational development. When I include accounts to show my educative relationships with my students in this story of my development, I try to hold on to a commitment not to violate those persons' freedom and autonomy as they speak for themselves in sharing their explanations of their own educational development.

I have learnt from others the importance of developing a rapport with one's audience. I have often told the story of the first paper I presented at the British Educational Research Association Conference in 1977. It was on the question, 'How do I improve this process of education here?', and attracted an audience of one. I talked at my audience for fifteen minutes, without any attempt to discover who this person was who had shown sufficient interest in attending my presentation. After fifteen minutes my listener thanked me and also suggested that I could perhaps develop my sense of audience, and Lawrence Stenhouse introduced himself! Since then I have shown some care at the beginning of lectures and papers to spend a little time trying to form a relationship with my audience. I have found this essential in encouraging conversations and correspondence in a shared sense of educational enquiry. In the next section I hope I am applying this learning, and that you do feel addressed directly.

Relating to You

What is my intention in writing to you?

I want to share my learning in a way which contributes to your understanding of education.

Why do I think education is important?

I think of education as something which is good, as something which helps you and me to live better lives than we would without it.

Why bother with educational knowledge?

Many, if not all, of us have passed through a school curriculum which embodies our society's beliefs about educational knowledge. Increasing numbers are going on to experience educational knowledge in further and adult education and in universities. With such large numbers of our future citizens experiencing such educational knowledge it seems important to understand its nature and growth and to be able to justify its inclusion in a curriculum.

Why bother with educational theory?

One of the distinguishing features of a profession is a body of theory which can help to justify and improve its practices. I hold the view that educational theory is a form of dialogue which has profound implications for the future of humanity because of the values it holds and because it is embodied in our practical lives in our workplaces and wider society. In other words, the educational theory I intend to show you is not simply an abstract and conceptual form of theory. It is a living theory embodied in practice. I place a high value on the educational theory of the teaching profession because it contains the values and understandings which constitute educative relationships with pupils and a possible, future society.

How will I try to persuade you that my educational knowledge is true?

First, I will offer you the story of my educational development in a University. This may challenge your preconceptions of a University as somehow divorced from the moral and political questions of the day. In showing you my educational development I hope to captivate your imaginations. The story contains three original ideas. If they don't ring true to your life's experience then this is a fundamental challenge to their validity. I hope to engage your feelings by inviting you to empathise with the values I am trying to live as fully as I can in my workplace and with my experience of their negations.

What do you care about?

I imagine that you are like me in enjoying loving relationships, that you value yourself and will defend your integrity against violations by others. I imagine that you might care about earning your living in the vocational sense, that you want to do something worthwhile for yourself and others in your productive work. I imagine that you care about understanding yourself and others in relation to the world we live in. I imagine that you express anger if you are constrained not to ask questions and express your opinions freely, and that you will act to overcome such violations. I feel that you care about injustice and would seek to overcome it. I imagine that you experience pleasure and communion when someone else affirms and values you.

Will what I say be significant for you?

I think it will only be significant in the way I intend if I can communicate in a way which touches what you care about. I do not want you to feel that I am thrusting ideas at you. Neither do I want you to feel that I am trying to impose anything on you. To captivate your imagination and have some influence on both the way you see education and on the way you act, I think my work must be offered as an invitation to engage. To do this it must embrace your feelings, and relate to how you see yourself and with the vision you have for a better world. I am hoping that what I have to show you about my educational development will captivate your imaginations.

How will I captivate your imagination?

By telling you a story which is entertaining with a serious intent. I want to make you laugh so that you can see how my laughter helped to reduce my anxiety and fear when being subjected to the abuse of power. Humour is part of the way I cope with the shocks of experiencing violations of trust, integrity, vocational commitment, truth, justice, freedom and democracy and has been helpful both in sustaining my persistence in the face of pressure and to my commitment to their fuller expression in my work. I also want to appeal to your curiosity, originality and desire for truth.

I think your curiosity will be engaged by three original ideas that might address and perhaps answer your questions, 'How do I improve what I am doing?', and 'How do I live my values more fully?'. I also want you to feel a desire to respond to my invitation to test the truth of my claim that you are like me in experiencing yourself as a living contradiction in your social context. What I mean by this is that you could be like me in holding certain values whilst at the same time experiencing their denial. The experience of this tension moves us to try to improve things by living our values as fully as possible.

What I have in mind are experiences which I think will captivate your imaginations because you care about the values being violated. If you value the freedom to question and express your opinions I think you will identify with my experience of constraints on this freedom. If you value social justice and equal opportunities I think you will identify with my commitment to resist those procedures which undermine them. If you value democratic decision making then I think you will feel engaged with my struggle to protect such procedures against authoritarian judgements and decision making. If you value truth you may recognise that those with the power to legitimate what counts as true sometimes work within procedures which permit the abuse of this power. See if I embody in my workplace support for the power of truth against the truth of power. In recognising that there is much learning to be done about how to protect these values and embody them more fully in our social practices, will you value my story because it is a contribution to such learning?

What are the three original ideas?

I have just given you the first one. It is the inclusion of your own 'I' as a living contradiction in answers to the question, 'How do I improve what I am doing?'. I think your answers to such questions could re-vitalise education.

The second idea is related to the way in which you try to improve your work. If you do not recognise what I said above about experiencing yourself as a living contradiction and recognise what I am about to say concerning the way in which you have already improved your practice, then I doubt if this book has much value. You see, I believe that you have already combined your capacities for action and reflection in a systematic approach to problem solving in which you will have wanted to improve something because you believe that your values could be lived more fully in your practice. I think you have already imagined ways forward, designed action plans, acted and gathered evidence on your actions, evaluated your actions in terms of their quality and effectiveness, and modified your concerns, ideas and actions in the light of your evaluations. The originality in this second idea is the integration of 'I' as a living contradiction in the form of the action reflection cycle.

The third idea concerns your description and explanation of your learning and educational development as you research your attempts to live your values more fully in your practice. I think your explanation is a living educational theory which, along with the theories of others, has profound implications for the future of humanity. I hope to convince you of the value of this idea by showing you its potential in the living accounts of other teachers, educators and managers.

What other ideas will you find in the text?

I am conscious of the anger of women in their understanding of the male-dominated hierachies of power and knowledge in our society. I identify with their sense of injustice partly because I have experienced the abuse of power in a male dominated regime of truth. I also see the urgent need for greater gender and racial equality. I try to move towards this gender equality through supporting the power of women's voices in their work as well as men's, and acknowledging their contribution to my own. These are expressed in the later part of the text. I have also tried to move towards racial equality as I hope the examples show.

In trying to ensure that my research is at the forefront of the field I attend seminars and conferences in the U.K. and abroad. Over the last twenty years I have witnessed a growing sense of crisis about the nature and growth of knowledge in the educational and social science research communities. Terms such as post-positivist, post-modernist and post-structuralist abound in the literature. They serve to stress the sense of crisis which appears when a research community moves beyond a particular paradigm and when no consensus has emerged about an alternative position apart from the consensus that no alternative has emerged!

I see my research as contributing to a new view of educational knowledge and educational theory. I think it embodies a form of rationality which has emerged from the dialectical tradition. I am thinking of a tradition which stresses educative conversations and processes of question and answer. This is a tradition which embraces contradictions and which engages with the social relations within which the knowledge is being produced and legitimated. It is also a form of moral enquiry which engages critically with its own justification in an aesthetics of existence. By this I mean that I see attempts by individuals to communicate the way in which they are giving a form to their lives as a form of art. The medium we are working on is ourselves. I love the way artists struggle to find authentic ways of communicating truths about what it means to be human. In seeing education as an art, I accept a responsibility for helping others to give a form to their own lives. Accounts of our own lives as educators do seem to be intimately related to the lives of those we teach. I mean this in the sense that in accounts of our educative relations we should surely expect our students to speak on their own behalf. I believe my students do.

What educational standards have I used to give a form and content to the book?

Part One is a description and explanation of my educational development in the enquiry, 'How do I improve my practice?'. It is a story of my educational research as I attempt to reveal a new form of educational knowledge and educational theory. My educative relationships in this research include my work with pupils, students and teachers. My story also includes the theories of other researchers and experiences of contradictions in institutional power relations. The educational standards which I think give a form to my educational development and hence the story in this book include a commitment to hold myself publicly accountable for my productive work whilst sustaining a commitment to academic freedom, autonomy and integrity, social justice, truth and democratic forms of social order.

Part Two shows some of the influences of my teaching and tutoring in the integration of original ideas from my research in the lives and case studies of other teachers and researchers. The educational standards I use to justify the inclusion of the case studies are that the studies embody the above values and make their own unique contribution to the extension of educational knowledge.

Part Three is focused on examples of the educative relationships of three teacher researchers who are speaking for themselves. As their University supervisor I have a tutorial responsibility to support their educational enquiries. The educational standard I have used to justify their inclusion is perhaps the most significant in education. I think my educative relationship can be felt in their accounts in a way which shows that my primary concern is to respond to their educational needs rather than to impose my own conceptual frameworks.

Part Four is included because of the increasing pressure of market forces on my work in education. I don't want to be misunderstood. I am not against a productive life in industry and commerce. Indeed I value highly my family's material well-being whilst feeling despondent at the suffering which millions experience in their poverty and lack of material resources. In particular I value the work of those who have provided access to the new forms of information technology. They have opened up great possibilities for enhancing communication around the world. What I want to contribute to, through my productive life in education, is a quality of life which shares material well-being as widely as possible whilst ensuring that the above values constitute and enhance the quality of our social order.

Just before I begin my story there is a concern I want to share with you about using everyone's real name. My closest colleagues and friends have advised me to change the names of those individuals who were involved in recommendations to terminate my employment, in judgements denying my originality and in matters concerning my academic freedom. The most telling reason they gave was that my naming the individuals may be interpreted by you, the reader, as the act of an individual seeking revenge and would hence distract your attention away from evaluating the contribution of the work to educational knowledge and educational theory. The reason I am prepared to take this risk is because I respect the integrity and authenticity of the work you are about to read. At no point do I believe it is motivated by anti-educational values. I believe it will be experienced as an invitation to respond in a way which will help to take the educational enquiry forward rather than as an attack upon any individual. Here is my story for you to judge. The visual representation of my story is intended to help you to relate to the story as a whole.

THE GROWTH OF EDUCATIONAL KNOWLEDGE AND
A LIVING EDUCATIONAL THEORY

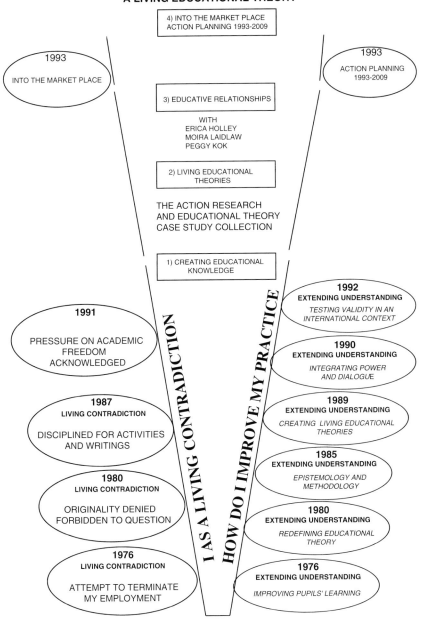

Background

The fact that you are reading this gives me some hope that you, like me, are life-affirming and want to live a good, pleasurable and productive life. I also think you must be aware of the energy released through the music, literature and drama of the 1960s. The educational, economic and artistic ferment of this period included questions about the meaning of human existence. I don't think that I was unusual in thinking about the certainty of my death and asking questions about what was worthwhile doing in the life remaining. I imagine that you have done the same but perhaps with very different choices and outcomes. I recall that my choice of education was focused on my thinking that it was a worthwhile vocation because it offered the possibility of my own continued learning. I could also help others to learn something significant about themselves and the world, to take conscious control over their own lives and to contribute to a more peaceful and productive world.

If you are making your choices in 1993 I know that they are more limited today than in the 1960s in the sense that in 1967 the economy was expanding, demand for graduates was high and we had a wide range of choice about where we worked. You may have had to be more practical and prudent than myself in that it was only after developing a sense of my vocation in education that I considered the need to earn money to live. I moved from Newcastle to take up my first teaching post in London in 1967. At the same time I married Joan, another teacher, and began my first job teaching at Langdon Park School in Tower Hamlets. You may recall that the Kray and Richardson gangs were active in the area at this time and their rather violent ways had perhaps some influence on the quality of human relationships in the area.

One of my most memorable experiences was being pinned against the wall of the school by a gang leader called Big Kamara, together with his gang, who informed me not too gently that he would slit my 'fuckin' throat' with his sharpened dog comb if I 'grassed' on his gang to the police. I have always blamed my predicament in this case on my Professor of Philosophy, Richard Peters. I had returned to the school after an early evening seminar with Peters on questions of the kind, 'What ought I to do?'. Peters would always answer that rationality and reason were the ways to overcome practical problems. I returned to the school to supervise a dance when I heard a dreadful racket coming from the front of the school. I asked myself Peters' question, and answered that I must go and reason with whoever was creating the disturbance. Hence I found myself against the wall with the possibility of a rather limited life-span.

My response at the time went beyond my previous understanding of rationality. In response to the threat to slit my fuckin' throat, I answered with a kind of demonic energy that, *'I've trained for five fuckin' years to teach you fuckin' bastards how to improve and make something of your fuckin' lives and I haven't come here to be fucked up by you fuckin' lot. So get out of my fuckin' way and I'll go to my fuckin' dance'* . I still look back with some relieved amazement that the group parted, Big Karmara stepped back, and I drove off, throat, life and limbs intact. As I drove away I remember thinking that perhaps my philosophy professor had got it wrong. Perhaps there was a different form of rationality in real life which I needed to understand.

Some 26 years later the only fundamental addition I would make to the above answer to the question of what am I working for, is related to my children, Rebecca and Jonathan. I recall vividly two significant experiences in the life-affirming decision to have children. The first emerged out of the earlier despair at facing the certainty of my death and feeling that there was no purpose to life. I suppose that most of us have all had to cope with both the feelings of being and nothingness. The life-affirming experience of the power of being came out of this despair with the understanding that I could create meaning and purpose for myself in whatever lifetime I had left. I am sure that my capacity to feel so whole-heartedly life affirming was influenced by my mother and father who provided, along with my brother Graham, a stable, caring and loving home-life. This life-affirming experience was strengthened when I fell in love with Joan.

Joan and I agreed to have a family, and she gave birth to Rebecca in 1975 and Jonathan in 1979. I feel a loving responsibility for them all which goes beyond my vocational commitment to education. Whilst Joan is economically independent, Rebecca and Jonathan are not. Part of my reason for working is to earn money to provide a secure material basis for their well-being. Whilst I have retained my sense of vocation in education, since moving to the University of Bath as a Lecturer in Education in 1973, I have continued to research questions about improving the quality and effectiveness of my practice. The rest of my story is concerned with my educational development as an educational researcher in the University of Bath as I attempt to contribute to knowledge of my subject, education.

A Working life in the University

The form of my story is the essence of my claim to have revealed a new form of educational knowledge. It is grounded in my commitment to live my values as fully as I can in my workplace and in the sense of existing as a living contradiction when my values are negated in practice. The story begins with a group of six teachers and their pupils as we worked together to improve the quality of the pupils' learning. The conversations show my interest in helping pupils to become more involved in their own learning and to help teachers to improve their practice and to understand the processes of improving pupils' learning. I then want you to experience the same kind of shock I experienced on receiving a letter terminating my employment and to identify with my experience of myself as a living contradiction. I am hoping that you will see, in the dialogical and dialectical form of my story, a contribution to educational knowledge which contains the three original ideas described above and the emergence of a new form that is being created by a University Academic in the process of researching his own educational development.

A number of my students and colleagues in other institutions sometimes comment that they have to search through different publications to get a sense of the developmental nature of my writing. I hope this present text helps in providing a coherent synthesis of my work. The story of my educational development is essentially a search for a new form of educational theory. My research programme can be followed through six of my papers published in 1977, 1980, 1985, 1989, 1991 and 1992, all of which are produced in this text. Here my educational development is also located in its economic and political context. For example, the extracts from the 1977 text which follow locate my concerns with the professional development of teachers and with improving the quality of pupils' learning. Yet as I was producing these ideas I was being subjected to the pressure of the full authority of the University that my employment was to be terminated.

In the 1980 and 1985 texts I set out my ideas on the need for school-based degrees to enhance the professionalism of teachers and explain the nature of a new form of educational knowledge which can be created by individuals from analyses of their own educational development. Yet at the time of writing these texts I was being subjected to the pressures of academic judgements on my research which sought to deny my originality, the quality of my writing and my academic freedom to question the judgements of those examining my work.

In 1989 I published my paper on creating living educational theories from questions of the kind, 'How do I improve my practice?'. You will see that this contains no mention of my experience in 1989 of having complaints made against me by two Professors of Education. In these experiences I was subjected to pressure from the Secretary and Registrar who claimed that my activities and writings were a challenge to the present and proper organisation of the University and not consistent with the duties the University wished me to pursue in teaching or research. What this experience finally did was to inspire me to recognise that the story of my educational development should include my understandings of how these experiences influenced that development. I published these accounts at the First and Second World Congresses on Action Learning, Action Research and Process Management in Australia in 1990 and 1992. There is, of course, the paradox that without these pressures I cannot see how I would have made a creative contribution to educational knowledge at all. I cannot however bring myself to thank the individuals responsible.

What all these pressures did, was to enhance my understanding of the particular regime of truth within my workplace and the wider society. I came to understand something of the University procedures which protected certain views against any challenge. I also came to understand and feel the pressures which could silence critics of dominant individuals and groups. You will see how far removed this growth of understanding was from my initial concern with helping teachers to improve the quality of pupils' learning. However it certainly helped me to understand what I had to do to gain academic legitimacy for teachers' claims to know their own professional development with their pupils.

The concern for educational knowledge and educational research methodology in my papers may lead you to think that I had lost contact with any interest in living educative relationships. I hope to remove any such thought in Part Two where I concentrate on the Action Research and Educational Theory Case Study Collection in the School of Education. Since my tutoring of Brian Green's M.A. dissertation in 1979 my research students have contributed their Ph.D., M.Phil., M.Ed., Advanced Diploma and Advanced Certificate programmes to the collection. Each one has acknowledged that they have used at least one of the original ideas from my research. They know the sustenance I have derived from their company, professionalism and research. I want you to know about this collection and something about its significance in relation to the work of authoritative researchers in the field. In relation to the story of my educational development it bears witness to the realisation of a possibility I put forward in the 1980 paper below about the need to support school-based degrees for enhancing the professionalism of teachers.

In Part Three I return to my original focus on the quality of educative relationships through the work of three researchers, Erica Holley, Moira Laidlaw and Peggy Kok. I want to show how they have contributed to my learning about the nature of educative relationships in classrooms with colleagues and pupils, in the University with students and in my own educative relationships. Erica gives new meaning to the idea of accounting for oneself. Moira shows how she enabled a student to formulate her own question of the kind, 'How do I improve the quality of my pupils' learning?'. Peggy mirrors back to me the conversations and reflections in which we both struggled to reconcile different educational values. She shows our educative relationship in action. There comes a moment in the conversations where I resist imposing my own view of the world on her and accept her right to create her own.

By refocusing on my original concern with the professional development of teachers and with improving the quality of learning of pupils and students I hope to continue to make a contribution to my subject, education. What I hope my story helps us not to forget is that some people can use institutional procedures which abuse power and trust and violate academic freedom and integrity. I hope that it also serves to stress the importance of keeping alive a commitment to resist such pressures and to help each other to live our values as fully as we can whenever such threats appear.

I think it would be foolish of me to omit from the story of my educational development a consideration of the direct influence of the market place which has been supported through legislation by Conservative Governments from 1979. So, in Part Four, I offer you what I have learnt from a group of senior local authority managers I have tutored for two years on their action research programmes. You will see how they are learning to cope with the penetration of market forces into local government. I fear that I will have much to learn about this penetration over the next few years. This tension has stimulated my action planning for the future and my concluding call that we should be supporting the creation of a General Education Council to protect the professionalism of teachers and the values of education.

Whilst I do not deny the complexity of my life in education, I think my claim to know my educational development has a coherent form with clearly defined standards of judgement which you can use to test its validity. From the basis of 'I' as a living contradiction I will be offering you a systematic enquiry in which the meanings of my values are clarified and developed in the course of their emergence in practice. I will be showing you how my cognitive range and concerns are being extended through the enquiry as I try to support the power of truth against the truth of power. In explaining my educational development in terms of my values and the extensions in my cognitive range and concerns I am offering you my personal educational theory as a new form of educational knowledge.

My academic colleagues at the University of Bath are making their acknowledged and scholarly contributions to knowledge in a way which will be recognised by academics throughout the world. They research. They present their papers at national and international conferences and publish their work in refereed journals. I do the same. Where I think my research is unique, in its form and content, is that I have systematically studied my own educational development in my workplace over the past twenty years.

Most academics I meet value most highly research which is acknowledged as establishing a new theoretical perspective on their subject. When such perspectives are first proposed it is not unusual for them to be greeted with scepticism by some influential members of the relevant research community. I think my claim to know my own educational development can integrate such scepticism and transcend the power relations which sustain it.

Any new form of knowledge is outside the dominant frameworks and may at first appear alien to your way of thinking. For example, as you read this book you will find that it has a dialogical rather than a conceptual form. This in itself is unusual as forms of knowledge are usually distinguished in terms of their conceptual frameworks and methods of validation. It is presented as a living rather than a linguistic form and embraces 'I' as a living contradiction. You may be familiar with Karl Popper's (1963) rejection of dialectical claims to knowledge on the grounds that they are based on nothing better than a loose and woolly way of speaking. He claimed that theories which contained contradictions were entirely useless as theories. His arguments rested on a two thousand year old tradition of Aristotelean logic which eliminated contradictions from correct thought because two mutually exclusive statements could not be true simultaneously. The alternative, dialectical tradition embraces contradiction as its nucleus and, in asking you to contribute to this tradition, I am appealing to your own experience of existing as a living contradiction in questions of the kind, 'How do I live my values more fully in my practice?'. Whilst the tradition of formal logic has rejected dialectical claims to knowledge, dialectics can embrace and integrate propositional claims to knowledge in the way I will demonstrate below.

Thus my claim to have produced a new form of educational knowledge is grounded in my experience of living contradictions in the workplace. It is presented as a story of my educational development as I try, through my educational research, to reconstruct the theoretical base of my subject, education. The claim has a dialogical form which shows a growth in understanding within academic, economic and political contexts. Whilst it embodies the values which, together with the growth of understanding, constitute my development as educational, you may think it falls short of my claim that it also represents a story of an individual's educational development as an aesthetics of existence. I say this because I think of education as close to a form of art in which individual artists are striving to give a form to their own existence in the face of the certainty of their death.

Perhaps I should say at the beginning of my narrative that it is a story of persistence in the face of pressure from some of my colleagues and from the institutional power relations they mobilised against me. The recognition by other colleagues that I had been subjected to such pressures came after some eighteen years in the University. This recognition came in May 1991 from a Senate Working Party established to investigate claims that my academic freedom had been constrained. I will elaborate on this later.

I know that this might sound strange, but this pressure has contributed directly to the originality of my contributions to educational knowledge. Without this pressure I would not have been driven to think about what I did or to engage with such a focus on the ideas of other academics on power, rationality and academic freedom. This is not to say that I am grateful for the pressure! In the face of the pressures below I think you will see that I could easily have felt bitter and allowed feelings of disgust to permeate my life. I think that I have avoided this and mobilised my energies into making positive contributions to education, through my research and with my students.

I hope my story captivates your imagination because the values I believe it embodies could move us to a better social order. It shows a commitment to resist threats to integrity, freedom and justice. It includes a political struggle to resist a threat to my employment and economic well-being. It confronts bias, prejudice and inadequate assessment in judgements by one academic on the work of another. It integrates ideas on power, dialectics, methodology and epistemology. It also includes an account which shows how the disciplinary power of a University was transcended when it was mobilised against my research. Above all I hope you see that I have fulfilled one of my ambitions as an academic and that is to make an original contribution to knowledge of my subject, education. Here, then, is my story and claim to know my own educational development, beginning with my first published work and a threat to my employment.

PART ONE

THE GROWTH OF EDUCATIONAL KNOWLEDGE AND LEARNING ABOUT POWER

Chapter One: 1976

Improving Learning in Schools—An In-Service Problem

The extracts in this Chapter were first published in a paper in the *British Journal of In-Service Education*, Vol.3, No.2, 1977.

In March 1976 at exactly the same time as receiving the letter terminating my employment as I outline in the next section, I produced a research report on the project I was evaluating. The report described my research with a group of six teachers from three schools who worked together for a year to improve the quality of learning for 11-14 year olds in mixed ability science groups. In 1977 the *British Journal of In-service Education* published an article of mine on 'Improving Learning in Schools - an In-Service Problem'. I argued that improvements in pupils' learning occurred through the creative power of individual teachers to transform their situation. I showed the teachers engaging in action learning where they isolated their own problems, produced their action plans, acted, evaluated the quality and effectiveness of their practice and modified their problems, ideas and actions in the light of their evaluations. Part of my work was to gather the evidence which the teachers could use to evaluate their practices.

The process of evaluation was based on the assumption that teachers could evaluate the contradictions between their intentions and practice when presented with objective evidence. I visited schools once a fortnight to observe the classrooms and to videotape and interview the pupils and teachers. The video tapes were viewed immediately after the lessons or at the next meeting of the working group. Transcripts of the interviews on the teachers' intentions and pupils' interpretations were given back to the teachers within a fortnight. When I read the conversations below I am conscious of my commitment to help teachers to enhance their professionalism and to improve the quality of their pupils' learning through research. In retrospect I wonder what an appropriate judgement on the contribution would now be by those academics who recommended the termination of my employment. I cannot help but contrast the quality of educative relationships the pupils experienced with their caring teachers, with the kind of relationship I experienced as a probationer lecturer with my senior academics.

What now follows are two extracts from the 1977 paper. The first extract illustrates how the process of self-evaluation of oneself as a living contradiction provided a basis for improvement for Roger Barrow, a science teacher in Wootton

Bassett School. The second extract shows enquiry learning in action with Paul
Hunt, a teacher at Dorcan School, Swindon.

First Extract

Roger: I was concerned with the fact that most of my teaching was being pitched in
the middle of the ability range and I wasn't really catering for individuals. I
also had the problem of designing courses for teachers who are not specialists
in particular fields. In the first instance I feel we must produce good work
schemes which increase the teachers' and pupils' confidence. When we
have built up our understanding of this situation, we can then move on to
the second phase of responding to the learners' questions.

Jack: You see the vital thing is getting the kids to ask questions?

Roger: I'm not sure everybody agrees. I feel that so much of what has happened in
science teaching has been a dull simulation, jumping through hoops at the
appropriate moment at the command of the teacher or the examiner. I've
come to realise over a period of time that we were chaining any creativeness
and inventiveness in science. I know someone has to work through all the
permutations and combinations but I think we have got to open out the
possibilities for originality. I think so much of what we do in science is
forced on us by exam syllabuses and kills all expression of opinion or
development of ideas.

I interviewed Paul, one of Roger's pupils:

Jack: What kind of things did you do yourself?

Paul: Well, we got all the apparatus and put it up ourselves and poured in the
mixtures ourselves and we did. Mr Barrow just helped us a little bit, if we
were stuck.

Jack: Really, yes. Did you ask any questions about the way you were doing this?

Paul: No.

Jack: You didn't. You just did it?

Paul: Yes.

Jack: But where did you get your ideas from then, if it didn't come from you?

Paul: Well, Mr Barrow had a little talk with us in the beginning and then he got all
our stuff out for us and we put it up and we went to go and get it and then we
did our experiments.

Jack: I see. As you were doing the experiments did you have any ideas of your
own that you wanted to test?

Paul: No.

Jack: I see. And if you've got questions of your own, like when I put that in front
of you, you said, you know, I've tried to separate it, is that because when
you're given substances like this, you were told how to separate it or not?

Paul: Mr. Barrow helped us a little bit.

Jack: Yes.

Paul: And he told us if we were doing things wrong. If we did we started again.

Jack: Yes. The thing I want to try to find out is do you have any ideas of your own that you'd really like to think about and test out?

Paul: No, not really.

Jack: You don't?

Paul: No.

Jack: What do think scientists do? Do you think all their problems are always given to them or do you think that some scientists really try to think out ideas of their own?

Paul: Yes.

Jack: Which one do you think?

Paul: That they try to think it out themselves. Trying to make things that can help people, medicines or something.

Roger interviewed his own pupils.

Roger: You remember that, and you had to try to save water yourself, didn't you? Yes?

Tracey: Yes.

Roger: Well, what did you do it stop to evaporating away?

Tracey: We put a dish on the top of a beaker with water in it and put ice in it.

Roger: Oh, yes. Why did you get that idea?

Tracey: I'm not quite sure.

Roger: You're not quite sure. Did you see other people?

Tracey: No.

Roger: Or did you work it out for yourself?

Tracey: No.

Roger: How did you get it then? You just don't remember.

Tracey: You told me.

Roger: I told you! Deary me. That's the second person who's said I told them, been splitting obviously. What was the ice doing then?

This process of evaluation has highlighted to Roger Barrow the gap between his intentions and his actual classroom practice. Within two months Roger modified his approach with the following result:

Roger: Now what I want to do is just ask you one or two questions about what we've been doing in science this term. First of all what did you do, what were you expecting when you discovered that you'd got science on your timetable? Did you have any idea what you would do?

David: No, not much. Well, some that we did in our other school was very different.

Roger: I see, what was different about it?

David: Well, it was more set, you know, they did more for you instead of now you have to do more for yourself.

Roger: You feel you've had to do more for yourself?

David: Yes.

Roger: Have you enjoyed doing more for yourself?
David: Yes. It's the independence of it . . .
Roger: The independence of it you enjoy?
David: Yes. Discovering the actual thing with nobody telling you what's going to happen.
Roger: You really enjoyed that, did you?
David: Yes, that's what I like about it.
Roger: You like that? Oh, splendid.

The following evidence clearly demonstrates how enquiry learning has actually taken place within a classroom where the children were working on a series of experiments highly structured by worksheets. The majority of the class could continue their activities with a minimum of supervision from the teacher. This allowed the teacher, Paul Hunt, the opportunity of fulfilling the role of 'consultant, advisor or tutor'. Paul taped his conversations with his pupils and in the following extracts he describes how the process of self-evaluation occurred in dialogue between himself and a small group of learners.

Extract Two

Four second year girls were measuring the acidity or alkalinity of oxides by adding drops of indicator (a green liquid) into a mixture of the powder and water. One pair obtained an orangey-red liquid indicating an acid and the other pair obtained a blue liquid indicating an alkali. They came to me, formulated their problem, 'We got different colours', and received permission to continue work to solve their problem.

By the end of a double lesson they succeeded, after three failures involving highly creative work, to obtain the same blue colour indicating that the oxide is alkaline.

Teacher: What was important about what you were doing?
Tracey: It's just that, well, when we got different answers, we couldn't see why we got different answers and so we wanted to get them so that they were the same.
Judith: We were excited . . . It would have been better if we'd had longer.
Teacher: I mean, why was what you did so valuable? What was its value to you?
Judith: I suppose it was our own little discovery.
Denise: We achieved something . . . we don't normally get so interested in lessons, but this time we just got interested because we wanted to find out the answer to it.
Teacher: Was it the answer, the so-called answer that was important or was it something else?
Tracey: Well, we were very pleased when we got the right answer, but I don't

know . . . well, every other experiment that I do is normally a complete flop and, well, this one seemed to be going quite well and so I got really interested in it.

Teacher: But for someone coming into the room, your experiment would have seemed more of a flop than the normal. Do you understand that? They would have seen one of you with a blue colour and one of you with an orange colour and said ,'Well, something has gone wrong . . . do it again . . . it's not right'. In fact it would have seemed a complete flop.

Tracey: Well, it came out of a . . . well, it wasn't exactly a flop, but it was more or less, but the reason was . . . it started off with a flop and we got it to a good experiment. Well, I thought it was.

Teacher: What do you feel you created in this room?

Sandra: Noise!!!

Judith: I suppose, you know, the atmosphere was, we were just more excited after it didn't work twice, so, you know, we just kinda, well, when the teacher come into the room and saw it was a flop, I don't think I could have seen it as a flop, because it was, you know, just a discovery which you wanted to take further. So if they saw it as a flop then I can't see why.

And subsequently:

Judith: Well, I suppose really it was that we were doing an experiment off our own bats, and it working was the most important thing because it was our achievement and not prompted by the teacher and it wasn't what everybody else was doing, so it was different and so we enjoyed it more than we would have before.

Teacher: Are there any questions that you want to ask me?

Judith: Well, in the next lesson, can we carry on?

Sandra: Yes, 'cos we didn't find out why. All we did was we finished the experiment, you know, just got the result the same, but we didn't find out why!!!

Teacher: Right! Yes. That's what you want to do. That would be good, you know, to find out what it was that made the oxide go, on the one hand blue and on the other hand red.

The dialogue shows how the evaluation process has encouraged the formulation of a new question; a sudden realization that another problem has arisen to which they were personally committed.

This personal commitment to the solution of a question which they had formulated produces a huge leap in their understanding of the scientific process, in their motivation and in the understanding of the concepts of acids and bases.

They continue their investigation:

Teacher: Denise, can you tell me about the experiment you are doing today?

Denise: Well, I get two test tubes, but I don't fill them up with the same amount of water and I measure up the same amount of oxide, one spatula, and 7 drops of indicator. Tracey uses dirty test tubes, Sandra uses exactly the same amount of water but different amounts of indicator but the same amount of water and oxide.

They say that the results might have been wrong the first week, for one of four reasons:

1. They used different amounts of water.
2. They used different amounts of oxide.
3. They used different amounts of indicator.
4. They used dirty tubes.

The experiments they devise use a sophisticated technique called 'a controlled experiment' where one variable (i.e. amount of water) is altered while all other factors are kept constant. This concept is notoriously difficult for a major proportion of children at this age when taught in the more conventional ways.

They obtained their results:

Teacher: Now you've said, 'It's nothing to do with the amount of water; it's nothing to do with the amount of oxide, or with dirty tubes, or the amount of indicator. In fact it doesn't seem to be to do with anything that you've tested.

Sandra: No.

Teacher: Now, what do you think was different about the experiment that you did last week which makes it different to the experiment you did this week?

Tracey: Well, I suppose what we could try, sir, is that we could have say, different amounts of water in the test tubes and different amounts of oxide and dirty test tubes and see whether it was all four of them.

They are saying, 'It wasn't one factor on its own that made the difference but it could have been caused by all these factors acting together':

Teacher: Yes, that is certainly true. It could have been. What about this idea? The oxide should turn the indicator a blue colour, but last week you had one tube that went red. Could it have been a dirty test tube which had acid in it?

Tracey: Wouldn't it go neutral, because a certain amount of acid and a certain amount of alkali in there . . . shouldn't it turn neutral, but we didn't. We got a very strong acid and one got a very strong alkali.

Teacher: You think about that.

Sandra: I don't get what you mean.

Tracey: I thought about it before I asked you!

Teacher: Well, think about it again. Sandra, you don't understand what we are driving at, do you?

Sandra: No.

Teacher: The mistake might have occurred last week because you had a dirty test tube and it had acid in it already. Now what would happen if you did all this in a test tube which was dirty to begin with, with a bit of acid? What might happen?

Sandra: What . . . what, you mean if we did an ordinary experiment and it turned acid and then we tipped it out without washing it, do you mean?

Teacher: Mm.

Judith: Well, then it would turn acid ,wouldn't it?

Tracey: Well, no it wouldn't. If you have got lead monoxide and that's, well we found out it was a very strong alkali. A strong alkali and a strong acid is going to make neutral isn't it?

Teacher: Well it depends . . .

Sandra: You've got to have virtually the same, haven't you?

Teacher: Yes it's a balance isn't it?

Sandra: Tracey said if you had a strong acid and a strong alkali - would make a neutral, but how is Tracey going to know how much acid is in there to add the same amount of alkali?

Teacher: Good point.

Judith: If we use a syringe, then we could put exactly the same in, so we know that it's balancing, or we know if it's stronger or weaker.

Sandra: But we don't know how much acid is in there.

A minute ago Sandra didn't understand the problem the other girls were raising. She has now grasped the idea of 'acids cancelling out alkalis' and of her own accord is appreciating the idea of balancing out different quantities of acids and alkalis whose 'strength' is unknown. A giant leap.

As I have said above I think the data shows my focus on understanding the professional development of teachers in relation to improving the quality of pupils' learning. My research interest at this point is in understanding the appropriate ways of conducting an enquiry of the form, 'How do I improve my practice?'. I am also interested in understanding the nature of the explanations ('why' questions) and educational knowledge generated in such enquiries. That is, I am interested in questions of methodology in the 'how' questions and questions of epistemology in the 'why' questions. As my enquiry continued I concentrated on these questions and give some answers in the 1980 paper which appears in Chapter Three below.

In the terms of my action research I was concerned that I did not understand an appropriate methodology for researching questions of the kind, 'How do I improve my practice?. I believed that by working with a group of teachers who were trying to improve their practice, I would come to understand an appropriate methodology. I acted, evaluated my actions and modified my concerns, ideas and actions in the light of the evaluations. I also believed that I would come to understand the nature of the educational knowledge created by individuals as they attempted to understand the processes of improving their practice. The results are described in the 1980 and 1985 papers below.

Before presenting the papers I want to draw you into the first of three experiences which have had a profound influence on my educational development. In the next chapter you will read a letter I received in 1976 terminating my employment. As you read the letter I am asking you to empathise with my existence as a living contradiction. At the moment I received the letter I was working on the above account. I think the account shows a commitment to search for a form of educational theory that can be related directly to the experiences, language and lives of those whose educational development the theory should have the capacity to explain. I take it that one of the tests of the validity of a theory is that it has the capacity to produce a valid explanation for an individual case subsumed by the theory. In explaining my own persistence in the face of the pressures which follow I think you should hold on to my view of myself as a creative academic. I see my productive life as being intimately related to revealing a form of educational theory which can be directly related to the educational development of individuals. If asked to explain why I think this enquiry is worthwhile pursuing I answer with my belief that educational theory is a form of dialogue which has profound implications for the future of humanity and I want to make a positive contribution to that future through my work in education. I do not think that any further justification is necessary or, in my case, possible. On reading my story, my students and colleagues have commented that they think that many people would have given up working in such circumstances. My explanation for why I continued, contains the determination not to put up with violations to my integrity and academic freedom, the challenges to my originality and the truth of power in imposing what counts as educational knowledge.

Chapter Two: 1976

Living Contradiction: I am a University Academic. I am not.

UNTIL RECENTLY, academics, on joining a University, would be offered a tenured appointment if they successfully completed a three year probation. On 21st January 1976 the Personnel Officer invited me to meet the Academic Staff Committee to assist them in reporting on progress:

The last meeting of the Academic Staff Committee considered a report on your progress to date with a view to confirming your appointment. The Committee felt that in order to assist them further in making a decision you should be interviewed by two members of that Committee and I should be obliged if you would report to the room of Professor R.E. Thomas, School of Management (Wessex House 3.14) at 10.00 a.m. on Wednesday, 4th February 1976 for interview by Professors Thomas and Broadbent. I expect the proceedings to take about 45-60 minutes.

Would you please bring copies of your publications or theses with you for possible inspection. Thank you.

As the University regulations required that a probationer be informed before the end of the second year if progress was unsatisfactory, and I was well into my third year, I attended the meeting with Professors Ray Thomas and Len Broadbent and a Professor Stephen Cotgrove with little concern that I would not be offered a tenured appointment. I would now ask you to use all your empathy and intuition in the feelings and thoughts which followed my reading of the following letter from the Personnel Officer on the 12th March 1976 which I received after the interview.

I am writing to inform you that the Academic Staff Committee made a recommendation to Senate that as you have not fully satisfied the requirements of your probationary contract, the University is unable to offer you a tenured appointment on the expiry of your probationary contract on 31st August 1976...

These recommendations have now been confirmed by Senate.

The Academic Staff Committee's grounds for recommending that a new appointment should not be offered are as follows:

1)   *That you have not given satisfaction in the teaching of prescribed courses assigned to you.*

2)   *That there is an absence of evidence to suggest that you have pursued research of sufficient quality for the assessors to be assured of your ability to perform adequately the duties of a University Lecturer; the objectives being to make acknowledged scholarly contributions to the advancement of your subject as well as to perform proper teaching and other administrative tasks.*

3)   *That you have exhibited forms of behaviour which have harmed the good order and morale of the School of Education.*

Can you imagine the strength and nature of my existence as a living contradiction in the feelings and responses I made to this communication? These judgements were made and communicated with the full force of the University. They were intended to terminate my employment as a University academic. Please focus your attention on the grounds given for terminating my employment. The University stated that I had not given satisfaction in my teaching. I had not pursued research of sufficient quality. **I had disturbed the good order and morale of the School of Education**. My judgements on my activities were that I was certainly a competent teacher, if not a good teacher, that my research into educational theory was progressing well and that the values embodied in my practice were making a positive contribution to the good order of the School of Education. I thus had to hold my positive judgements together with the University's negative judgements. You can imagine my tension in living this contradiction. My determination to resist the negative judgements and the power relations which legitimated them led me to make the submission below to the Vice-Chancellor on the 29th March 1976.

I am writing to you in your capacity as Chairman of the Academic Staff Committee, to appeal against the decision of Senate to confirm the recommendation of the committee that I should not be offered a new appointment.

Fresh evidence will be submitted to the Committee in the immediate future, concerning my teaching, research and behaviour.

Between receiving the letter of the 12th March and appealing on the 29th March I received support from a number of colleagues, students and external academics. I could not have survived if I had been left on my own. Indeed, one of the most depressing moments I can still vividly recall was the response to my request for help from Dr. Leslie Palmier, the Chairman of Bath University Association of University Teachers. He advised me that my attempt to resist the University was hopeless and that I should look for other employment. In marked contrast to this advice was the support I received from Geoff Whitty, Mary Tasker and Cyril Selmes, three of my colleagues in the School of Education, and Paul Hunt, the education student mentioned above. Geoff Whitty in particular provided bedrock support. He advised me to contact the Campaign for Academic Freedom and Democracy. I went to see John Griffiths, a Professor of Public Law at the London School of Economics. After looking at the letter of the 12th March and the procedures for probationary lecturers he agreed to write to the University on my behalf. Geoff organised petitions around the School to confront the judgements that I had disturbed the good order and morale of the School of Education. Paul Hunt organised petitions from students and teachers in local schools which confronted the negative judgements on my teaching. Geoff advised me to send my research papers to Michael Young at the Institute of Education of London University and to a Dr. David Hamilton, a Visiting Professor at the Center for Instructional Research and Curriculum Evaluation of the University of Illinois, who was a well respected educational researcher. All this had to be organised between the 12th and the 29th March. I look back with gratitude and some incredulity at what others were prepared to do on my behalf. One political lesson is very clear. The exercise of institutional power requires organised resistance if it is to be overcome. As an individual, without this support, I would have been overcome.

The Vice-Chancellor replied on the 30th March
Thank you for your letter date 29th March. It is likely that Senate would want the Academic Staff Committee to consider any new evidence you may care to put forward but, for your guidance, I should say that I doubt if it would be sufficient for you merely to re-submit in a different form data which the Committee has already considered. However, the form in which you present your views is a matter for you to decide.

I responded on the 1st April:
Further to my letter of 29 March, I enclose fresh evidence relating to my teaching, research and behaviour. I would hope that there is sufficient fresh evidence for the Academic Staff Committee to reconsider its recommendations to Senate that a new appointment should not be offered to me.

In the letter to Mr. Horner, I state the grounds, and gave the evidence to substantiate my grievance appeal to Council. I should be grateful if you could submit this evidence to the academic staff committee, as a matter of urgency.

I have included copies of all correspondence in my possession relevant to my case....

I do think that serious charges have been made against me, which I am anxious to answer as soon as possible. I hope that you will be able to assist me in obtaining a hearing for what I see as a serious miscarriage of justice.

The submissions included the following letter from John Griffiths. Given his position as a Professor of Public Law I think it carried significant force to the University.

I ask you to consider the following submissions which suggest to me that he (Mr Whitehead) is being treated with less than justice.

1. *The first ground given was that Mr. Whitehead had not given satisfaction in the teaching of prescribed courses. But here again he is not told where and how he is deemed to have failed. So how can he answer or produce fresh evidence on this charge?*

2. *The second ground given was that there was an 'absence of evidence' about his pursuit of research. I note that it is not said that the research he has undertaken is of insufficient quality. What then is the nature of the evidence of his 'pursuit of research' that the Academic Staff Committee requires but finds absent? Unless he is told this, he cannot meet this criticism, or be sure he is producing the most relevant fresh evidence. 'Absence of evidence' may be a good ground for acquitting a man of fault but it cannot be a ground for proving him culpable.*

3. *The third ground given by the Academic Staff Committee was that he had exhibited forms of behaviour which had harmed the good order and morale of the School of Education. The Academic Staff Committee have refused to substantiate this. This refusal is manifestly unjust, as it is wholly unspecific. The ground might relate to his political opinions, to his personal morality, to his style of dress. Moreover the accusation is that his 'forms of behaviour' have actually harmed the School of Education. He is surely entitled to know how he has done so. It is an elementary rule of natural justice that a man shall be told the offence with which he is charged and which, in this instance, has been found proved against him. How, otherwise, can he produce fresh, or indeed any, evidence? ...*

The Personnel Officer wrote to me on the 18th May:

The Academic Staff Committee met last Friday (14th May 1976) to consider the appeal indicated in your letter to the Vice-Chancellor of the 29th March 1976.

I confirm that (I quote from my written version of the statement which I read to you last Friday) the Academic Staff Committee thinks there may be further evidence to consider and has decided to meet again on Wednesday 26th May commencing at 9.15 a.m.

The Vice-Chancellor would like you to be available during that morning in case the Committee wishes to see you. If you would care to provide telephone numbers where you may be contacted quickly during the morning, this would assist us and possibly save your time...

I met the Committee along with Professor 'Bunny' Dowdeswell, my Head of School and the Professor responsible for submitting the original evidence to the Academic Staff Committee on which was based the recommendations and judgements in the letter of the 12th March terminating my employment. Whilst I only have a vague recollection of this meeting I am sure that I communicated a sense of justified outrage.

The Secretary and Registrar wrote to me on the 14th June 1976 :

On the advice of the Academic Staff Committee, Senate has given further consideration to your position in the University, and has resolved to extend your period of service as a probationary lecturer for one further year to 31st August 1977. I should be glad if you would confirm that in the circumstances, you will not now wish to proceed with your request for a hearing of a grievance relating to the procedure for notifying criticisms.

You will be considered again for a permanent appointment in the early part of 1977 in accordance with the usual procedures, and I am instructed to make it quite clear to you that it is by no means certain that such an appointment will be offered; the decision will be made at the appropriate time on the basis of the evidence before the Academic Staff Committee on your attainment in teaching, research and administration, and the committee must be satisfied that you have shown the necessary ability to perform the duties of a lecturer in the University.

In particular, the Committee will have regard to the following criteria:

1) *The presentation of the conclusions of your research in publishable form, to the satisfaction of referees.*

2) *Your work in the development of the Science and Technology Centre for teachers.*

3) *Your teaching ability.*

4) *Your co-operation in the efficient running of the School.*

Professor Dowdeswell will give you all possible guidance and assistance.

Without any further problems I received an offer of tenure from the Personnel Officer on the 11th February 1977.

I am writing to inform you that Senate recently approved a recommendation from the Academic Staff Committee that you be offered a permanent appointment in the University with effect from the 1st September 1977.

At the time I did not relate these experiences to my educational research. The paper described in Chapter Three was written in 1979 and published in the *British*

Journal of In-Service Education in 1980. It contains no reference to the above experiences which have had a profound influence on my educational development in the workplace. What it does contain however is the evidence of the three original ideas described in the introduction in terms of individuals experiencing themselves as contradictions when some of their values are negated in practice. It contains the action reflection cycle and the view that a new form of educational theory is being constituted by the explanations which individual educators produce for their own educational development as they answer questions of the kind, 'How do I improve my practice?'. It also contains the imaginative proposal that school-based degrees could be awarded for teachers' analyses of their own work with their pupils. The successful implementation of this idea can be seen in the completion of Ph.D., M.Phil., M.Ed., Advanced Diploma and Advanced Certificate programmes described in Parts Two and Three. When you read Parts Two and Three do bear in mind the comprehensive rejection of my ideas by the examiners of my Ph.D. submissions in 1980 and 1982. Details of the rejection follow my 1980 paper on the knowledge base of educational theory. At this point I am still being driven by my commitment as an educational researcher to make an original contribution to knowledge of education.

Chapter Three: 1980

In-Service Education: The Knowledge Base of Educational Theory

This paper first appeared in the *British Journal of In-Service Education*, Vol.6, No.2, 1980.

As a science teacher in London Comprehensive Schools (1967-73) I have faced the practical problems of attempting to improve my educational practice. As a lecturer in education at Bath University (1973-79) I have faced the theoretical problems of attempting to make a scholarly contribution to educational theory. I am conscious of a gap between the theory and the practice of education. The nature of this gap has been the focus of concern of several academics over recent years (Clark, 1976; Dunlop, 1977; Walking, 1979). The conclusions of these theorists is that the dominant 'disciplines' approach to educational theory is fundamentally mistaken.

I am sure that all the readers of this journal will be familiar with the view of educational theory which holds that this theory is constituted by the disciplines of education. The dominant disciplines over the past twenty years have been the philosophy, psychology and sociology of education. What this has meant for in-service education is that teachers have been brought to see educational theory, not in terms of explanations for their own educational practice, but in terms of the conceptual frameworks and methods of validation of the disciplines of education.

The purpose of this paper is to argue for a view of educational theory which is based in the educational practice of individual educators. I shall argue that a form of in-service education, which is based on a teacher's practice, should be the knowledge base of educational theory. My central point is simple. I am saying that by reflecting on their practical attempts to answer questions of the form, 'How do I improve this process of education here?', individual teachers will be able to construct explanations which correspond to their educational practice. I am saying that it is the aggregate of these explanations which constitute educational theory. In order to produce such a theory changes will be needed in the way university academics think about educational theory. I will explore the nature of these changes together with their implications for the increasing number of in-service degrees by independent study which are being developed by our Colleges of Higher Education and our Polytechnics.

I do not wish to create the impression that I believe that the disciplines of education have nothing of value to contribute to the construction of educational theory. What I am about to argue is that educational theory, if it is believed to be constituted solely by the disciplines of education, is simply mistaken. I shall argue that this view of theory should be replaced by one which is focused upon explanations for the lives of individual educators in their educational practice. Allen (1978), in his criticism of the ideas of Paul Hirst, makes the point that when an educator has integrated the forms of knowledge into his practice an explanation for his practice will not consist of one of these forms. A different form of explanation will be required to allow an understanding of educational practice. I am suggesting that one such form can be produced from explanations for the lives of individual educators.

What Knowledge is to Count as Theory of Education?

If my view of educational theory is accepted then a change will be needed in the knowledge sustained by university academics. I have chosen to focus on the changes needed by these academics for two reasons. The first is that these academics have a dominant influence on what is to count as knowledge. The second is concerned with the failure of many of these academics to explore blatant contradictions in their epistemologies. I assume that my first reason is accepted without the need for any expansion. My second point is directed at those researchers who continue to pursue educational research as if they were generating knowledge which was value-free.

The practical activity of education is value-laden. To pick out a process as education requires value judgements. This simple fact must surely be taken seriously by those researchers who pursue educational research from within the disciplines of education as if it were value free. Such academics are not only mistaken but unfortunately, because of their status, have the power to prevent alternative views from being developed. As a person who has experienced at first hand the political judgements of academics as to what is to count as valid knowledge I can only regret that the value of intellectual integrity is not always the value which is applied in the way these judgements are made. The most recent case to be exposed was that of Sir Cyril Burt in his attempts to prevent the dissemination of views which ran counter to his own.

A Theory of Practice Derived from In-Service Education

My own attempt to understand the nature of an educational theory, which could be constructed directly from practice, consisted of a return to the classroom and a case study of my own practical and theoretical explorations of my problem, 'How do I improve this process of education here?'. I gathered data on my practice with video tapes of the exchanges between myself and the pupils and between the pupils themselves. The reasons I gave for changing my practice were focused upon the fact that I experienced the negation of some of my educational values in my practice. For example, when I was teaching all my 30 pupils the same thing at the same time I could not allow my pupils any freedom to choose any aspect of their learning. I also could not allow my pupils to pursue enquiries which did not conform to the logic of my lesson. In many cases this meant stifling the imaginative episodes of my pupils' thinking. The explanation I gave for my attempts to change my practice was given in terms of a struggle to live my educational values in my practice. By this I mean that the structuring principles in my explanation were educational values. I could say, following Peters (1966), that I hold the educational values of freedom, equality, respect for persons, worthwhile activities and the consideration of interests. This does not however give a clear definition of meaning.

To communicate my meaning to you I must point to my practice to show you my values in the practice. Linguistic definition is inadequate as a medium for the clear expression of educational values. These values can only be fully understood in relation to practice. This fact exposes a limitation in the assumption that Journals of Education can communicate the nature of educational theory purely in linguistic form. This point cannot be over-emphasised. What I am saying is that linguistic definition needs to be supplemented by ostensive definition for a clear communication of the nature of educational values. The necessity of 'pointing to practice' (ostensive definition) prevents the separation of theory from practice in the constitution of educational theory. Both the meaning of the explanations, which are constitutive of theory, and the methods of testing the validity of the explanations require ostensive definition.

If this view of educational theory is accepted then one implication is that articles on the production of educational theory will have to be supplemented with other data, for example on video or audio tape, than that presented in linguistic form. A further implication of this idea is that *criticism,* which has a primary role in the testing of theory, will be directed not only at linguistic statements in the explanation but at the individual who is offering the explanation for his or her own form of life.

I will now make some suggestions on the nature of In-Service Education which could provide an epistemological basis for the construction of an educational theory based on educational practice.

First it must be school focused in the sense that it is grounded in the actual educational practice of the educator in the classroom with his/her pupils. The primary task of the providers of in-service support is to elicit an open response by the teachers on the nature of their problems. It may be said, in criticism of this approach, that the teacher may not identify his problems correctly. The implication being that the provider of the support can in fact identify the problems correctly. This may in fact be the case but to impose the provider's problems onto the teacher is, I suggest, the route to certain failure. The emergence of a set of shared problems is the most crucial element in the provision of in-service support. In my experience, these problems emerge over time, not often in an hour, or a day, but sometimes over months. The definition of the shared problems, and the deepening understanding of the participants, of the nature of each other's problems, usually happens as the providers and the teachers become increasingly aware of each other's practices, what each has to contribute to the joint exercise and, most importantly, how far the teachers can trust the providers and each other. Everyone who has engaged in school-focused in-service education will know that this is a most delicate area, at the centre of which is the process of evaluating the in-service activity. In a trusting atmosphere teachers will engage in the most savage self-criticism of their own practice. Once, however, the hierarchical nature of political controls appear in the evaluation, and by this I mean the participation, in the in-service support, of heads, advisors, inspectors or lecturers, who are viewed by the teachers in terms of their institutional power rather than as critical friends whose primary concern is to support them in their attempts to improve their practice, then the openness is replaced by a defensiveness which prevents any movement forward in the teachers' educational practice.

In the case of my own research, reported in this Journal (Whitehead, 1977), the in-service support lasted over a period of two years and resulted in the teachers bringing about highly significant changes in their practice. By highly significant I mean that they were able to move from a position in which their educational values were negated, to a position in which their values were realised in their practice. The point that educational change can be understood in terms of attempts by individuals to overcome their experience that some of their educational values were being negated is perhaps the single most important idea to emerge from my research and it undermines the epistemological basis of the disciplines approach to educational theory. It undermines this approach at its strongest point: that is its *logic*. What it does is to demonstrate that education is a process in which individuals are changing and that the logic which can comprehend change, in terms of negating the experience of a negation, is a dialectical logic. The formal logic of the disciplines approach does not include a dialectical logic. I will illustrate the importance of this idea by asking you to reflect on your own attempts to improve a process of education for your pupils. I am assuming that your attempts to improve your practice are rational and have the psychological form of the explanation below. If your reflections indicate that the explanation should have a different form and content then my assumption is mistaken and the construction of an educational theory of the form advocated above will not occur.

An Explanation for my Educational Practice

1)   I experience a problem because some of my educational values are negated.
2)   I imagine a solution.
3)   I act in the direction of the imagined solution.
4)   I evaluate the actions.
5)   I modify my actions/ideas in the light of my evaluations.

I take it that this is the traditional model of rational problem solving with the addition of the first point about problem formation. This addition is crucial for establishing a logic of educational theory which contains formal logic within a dialectical form of enquiry. What is new about this form of explanation is that the structuring principles of the explanation are educational values as they are expressed in an individual's form of life. What is also radically different in this form of explanation is that the 'I's of individual educators are contained in the explanation as conscious and causal agents of change. This inclusion transforms the traditional view of a scientific explanation of human action. I am saying that the scientific study of educational practice should not conceptualise the individuals who constitute the practice in terms of concepts or abstract generalities. Rather I am saying that they should be understood in terms of their qualities of being individuals. In my view, educational theory, as general, will exist in the aggregate of explanations for the form of life of individual educators in their educational practice. The responsibility for the construction of educational theory, on the base of this form of in-service education, rests with the educators themselves and the providers of the support. The providers have the difficult task of developing the support services which will enable the teachers to explore the practical and theoretical implications of questions of the form, 'How do I improve this process of education here?'.

In submitting my ideas for your critical judgement I am asking you to reflect on the way you attempt to educate your pupils and students and to compare the explanation you give for your own practice with my own. I have claimed that you become conscious of a problem when you experience the negation of some of your educational values. You then imagine a solution. In the disciplines approach it is held that the first step in your attempts to solve a practical educational problem must be to break it down into its logically distinct components (Peters, 1977). I am claiming that the first step in your own attempts to solve your problem was to imagine a solution which you then acted upon, evaluated and modified. In this process you may have drawn upon the insights from the different disciplines and tried them out in your practice. I have argued that the explanation which you give for your own practice is what should constitute educational theory. Whilst it is impossible to present, in such a brief article, the detailed working out of such a theory, I will explore what I see to be the implications of such a view for some of the in-service degrees by independent study which are currently being designed in our Colleges of Higher Education and our Polytechnics.

School Based Degrees
In an attempt to improve education within schools several of our Institutions of Higher Education are looking at the possibility of designing degrees which are 'school-focused' in the sense of being based upon the graduate teacher's educational practice. It is my contention that these degrees offer the possibility of beginning the production of a new form of educational theory. In my own experience of in-service education I have encountered scores of teachers in the Avon area who wish to engage in a course of study which would emerge from their own attempts to improve their practice and whose content could gain universal recognition as of a first degree or higher degree standard. The way in which this could be achieved is quite simple. I am however under no illusion that the political problems of overcoming the powerful interest groups who are determined to continue their support for the disciplines approach, will be immense. What could be done is that teachers, selected by the Institution of Higher Education, the Local Authority or by self selection could enrol on a degree course which was designed as a programme of independent study into questions of the form, 'How do I improve this process of education here?'. The teacher's programme of work could be agreed as realistic and validated by the same procedures which have been established by the North East London Polytechnic (Burgess and Adams, 1980). To satisfy the university requirements, that the work of the student should make a scholarly contribution to the study of his/her subject, the teacher must present an explanation for his/her practice. The criteria of judgement of the explanation would include a demonstration of the influence of her or his activities on the process of improving his or her own educational practice.

In the Schools Council Mixed Ability Exercise (Whitehead, 1976), one of whose aims was the development of a network of in-service support for teachers, I constructed several explanations for the lives of the teachers involved in the exercise. A group of the participants, including advisors from the L.E.A. and Schools Council, formed an 'Evaluation Group', and subjected my explanations to criticism. I found that I had to modify the nature of my explanations because of the power of the rational arguments which were critical of my explanation. I had used models and a language which were inappropriate for the construction of an explanation for the lives of the teachers. A reconstructed explanation was accepted by the participants as corresponding to the lives of the teachers. I make this point to emphasise the importance of an Evaluation Group in providing critical support for the construction of explanations. To assist teachers in their in-service degrees by independent study I am sure that it will be necessary to form Evaluation Groups for the purpose of subjecting the teacher's explanations for his/her own practice to critical scrutiny.

The normal procedures which Universities use in their system of external examiners could be used in the final assessment of the quality of the teacher's contribution to the production of educational theory. As I have said the procedures are simple. They are grounded in the values of rationality itself. The view of educational theory which dominates our universities claims the mantle of rationality. I am saying that a simple reflection by you, on the nature of the rationality which is involved in your attempts to educate your pupils and to improve the process of education, will demonstrate the irrationality of a position which refuses to allow the production of educational theory to be structured on the basis of the attempts of individual educators to live their educational values in their practice. It is my contention that the providers of in-service support have a responsibility to education to ensure that those universities who have failed to uphold, in their school and Institutes of Education, the tradition of intellectual integrity, should not be supported until they have adopted a rational approach to the production of educational theory.

And now forward from 1977 to 1980. I will now ask you to identify again with my experience of existing as a living contradiction in the workplace. I have asked you to test the validity of the explanatory principle, in my claim to know my educational knowledge, that I value my work as a University Academic in making original contributions to educational knowledge. In my early work with teachers and pupils in the 1977 paper I showed that I valued their capacity for asking questions and believed in their freedom to pursue their enquiries. I also valued my own capacities and freedom to do the same. I held these values together with the judgements of my examiners which appear in the next Chapter, that I had not shown a capacity to conduct original enquiries nor a capacity to test my own ideas or those of others. I had to hold the values together with an instruction that I was not free to question the competence of my examiners under any circumstances. When you read later of a Senate Working Party's conclusion that I had been subjected to pressures which might have constrained a less determined individual, do look back on the judgements which follow, to see if you agree that two explanatory principles in my educational development have been my commitment to expressing originality and to the academic freedom to ask questions and to report my enquiries in a public arena.

CHAPTER FOUR: 1980

LIVING CONTRADICTIONS: I AM A CREATIVE ACADEMIC. I AM NOT. I CAN QUESTION THE JUDGEMENTS OF OTHER ACADEMICS. I CANNOT.

YOU MAY have a degree and recall your graduation ceremony. I remember mine at the University of Durham in 1965. My parents expressed their delight. I was pleased to receive a degree but I recall the distinct feeling that there must be more to education than my specialised degree in Science. It was later that I experienced the delight of believing that I had learnt something worth while, on receiving my Academic Diploma in the philosophy and psychology of education from the University of London in 1970. In my examination papers I experienced little anxiety about my knowledge and was committed to the disciplines approach to educational theory which underpinned the papers. I felt a more subdued relief on receiving my M.A. degree in the psychology of education in 1972. The relief came because I had taken a risk in rejecting the whole basis of the M.A. programme in my examination papers. I rejected its basis because I could not directly relate the explanations from any of the different schools of the psychology of education to my understanding of my educative relationships with my pupils. Whilst I could not articulate clearly an alternative view of educational theory to the disciplines approach which underpinned the papers I could no longer accept the approach. I know that my responses to the questions reflected my own sense of confusion yet I took the risk of embracing and expressing the inchoate nature of my thinking.

I wonder if you share my view that a University graduation ceremony should be a celebration of learning. It should be a recognition of intellectual achievement and something to recall with the pleasure of such achievement. It is usual for most academics to have received a Ph.D. Degree for making original contributions to knowledge of their subject.

I submitted two doctoral theses to the University of Bath for examination in 1980 and 1982. The examiners were required by the University to judge the theses in terms of criteria which included the following:

1) *Has the candidate shown that he is able to conduct original investigations and to test his own ideas and those of others?*

2) *Does the thesis contain matter worthy of publication?*

All examiners of research degrees were informed before making their judgements that the results of the research and study must be satisfactorily presented in the thesis,

*'which should include matter worthy of publication **although it need not be submitted in a form suitable for publication'*** (my emphasis).

Bearing in mind the problems I outlined above when I recounted the story of my near-dismissal, I think you will understand why I made the point about the assessors of my work in the following letter to the Secretary and Registrar on the 25 October 1977.

I shall be submitting a thesis to the University some time after August 1st 1978 for the degree of Doctor of Philosophy. According to the University regulations I believe that I need to inform you of my intentions at least six months before my proposed date of submission and pay a fee of £10. This fee is enclosed.

The university regulations also state that assessors will be appointed. Whilst I would not normally comment on the appointment of assessors by the University I have had an unfortunate experience with assessors within the University which leads me to make the following submission. In the past I have been questioned by University Assessors on the quality of my research. As part of my academic training I learnt the importance of judging a person's understanding of a piece of work through the quality of the questions asked. In my own case, I was asked questions which demonstrated the questioners' lack of familiarity with my field of enquiry. I would ask that the University appoints assessors who have published research in a field closely connected with my own. That is:- educational theory and the process of improving education within comprehensive schools.

The Secretary and Registrar responded on the 2nd November 1977:

Thank you for your letter dated 25th October advising me of your intention to submit for the degree of Doctor of Philosophy under the provision of Regulation 18.5 Method B.

In accordance with the provisions of that Regulation I shall advise the Chairman of the Board of Studies for Education that he should ask the Board to recommend to Senate the appointment of members of staff to advise you on the presentation of the work. I will also draw his attention to your comments on assessors.

I then made a request to the University to take care in ensuring the competence of the examiners, to which the Secretary and Registrar replied:

Thank you for your letter of 8th May regarding the submission of your Ph.D thesis.

External examiners are appointed by the Council on the recommendation of Senate, and Senate is advised by the appropriate Board of Studies.

It is therefore a matter for the Board of Studies for Education in the first instance to satisfy itself of the competence of the examiners. I understand that you have already written to the Chairman of the Board to make your point, and I am sure every consideration will be given to it.

Once the examiners have been appointed, their competence cannot in any circumstances be questioned. (My emphasis)

The Thesis I submitted had the title *'Educational Practice and its theory - an analysis of a research programme on the enquiry, "How do I improve this process of education here?".'* The following abstract should give you an idea of the point of the thesis.

Abstract

This thesis presents a claim to know an individual's educational practice. On the basis of this claim it is argued that the dominant concept of educational theory is too limited to produce an explanation which corresponds to an individual's educational practice. A psychological form, for a dialectical materialist's approach to the production of educational theory, is presented as an alternative to the dominant concept of educational theory. The alternative is based upon an exploration of the implication of the practical educational problem, 'How do I improve this process of education here?'. These implications include the fact that the problem was formulated within the political and economic realities of the division of labour in society.

The examiners appointed by Senate on the recommendation of the Board of Studies for Education were Professor Jeff Thompson who had recently joined the School following the retirement of 'Bunny' Dowdeswell, Professor William Taylor, now Sir William and recently retired as Chair of the Council for the Accreditation of Teacher Education, and Professor Jack Wrigley from the University of Reading.

The viva-voce examination was held on the 14th October 1980. The Examiners' Report to the Board of Studies for Education recommended that the Degree of Doctor of Philosophy should not be awarded and that I should not be permitted to resubmit my thesis. The Board of Studies accepted the recommendation. Just as I asked you to focus your intuition on identifying with my existence as a living contradiction as you read the letter of March 1976 terminating my employment I now ask you to use all your intuition and insight to empathise with my response to hearing the following judgements on my research which were again made with the full force of the University.

The examiners were agreed that I had not shown that I was able to conduct original investigations and to test my own ideas and those of others.

They were agreed that the thesis did not contain matter worthy of publication.

They were agreed that I should not be permitted to re-submit my thesis.

I held a view of my thesis as an original contribution to educational knowledge which contained matter worthy of publication. Today, after some thirteen years examining with other internal and external examiners, Masters Degrees and M.Phil. and Ph.D. degrees which contain the same ideas as those which my examiners rejected, I am now more certain of these judgements. I had to hold together the view of myself as an original researcher together with the University judgements that I was not. I had to hold together my view that the thesis contained matter worthy of publication together with the University view that it did not. I also had to hold together my questioning of the competence of the examiners' judgements with the University's instruction that I could not question the competence of the examiners under any circumstances.

I had informed the University of the dialectical basis of my work and the need to take care in the appointment of examiners. The University exercised this care by appointing Professor William Taylor. In 1978 Professor Taylor published the following views on the 'New Criticism' in education - the field of my research.

'In commenting upon and expressing disquiet about the implications of the ideas of these authors, I do not wish to identify myself with those who dismiss their work as of little consequence. Whether we agree or disagree with their mode of analysis and conclusions - and my own disagreement is almost total - we cannot ignore the attraction of their ideas for large numbers of students and teachers, or their influence on the development of curriculum study..... the New Criticism, in directly opposing the values of bourgeois society and the 'liberal ideology', undermines institutional structures and practices that sustain possibilities of individual freedom and democratic pluralism, and is very imprecise about the structures and practices that would characterise post-capitalist social and political life.' (Taylor, 1978).

On the 11th November 1980, I wrote to the Secretary and Registrar asking for information on which examiner the University believed to be an authority in the field of my research:

I wish to draw your attention to your letters of 2/11/77 and 13/5/80, in which you noted my points about assessors and said that you were sure that the Board of Studies for Education would give every consideration to my request concerning the competence of my examiners. My reason for writing to you on the 13/5/80 was to alert you to the central importance of dialectical materialist epistemology in my claim to have made an original and substantial contribution to knowledge. One of my advisers had written a report in which he acknowledged his lack of competence to judge the validity of the epistemological base of my work.This adviser is a recognised authority in the field of education. I felt that I ought to point out that the examiners (or at least one examiner) should be competent to judge my claim to have made an original and substantial contribution to knowledge, a claim made from within the tradition of dialectical materialist epistemology.

Following my viva voce on 14th October, I was informed by the Chairman of the Examination Board that the examination of my thesis, 'Educational Practice and its Theory', was continuing. I was informed on the 20th October that the examiners had arrived at a decision. In the light of the nature of my examination I am curious to know which of the examiners was appointed by the University as an acknowledged authority in the field of my work. Could you please supply me with this information?

The Head of the School of Education informed me that Professor William Taylor was the University's choice as the acknowledged authority in the field of my research. The University appointed an examiner whose disagreement with the mode of analysis and conclusions of my field of research was almost total and who believed that it undermined institutional structures and practices that sustain possibilities of individual freedom and democratic pluralism. It should surely be permissible to raise just the hint of a question about the possibility that such an examiner might be just the tiniest bit biased against the mode of analysis he is in almost total disagreement with.

The Secretary and Registrar wrote to me on the 14th November 1980 with a splendidly clear re-affirmation of the instruction that I could not raise any question about the competence of the examiners.

I wish to acknowledge your letter of 11 November.

Clearly, in any matter related to your submission for a higher degree I must treat you in the same manner as I would treat any other candidate for a degree.

I must re-iterate that no question may now be raised about the competence of the examiners, and I must also say that I cannot enter into any discussion as to what may have been said in the viva voce examination.

I wrote to the Secretary and Registrar to request a review of the results of the examination on the 3rd December 1980.

In the absence of my Head of School I am writing to you to request a review of the matter of the results of my candidacy for the degree of Ph.D. I informed my

Head of School on November 27th of my request for a review and I have given to his secretary my reasons in writing. I simply wish to record that my request was made on 3.12.80.

The procedures, under University Regulations 17.5 'Duties of Boards of Studies', are unclear. May I call witnesses to the hearing? Could you assure me that all the evidence considered by the Board will be open to myself and my adviser to challenge?

The Secretary and Registrar replied:

Thank you for your letter of 3 December. I believe the Board of Studies for Education will be meeting to review the result of your Ph.D. submission later this month.

I should perhaps make it clear that the purpose of the meeting is to consider whether any of the matters which you raise were not known to the Board of Examiners, and are such that, if they had been known, they could have influenced the Board's decision. If the Board of Studies sees fit, it can bring the attention of the examiners to these matters. There is no question of the Board having before it any evidence other than your own. There would be no point in calling witnesses unless there were some dispute on a matter of fact.

I think the following grounds for requesting a review speak for themselves. The majority of the members of the Board of Studies hearing the request for a review were my colleagues in the School of Education. Some of them still are. In my judgement there is something profoundly anti-academic in the refusal to permit me to resubmit the thesis. Here is the paper I submitted to my colleagues requesting a review of the results of the examination.

My request for a review of the results of the examination of the thesis, "Educational Practice and its Theory" submitted to the Board of Studies for its meeting on December 17th 1980 .

The matters I will raise, when heard in person by the Board of Studies, are included within the following points:

My thesis is that educational theory can be produced from the explanations which individuals give for their own educational practice. The thesis contains an explanation for my own educational practice. The standards of judgement which can be used to criticise the explanation as a dialectical materialist's claim to knowledge, are presented in the thesis. These standards are defined in terms of,

1) scientific criteria
2) ethical criteria
3) aesthetic criteria
4) use value.

I am disturbed by the discrepancy between the judgements of my advisers and the examiners on the presentation of my thesis. I do not question the right of the examiners to disagree with the judgements of my advisers. What I do suggest is that there is an intimate relationship between the form of presentation and the content of the claim to knowledge, in the epistemology of dialectical materialism. I further submit that, as there is a strong possibility that the form of the presentation did not present my thesis in a way which enabled the examiners to clearly see its nature, I should be permitted to re-submit my work in a form which clearly reveals the thesis to the examiners.

Material placed before the Board in relation to the examiners' judgements (on the following five criteria used by the examiners in judging the thesis).

1) Has the candidate shown that he is able to conduct original investigations and to test his own ideas and those of others?

I claim that I have shown that I am able to conduct original investigations and to test my own ideas and those of others in the following areas:

A) *The presentation of a dialectical materialist's claim to know the art of education. This presentation included an examination of different claims to knowledge in terms of propositional knowledge (Know-that), procedural knowledge (Know-how) and knowledge with a direct object (Know-this). The examination included a dialectical materialist's testing of the epistemological positions of P. Hirst and L.A. Reid with particular reference to the claim to know the art of education.*

B) *The presentation of a dialectical materialist's movement through four methodological approaches to the social sciences. I claim that this is an original investigation to discover the mode of enquiry and the logic of an appropriate methodology, for use in the investigation of the practical educational problem, 'How do I improve this process of education here?'. I claim to have tested, in a dialectical materialist's way, the modes of enquiry and the preferred logics of the methodological approaches of the Analytic Scientist, the Conceptual Theorist, the Conceptual Humanist and the Particular Humanist (Mitroff and Kilman, 1978).*

C) *The presentation of a dialectical materialist's movement, from the epistemology of Objective Knowledge (Popper), through the epistemology of Personal Knowledge (Polanyi) and into the epistemology of Dialectical Materialism. I claim that this is an original investigation to discover a valid epistemological base for use in the claim to know an individual's educational practice.*

D) *The presentation of the discovery of a psychological form for a dialectical materialist's approach to the production of educational theory. This presentation involved the explication of the units of appraisal and the standards of judgement, which could be used to test such an approach, from within the dialectical materialist's position. I claim that this is an original investigation which involved the testing, in a dialectical materialist's way, of the units of appraisal and the standards of judgement which have been used in the epistemologies of Popper, Lakatos, Kuhn, Polanyi and Rubens.*

2) Have I shown that I understand how my special theme is related to a wider field of knowledge?

I claim that I have shown, in a dialectical materialist's way, how my special theme is related to a wider field of knowledge. My claim to know an individual's educational practice not only undermines the disciplines approach to educational theory but can form the basis for the production of a dialectical materialist's alternative. The special theme is the existence of 'I' as a living contradiction in my claim to knowledge. I claim that I have examined the assumptions in the linguistic school of the philosophy of education, the behaviourist, cognitive theorist and humanistic schools, of the psychology of education, and the structural functionalist, phenomenological and Marxist schools of the sociology of education. I also claim to have tested these assumptions, in a dialectical materialist's way, and found that they explicitly exclude or omit the existence of 'I' as a living contradiction from the explanations of human action.

3) Does the thesis contain matter worthy of publication?

Matter already published from the thesis or accepted for publication.

a) *Improving learning in schools - an in-service problem.*
   British Journal of In-Service Education. Vol. 3, No. 2, Spring 1977.

b) *Evaluation and Learning in Secondary Schools (with Joan Whitehead) in Outcomes of Education. Ed. Burgess and Adams. Macmillan 1980.*

c) *In-Service Education - The Knowledge Base of Educational Theory. British Journal of In-service Education. Vol. 6, No. 2, Spring 1980.*

d) *A Practical Example of a Dialectical Approach to Educational Research in Human Inquiry. Ed. Reason, P., and Rowan, J. To be published by Wiley (1981).*

e) *Educational Evaluation and the NAIEA. Accepted for publication in the Journal of the National Association of Inspectors and Educational Advisers Spring 1981 issue.*

Transforming Education Now. A publication accepted by the Inspectorate of Mauritius, 'to help form the nucleus of a Resource Centre for the Inspectorate'.

4) Are the style and general arrangements of the thesis satisfactory?

The Board of Studies for Education appointed Professor Austwick and Professor Hoyle as my advisers. I presented my initial draft to Professor Austwick in September 1978. In January 1979 Professor Austwick returned the draft and read out a report from Professor Hoyle. He then gave me a copy of the report. Having acted upon the advice, given by Professor Hoyle, I gave Professor Austwick the rewritten thesis in September 1979 and asked for his advice on the relationship between the epistemology and the presentation of my thesis. This was a crucial problem in the presentation of a dialectical thesis on educational practice and its theory. Professor Hoyle assessed the thesis. I received no further advice and submitted my thesis to the Registrar in March 1980. The advisers reported to the Board of Studies of May 14th 1980 that the work presented was worthy of examination.

5) Were the results of the oral examination satisfactory?

I claim that the results of the oral examination could not have been satisfactory. The examination was conducted solely within an epistemological position which was incompatible with my claim to have made an original and substantial contribution to knowledge. I claim that the examiners did not ask one question which examined the thesis from within its own epistemological position. After one hour and forty minutes of questioning the Chairman of the Examiners asked if I had any questions to put to the examiners. I asked the examiners to examine the thesis using the criteria I had explicated in my claim to have made an original and substantial contribution to knowledge of my subject. One examiner replied that the University had its own criteria. The viva voce then terminated. On going to my Head of School, the following day, to express my dissatisfaction with the viva voce, I was told that the external examiners had taken the thesis away and that the examination was continuing.

I may also wish to raise the following matters.

1) The report of the 1980 International Conference of the World Education Fellowship.

I presented an outline of this thesis to the conference in August 1980. The conference report clearly shows the part which the video tapes play in the claims to knowledge and in the testing of the claims to knowledge. It is an indication that the examiners were operating from a different epistemological position in that they did not see fit to have video facilities available nor did they ask questions which required reference to the tapes. I requested that the examiners should examine the thesis from within its own epistemological position and this met with the response, 'The University has its own criteria'.

2) At the meeting of the Board of Studies of November 26th, a member of the Board proposed an amendment to the report. He also stated that the examiners' report did not contain sufficient information on which he could satisfy himself of the examiners' report. This member proposed that I be allowed to re-submit my thesis. The Board was advised that its function was to receive the report as a whole. It was not advised that the Report could be referred back to the Board of Examiners for reconsideration of the recommendation that the candidate be not allowed to re-submit.

3) I had written to the Registrar and the Chairman of the Board of Studies to emphasise that this work should be judged as a contribution to the epistemological tradition of dialectical materialism.

4) I had not been able to discover who the Board of Studies nominated to the Board of Examiners as an acknowledged authority in the field of my work.

5) I may wish to raise the matter of the views of the internal adviser on the nature of his research.

6) I submitted, to a staff meeting in the summer 1980, a proposal for a module on the M.Ed course.

7) I claim that the use value of my thesis can be seen in the MEd and MA dissertations of:

B. Green M.A. London University 1979
C. Bell M.Ed. Bath University 1980
C. Peters M.Ed Bath University 1980
J. Vowles M.Ed Bath University 1980
J. Hayes   M.Ed Bath University 1980
The M.Ed submissions of D. Foster and P. Denley.

On the 17th December 1980 a special Board of Studies met to hear my appeal. Here is an extract from the minutes of that meeting.

The chairman explained that Mr. Whitehead was appealing against the Examiners' Report on his examination for Ph.D. The Board would have to decide whether the appellant had produced fresh evidence that was not available to the Examiners at the time of his examination which could have materially affected the result.

Mr. Whitehead, accompanied by Mr. T. Adam, School of Engineering, were invited into the meeting. Mr. Whitehead made a statement to the Board outlining the matters he considered to be new evidence which the Examiners either did not have, or took no account of during his examination.

The Board was given the opportunity to question Mr. Whitehead on his statement. Mr Whitehead and Mr. Adam then withdrew.

After considerable discussion the Board voted on the matter and rejected the appeal on the grounds that the evidence presented was insufficient to refer the matter back to the Examiners.

Four members of the Board abstained from voting because they considered there was an absence of clear guidelines in the matter of an appeal against a Ph.D. examination.

The Board expressed concern over the regulations governing Staff Candidature (particularly under Regulation 18.5 Method B) and agreed to discuss the subject at a future meeting.

I spent the next twelve months working on ways of re-presenting my thesis in a way which could be presented as a new submission to the University rather than a re-submission. This thesis, entitled 'A dialectical approach to education', was examined in 1982 and again rejected. The Abstract will give you some idea of the contents of the work.

Abstract

The past twenty years have seen the emergence, dominance and partial decline of an approach to educational theory which has become known as the 'disciplines' approach. The principle of differentiation in this approach is contained in the statement of R.S. Peters that '... Though it (educational theory) must be presented in a differentiated way the different disciplines must also mesh in with and be seen to mesh in with each other in relation to matters of educational policy and practice'.

This thesis seeks to replace the principle of differentiation of the 'disciplines' approach with a 'dialectical' alternative. The alternative is presented in terms of an individual's claim to know his own in-service educational development.

To show that the approach has some universal potential its implications are explored in the in-service educational development of a manager in a local Authority Youth service, a teacher and an educational researcher.

The dialectical approach is shown to have some emancipatory potential. It also throws some light on the problem of finding a way of integrating the contributions of the different disciplines of education in the solution of a practical educational problem.

In May 1981 I wrote to the University to give notice of my intention to submit a thesis and the Secretary and Registrar replied that Senate would appoint an adviser or advisers to assist me with the presentation of my work. Senate appointed Professor Jeff Thompson to assist me. Given the dialectical basis of my work this was an interesting choice. I recall with a mixture of amusement and irritation his suggestion that I remove a section dealing with the significance of Marxist thought from my thesis.

Senate appointed Professor John Nisbett from Aberdeen University - Education, Professor Stephen Cotgrove, a sociologist at Bath and Richard West, now a Professor of Education.

Following a viva-voce examination on the 4th November 1982 the examiners reported to the Board of Studies on November 24th recommending that the award of Ph.D. should not be granted.

The examiners were agreed that:

I had not fully satisfied the criteria that I should show that I was able to conduct original investigations and to test my own ideas and those of others.

The thesis did not contain matter worthy of publication.

I should not be permitted to resubmit the thesis 'A dialectical approach to education'.

The Board accepted the examiners' recommendation that the award of Ph.D. should not be made and that I should not be permitted to resubmit.

Requests for a review of results have to be made in writing up to fourteen days after being informed of the decision. At the time of this second failure I was due to be assessed by the University to see if I should pass beyond the efficiency bar. The advice I received from the Association of University Teachers was that I should wait until I failed to pass the bar and then bring a grievance which would include the case of the second Ph.D.. In the event my work was judged as satisfactory and I passed the efficiency bar. I now regret the decision not to request a review of the results. I recorded a decision at the time to fight my case in the academic and other public arenas.

I think it worth recording that one of the examiners in this later examination had previously been a party to the recommendation to terminate my employment on the grounds that there was an absence of evidence to suggest that I had pursued research of sufficient quality for the assessors to be assured of my ability to perform adequately the duties of a University Lecturer. Should I not be permitted to raise the possibility that this examiner, having been party to the recommendation to terminate my employment, could have perhaps been a little prejudiced in the matter of examining my research?

****

The 1985 paper which follows in the next chapter makes no references to these experiences even though it is explicitly concerned with an analysis of my educational development. You will see that I am still treating my educational development as if it is solely concerned with reaching understanding of a form of educational knowledge which is independent of the context within which it is being produced. It was written in 1983 following the rejection of my second Ph.D. submission on grounds similar to the first rejection. Again the judgements were made that the thesis contained no matter worthy of publication and that I should not be permitted to re-submit. The paper is focused on the epistemological issues related to an individual's claim to know his or her own educational development. In terms of action research I am concerned in the paper to explicate the methodological and epistemological assumptions in my claim to educational knowledge. I think you will clearly see the development from my 1980 paper in extending my cognitive range and concerns into the work of academics such as Eward Ilyenkov, Michael Polanyi and Jürgen Habermas. I relate their ideas on logic, personal knowledge and social validation to the three original ideas from my own research. If you had any doubts about the primary, explanatory principle for my own educational development being my commitment to reconstruct educational theory, this paper should dispel them. Following this 1985 paper I will describe how my enquiry was pushed forward through violations of my value of integrity, truth and justice, in another experience of existing as a living contradiction.

Chapter Five: 1985

An Analysis of an Individual's Educational Development: The Basis for Personally Oriented Action Research

This paper first appeared in *Educational Research: Principles, Policies and Practice,* edited by M. Shipman and published by Falmer Press.

My purpose is to draw your attention to the development of a living form of educational theory. The theory is grounded in the lives of professional educators and their pupils and has the power to integrate within itself the traditional disciplines of education. Educational theory occupies an ambiguous position in the educational profession. Its importance is due to the fact that a profession supports its skills and techniques with a body of systematically produced theory. On the other hand, teachers tend to decry educational theory because of its lack of relationship to their practical skills and techniques.

My purpose in writing this chapter is to outline how I think a professionally credible educational theory could be generated and tested from a form of self-reflective inquiry undertaken by participants in educational contexts in order to improve the rationality and justice of:

(a) their own educational practices,
(b) their understanding of these practices,
(c) the situations in which the practices are carried out.
    'It is most empowering when undertaken by participants collaboratively, though it is often undertaken by individuals sometimes in co-operation with 'outsiders'. (Carr and Kemmis, 1983).

I am assuming that a teacher action-researcher, who is interested in contributing to knowledge of the process of improving education within schools, will be faced by an academic community which will examine the legitimacy of the claim to knowledge. I am also assuming that a teacher-researcher is concerned to establish a direct relationship between the claim to know what he or she is doing and the pupils' educational development.

The educational analysis which follows is focused upon the nature of the validity of an individual action-researcher's claim to know his or her own educational development. The analysis outlines a form of educational theory which can be generated from professional practice and which can integrate the different contributions of the disciplines of education. Let me say at the beginning how I see the relationship between my own research and teacher action research. In my work in a University I am paid to make scholarly and acknowledged contributions to knowledge of my subject, education. I characterize my attempts to make this contribution as a form of academic action-research. In my investigation of my own claims to know my own educational development I have explored the nature of a form of educational theory which is directly related to educational practice. My particular concerns have focused upon the academic legitimacy of an individual's claim to know his or her own educational development. I think that my findings will be of use to those teacher-researchers who wish to justify their own claims to knowledge to the academic community.

The approach to educational theory I am suggesting we adopt rests on a number of assumptions concerning both the idea of a 'living form of theory' and the personal and social criteria which can be used to criticize the theory. I use the term a 'living form of theory' to distinguish the suggested approach from the 'linguistic form' in which traditional theories are presented for criticism. In a living approach to educational theory I am suggesting that teacher action-researchers present their claims to know how and why they are attempting to overcome practical educational problems in this form:

> I experience a problem when some of my educational values are negated in my practice.
> I imagine a solution to my problem.
> I act in the direction of my solution.
> I evaluate the outcomes of my actions.
> I modify my problems, ideas and actions in the light of my evaluations.

For educational theory to be directly related to educational practice it must have the power to explain an individual's development. One of the major problems which has led to the discrediting of traditional forms of educational theory was that they could not produce adequate explanations for the educational development of individuals. A theory should also be able to answer questions concerning why things happen. In the approach to educational theory advocated here the 'why' questions are answered in terms of 'value'. Like Ilyenkov (1982) I take 'value' to be a human goal for the sake of which we struggle to give our lives their particular form. In relation to the enquiry I take it that the experience of the negation of educational values moves the enquiry forward and that the values are taken, by the holder, to be held with universal intent.

Questions concerning the academic legitimacy of a claim to knowledge are often focused upon the criticism of a particular piece of work. The work being criticized can be a single hypothesis or theory (Popper, 1972) or a research programme (Lakatos, 1972). Whatever is being criticized is known as the unit of appraisal. In criticizing a claim to knowledge it is important to be clear about the unit and the standards of judgment which can legitimately be used in the criticism. There is some dispute amongst philosophers about the nature of the standards which can be used to criticize a claim to knowledge.

The unit of appraisal in my conception of educational theory is the individual's claim to know his or her own educational development. Although this unit may appear strange to most educational researchers I think that it is clearly comprehensible. The standards of judgment are however more difficult to communicate. I use both personal and social standards in justifying my own claims to know my own educational development. In using personal criteria I draw upon the work of Michael Polanyi. I am grateful for *Personal Knowledge* (1958) because in my case Polanyi fulfilled his purpose of *'stripping away the crippling mutilations which centuries of objectivist thought have imposed on the minds of men'*. The personal criteria I use in making a claim to know my own educational development include Polanyi's values of respect and commitment.

'To claim validity for a statement merely declares that it ought to be accepted by everyone because everyone ought to be able to see it . . . The affirmation of a scientific truth has an obligatory character; in this it is like all other valuations that are declared universal by our own respect for them'.   (Polanyi and Prosch, 1975)

'It is the act of commitment in its full structure that saves personal knowledge from being merely subjective. Intellectual commitment is a responsible decision, in submission to the compelling claims of what in good conscience I conceive to be true. It is an act of hope, striving to fulfil an obligation within a personal situation for which I am not responsible and which therefore determines my calling. This hope and this obligation are expressed in the universal intent of personal knowledge.

. . . Any conclusion, whether given as a surmise or claimed as a certainty, represents a commitment of the person who arrives at it. No one can utter more than a responsible commitment of his own, and this completely fulfils his responsibility for finding the truth and telling it. Whether or not it is the truth can be hazarded only by another, equally responsible commitment'. (Polanyi, 1958).

In grounding my epistemology in *Personal Knowledge* I am conscious that I have taken a decision to understand the world from my own point of view, as a person claiming originality and exercising his personal judgment responsibly with universal intent. This commitment determines the nature of the unit of appraisal in my claim to knowledge. The unit is the individual's claim to know his or her own educational development.

The social criteria I use to criticize my claim to knowledge appear to conform to Habermas' view on what claims to validity I am making if I wish to participate in a process of reaching understanding with you. Habermas (1979) says that I must choose a comprehensible expression so that we can understand one another. I must have the intention of communicating a true proposition so that we can share my claim to knowledge. I must want to express my intentions truthfully so that we can believe what I say. Finally, I must choose an utterance that is right so that we can accept what I say and we can agree with one another with respect to a recognized normative background. Moreover, communicative action can continue undisturbed only as long as participants suppose that the validity claims they reciprocally raise are justified.

From this I take it that the action-researcher has a responsibility to present a claim to knowledge for public criticism in a way which is comprehensible. The researcher must justify the propositional content of what he or she asserts, and justify the values which are used to give a form to the researcher's life in education. The researcher must be authentic in the sense of wanting to express his or her intentions truthfully. Habermas says, and I agree, that a claim to authenticity can only be realized in interaction:

'in the interaction it will be shown in time, whether the other side is "in truth or honestly" participating or is only pretending to engage in communicative action.'

The personal and social standards I use to judge the academic legitimacy of my claim to knowledge are the values I use in giving my life its particular form in education. In judging my own claim to educational knowledge I use the following logical, scientific, ethical and aesthetic values. In such a brief space all I can hope to do is to sketch out the general principles of my position and to draw your attention to the locations where the position is being worked out in more detail in practice. The most difficult problem to be overcome in presenting my ideas to others in a comprehensible way concerns the logic of my position. As a dialectician I am aware of the attacks on dialectical logic by such eminent Western philosophers as Karl Popper. Popper (1963) dismissed the use of dialectical logic in the presentation of theories as based on nothing better than a loose and woolly way of speaking. His case rests on the way he thinks about contradictions. The point at issue has been clearly put by Ilyenkov (1977):

'Contradiction as the concrete unity of mutually exclusive opposites is the real nucleus of dialectics, its central category . . . but no small difficulty immediately arises as soon as matters touch on 'subjective dialectics', on dialectics as the logic of thinking. If any object is a living contradiction, what must the thought (statement about the object) be that expresses it? Can and should an objective contradiction find reflection in thought? And if so, in what form?'

Formal logicians such as Popper (1963) hold that any theory which contains contradictions is entirely useless as a theory. This view is based upon a linguistic presentation of theory. In this paper I am drawing your attention to the locations (Note 1) where a living form of educational theory is being produced. The theory is embodied in the lives of practitioners who exist as living contradictions. The inclusion of 'I' as a living contradiction within a theoretical presentation creates problems if we attempt this presentation in a purely propositional form because the propositional logic holds that we cannot have two mutually exclusive statements which are true simultaneously.

In my own development I am conscious of attempting to overcome the experience of myself as a living contradiction in order to minimize the tensions between, for example, values negated in practice and the current practice. I am also conscious of the need to give a form to my life and of the need for meaning and purpose. If I attempt to describe my development in a purely propositional form I will fail to communicate my meaning because of the existence of 'I' as a living contradiction in my development. The central problem is how to present a dialectical claim to knowledge in a publicly criticizable form. My own presentation is in the form of ten research reports (Whitehead 1982) produced over the past ten years as I have explored my existence in terms of 'I' as a living contradiction in the School of Education of the University of Bath. I would also draw your attention to the work of colleagues and students of mine, past and present, who are struggling in a similar way to improve the quality of education (see Note 2). By drawing your attention to where the theory is being generated and tested in practice, I hope to emphasize that it is being generated and tested in practice and that it is embodied in the form of life of practitioners rather than existing in a propositional form within textbooks on library shelves.

This is not to deny that the propositional form can have significance for the genesis of educational theory. On the contrary, the standards I use to justify my claim to know my own development as a scientific form of life are drawn from Popper's (1972) views on the logic of scientific discovery. The main difference between the traditional view of educational theory and the dialectical approach is that the traditional view was presented in a propositional form which excluded dialectical logic. The dialectical approach is presented in terms of the forms of life of individuals in education and shows how propositional forms exist within the forms of life.

In using Popper's work I check to see whether or not the claim to know my own educational development conforms to the cycle of experiencing and formulating problems, imagining a solution, acting on the imagined solution, evaluating the outcomes and modifying the problems and ideas. This capacity of the dialectical approach to integrate within itself the insights from a propositional form is what gives the approach its power to integrate the concepts of the disciplines of education. I think that this power rests upon the imaginative capacity of individuals to relate the concepts to their practical concerns. For example, as the individual encounters personal and social constraints in his or her attempts to improve the quality of education in schools, the concepts from the psychology or sociology of education might prove useful in helping to overcome the barriers to improvement. The form I suggested above for the presentation of our claims to know our own educational development has the capacity to allow the inclusion of the concepts from the disciplines of education whilst being itself irreducible to the form of any of the present disciplines of education.

As the individual presents a claim to educational knowledge the academic community will be able to judge whether or not the work demonstrates an understanding of contemporary accounts in the different disciplines of education. It might also be the case that the claims to educational knowledge could point out deficiences in the present state of development of the disciplines of education.

Because of a desire to give a correct account of the nature of educational theory I want to hold up the value-laden nature of my claim to knowledge for public criticism. I want you to understand and accept for good reasons the normative background of my ethical values.

I recognize a major problem, almost as great as the problem of contradiction, as soon as I attempt to communicate the ethical values in my claim to know my educational development. The problem is grounded in the principle known as the autonomy of ethics. This principle, usually attributed to Hume (1738) and upheld by linguistic philosophers, holds that statements of value and statements of fact form logically independent realms of discourse. In my educational development, matters of fact and matters of value are integrated in my experience of practical problems of the kind, 'How do I improve this process of education here?'. How then do I present a claim to know my educational development in a way that truly represents this integration?

I can talk about the ethical values I use in making decisions which give a form to my life in education. I can use value-words such as those of consideration of interest, worthwhile activities, respect for persons and democratic forms of social control (Peters, 1966). The meanings of my ethical values are however embodied in my educational practice. Their meanings emerge in the course of my attempts to overcome their negation (Feyerabend, 1975). In order to communicate these meanings I think that it is necessary to present visual records of that practice. I must show you where I am experiencing the denial of my educational values, give a public formulation of my problems in terms of the denial, and I must present a programme of activities which I believe will overcome the denial. I must show you my actions and hold up my evaluations of those actions for your criticism. In this way it is possible for an individual to hold up a claim to know his or her educational development as an ethical form of life for public scrutiny. The individual can thus generate a personal form of educational theory and submit it for public test.

However, since the meaning of values cannot be expressed in a purely linguistic form of discourse, they must, as I have said, be shown in action. Hence, it will be necessary for whoever is validating the claim to knowledge to use ostensive, as well as linguistic, criticism, in judging this aspect of the claim to knowledge. In judging the legitimacy of a value-laden claim to knowledge the individual is faced with the problem of justifying one set of values against another. In recent Islamic publications (Abdullah, 1982), for example, the Western view of democracy has been declared inimical to educational theory viewed from an Islamic perspective. My own justification for my educational values is grounded within Polanyi's view of personal knowledge. Given that I am using a particular set of values in attempting to give my life its particular form in education, I am committed to examining the implications of attempting to overcome the experience of the negation of these values, in a way which fulfils Habermas' views on the validity claims I must fulfil if I am to reach an understanding with you. If our values conflict it seems to me inevitable that we are engaged in a political struggle. Conflict is most intensive when particular forms of life cut across those of others to the extent of one form negating the value-laden practice of another.

In the justification of a claim for scientific status for the individual's claim to know his or her own educational development I advocated the use of criteria from the work of Popper. To judge the logical status of the claim I suggested the use of a dialectical logic based on the work of Ilyenkov. To judge the ethical status I explained that my values were embodied in practice and that public criticism of the ethical base of my claim would require a form of ostensive criticism in which I must present visual records of my practice. I recognize that the cultural relativity of ethical values presents a serious problem for educators in a multicultural society who are asked to justify their own educational values. How the problem is being resolved must be shown and criticized in practice.

The final criterion is concerned with the notion of authenticity. This is a difficult concept to define because I think of education as a form of art in the sense that the individual is attempting to give a form to his or her life in a way which does not violate the integrity of other individuals. The aesthetic standard I use in judging the authenticity of the claim to knowledge requires an approach I have termed, following Holbrook (1979), 'indwelling'. Its use involves an ability on the part of the reader to empathize (through written, aural and visual records) with another individual's form of life as it is presented in a claim to knowledge and, through 'delicate intuitions, imagination and respect' (Russell, 1916), to judge whether or not the form of life can be seen in terms of the quality of human relationships in which the unity of humanity appears to be possible.

Just as the artist attempts to give a form to his or her material, so teachers, who are practising the art of education, are giving a form to their own lives in education and assisting their pupils to do the same. When the artist presents his or her work, the appreciation of it will come as the viewer spends time 'reliving the work of its creator' (Lipps in Holbrook, 1979). In a similar way, in judging the aesethetic form of a claim to know another individual's form of life in education, the reader must attempt to identify with the process in which that individual struggled to give a form to his or her life in education. In affirming or rejecting the claim to knowledge as embodying an aesthetic form of life it is necessary, I think, for the reader to judge whether the quality of the actions presented in the claim to knowledge has violated the integrity of an individual or the unity of humanity as a whole. I say this because education has, for me, significance not only for its personal influence but also for its role in the world as a whole.

In offering the unit of appraisal and the standards of judgment which I think can be used by educational action-researchers to establish the academic legitimacy of their claims to knowledge I wish to emphasize that the logic of education proposed by Hirst and Peters (1970) is mistaken:

'. . . facts are only relevant to practical decisions about educational matters in so far as they are made relevant by some general view of what we are about when we are educating people. It is the purpose of this book to show the ways in which a view of education must impose such a structure on our practical decisions.'

In my view of educational theory the theory is essentially transformatory. Structures may exist in the process of transformation but they must not be *imposed* on the individual. The idea of imposing a structure is inconsistent with the view of educational knowledge proposed above. I would remind readers that they should always bear Polanyi's point in mind and approach their own claims to knowledge in a creative and critical way as individuals who have made a decision to understand the world from their own point of view, and who are claiming originality and exercising their judgments with universal intent. For the sake of the development of the profession of education they should also feel obliged to offer their claims to knowledge in an open forum for rational criticism.

Every educational action-researcher has a part to play in the development of the profession. Teacher action researchers must be prepared to make public the educational theory which is embodied in their practices. Academic action researchers must be prepared to help to establish the standards of judgment which are appropriate for judging the validity of such claims to knowledge. Administrator action researchers must be prepared to show in what sense their activities are sustaining or improving the quality of education with the pupils in their institutions. My own work is concerned with assisting teacher action researchers to justify their professional claims to know what they are doing through the provision of standards of judgment which themselves can stand the test of public and rational criticism. One reason for writing this Chapter is the hope that it will lead you to contact some of those action-researchers who are participating in the programme or who are described in the bibliography and notes. Through such contact we hope that a shared form of educational theory will be generated and tested in our professional practices. We believe that this will lead to improvement in the quality of education in our educational and other social institutions.

Notes

1) *The Need for a Conference.* The past five years have seen an upsurge in the potential of action research as a way of relating practical and theoretical work in education, and thereby improving the quality of classroom learning. A number of our higher degree students have submitted dissertations using an action research approach and an increasing number of students are registering with us because of the work we do in this area. Because of the work either completed or in progress we are now able to organize a one-day conference which we hope will bring teachers, academics and administrators together. We hope to develop a network of action researchers and also to contribute to in-service days and to DES courses which could help teachers to explore the nature of their educational practice.

2) *The ideas in this Chapter.* These have developed over a number of years through the collaboration, criticism and support of colleagues and students. In particular I have benefited from the support of Dr. Cyril Selmes and Mary Tasker in the School of Education at the University of Bath and from the unpublished Masters Degree dissertations, listed below, of students who have worked with me to improve the quality of education in both theory and practice.

BARRETT, M., (1982), *'An approach to the in-service professional development of teachers'*, University of Bath.

FORREST, M., (1982), *'The teacher as researcher - the use of historical artefacts in primary schools'* , University of Bath.

FOSTER, D., (1982), *'Explanations for teachers' attempts to improve the quality of education for their pupils'*, University of Bath.

GREEN, B., (1979), *'Personal dialectics in educational theory and educational research methodology'*, University of London.

HAYES, G., (1980), *'An investigation of educational practice in the classroom'*, University of Bath.

PETERS, C., (1980), *'Research into the evaluation of youth work'*, University of Bath.

In Chapter Six I am going to ask you, for the third time, to identify with my experience of existing as a living contradiction. On the 1st May 1987 I had to appear before a disciplinary hearing which was chaired by Mr. Richard Mawditt, the Secretary and Registrar. It met under the authority of the University Council to hear complaints from Professors Austwick and Thompson about my activities and writings. The University was represented by The Secretary and Registrar, The Personnel Officer and The University Solicitor. You will see from the correspondence in the next chapter that it is claimed by the Secretary and Registrar that my activities and writings are a challenge to its present and proper organisation and not consistent with the duties the University wished me to pursue in teaching or research. This claim and the power of the University which backed it mobilised a most ferocious response in me. I felt disgust towards those two professors because they did not discuss their complaints face to face before making them to the University and I felt outraged at the University's procedures which permitted my academic work to be judged by a group which contained no academic member of staff.

I was moved by the experience to extend my cognitive range and concerns further into issues of morality, rationality and power through studying the work of Alastair MacIntyre, Richard Bernstein, Michel Foucault and Jürgen Habermas. The force of this third experience marks a transformation in the central concerns within the story of my educational development. Whilst I am still motivated primarily by a concern to reconstruct educational theory I now begin to ground the analysis of my educational development in a relationship between the traditional, propositional forms of academic knowledge, represented in my papers, and in my understanding of my form of life as a living contradiction in the workplace. Before I explored the implications of this transformation in the 1990 and 1992 papers below, I published a paper on creating living educational theories from questions of the kind, 'How do I improve my practice?'. I have been delighted to examine a number of higher degrees in other Universities which have acknowledged the value of this idea of a living educational theory. This delight followed my fury at being subjected to the pressures about to be described in Chapter Six.

Chapter Six: 1987

Living Contradiction: My Writings are Consistent with my Duties as a University Academic. No, they are not.

FOR THE THIRD time I experienced myself as a living contradiction in the workplace. The passion to continue with my contribution to educational knowledge and determination to stand firm in the values of academic integrity, freedom and justice stimulated my imagination to think of an action plan and moved me to act in support of my values.

In April 1987 I was informed by the Secretary and Registrar that two Professors of Education, Jeff Thompson and Ken Austwick, had complained about my activities and writings to the University. On 1st May 1987 the Secretary and Registrar held a meeting, under the authority of the University Council, to hear the complaints. The constitution of this meeting was The Secretary and Registrar, The University Solicitor, The University Personnel Officer, an AUT friend and myself. Following this meeting, in June 1987, The Secretary and Registrar informed me that my activities and writings were a challenge to the present and proper organisation of the University and not consistent with the duties the University wished me to pursue in teaching or research. I was also instructed that I must be loyal to my employer.

As in the previous experiences I was faced with judgements being made in the name of the University. I held the above judgements together with my judgements that I was a creative academic whose educational research was contributing to the good order of the University and who had the academic freedom to research his chosen field and to tutor his research students as determined by his academic integrity. The experience of this disciplinary hearing marked a fundamental change in my perception of my educational development. From this meeting onwards I worked at integrating my experiences of institutional power relations and my understanding of these relations within the story of my educational development. I returned to the documents which related to my fight over tenure and the regime of truth which made and upheld the judgements on the two Ph.D. submissions. I began to understand the dialogical form of the correspondences relating to these cases and saw that I could reconstruct the story of my educational development in a more comprehensive way than my 1985 paper above. The story could integrate my learning from the above experiences of existing as a living contradiction. What follows now is the story of the experiences which finally moved me to integrate my understanding of power relations within my workplace, within a dialogical form, in the story of my educational development.

At the meeting of 1st May 1987 the Secretary and Registrar explained that the complaints from Professor Thompson were focused on three issues. These were the contents of a paper I had presented to an M.Ed. Seminar at Bristol University on 4th February 1987, a letter I was held responsible for sending to the *Times Educational Supplement* (13/2/87) and his allegation that I did not accept his authority as Head of School. The complaint from Professor Austwick was that I had deliberately flouted an instruction he had issued in a letter to a student of July 1986, and that I had published information without authority.

I attended the meeting of the 1st May with the Secretary and Registrar acting on behalf of the University Council, the Personnel Officer, the University Solicitor, and my AUT friend, Rod Brunt.

Following the meeting I made the following notes and sent them to the Personnel Officer.

I have checked through the accounts made by Rod Brunt and me during the disciplinary meeting on Friday 1st May. Could you let me know if you think there are any errors of fact in the background and notes.

Notes on the Meeting

The meeting began with Mr. Whitehead being informed that this was a properly constituted meeting with Mr. Mawditt representing Council as Secretary and Registrar. Mr. Mawditt assured the meeting that only recent behaviour would be considered.

Three Charges were brought by the University Against Mr. Whitehead.

1) The first was based on Professor Thompson, 'holding Mr. Whitehead responsible for a letter which appeared in the <u>Times Educational Supplement</u> on 13.2.87'. This letter was held to be evidence of 'incompetent and perhaps mischievous behaviour'. The Secretary and Registrar stated that this was not the first time the University had received evidence which called the competence of Mr. Whitehead's work into question. He referred to correspondence from Professor Wragg of Exeter University in 1983.

A letter from Professor Thompson of the 4th March 1987 to Mr. Whitehead, all members of staff, the Vice-Chancellor and the Secretary and Registrar, clearly held Mr. Whitehead responsible for the letter to the <u>Times Educational Supplement</u>.

2) *The second charge was unspecified. Professor Thompson had complained about a paper on 'A Living Educational Theory', presented by Mr. Whitehead, to a Higher Degree Seminar at Bristol University on the 4th February 1987. Professor Thompson was 'aggrieved by matters in the paper', specifically on pages 5 and 6. He was also 'aggrieved that his authority was not accepted by Mr. Whitehead'. Mr. Johnson explained that he had thought of recommending action over the paper. It was, however, 'following the letter to the <u>Times Educational Supplement</u> that the position is now unacceptable'.*

3) *The third charge followed the request from Professor Austwick that action be taken against Mr. Whitehead. The charge was that Mr. Whitehead had deliberately flouted an instruction and had 'used information without authority', in papers to conferences and at meetings which was 'disabling his employer from giving facilities', not only to his employment but to the employment of others.*

   The instruction to Mr. Whitehead was contained in a letter sent by Professor Austwick to a student in July 1986. As the student's supervisor Mr. Whitehead had been given a copy of the letter.

   The information, papers, conferences and meetings were unspecified. Reference was made to a confidential letter from the Wiltshire Authority relating to this charge. Mr. Whitehead requested that he see the letter and be given a copy. Both requests were refused.

   Mr Whitehead requested a copy of all statements made by Professor Thompson and Professor Austwick which had played any part in initiating the formal action. Mr. Johnson explained that Mr. Whitehead would receive a letter which would contain details from these statements in relation to the charges being brought.

   In the discussion which followed Mr. Whitehead took up Mr. Johnson's suggestion that it might be wise for all parties to have a meeting before a formal letter was sent to Mr. Whitehead. Mr. Mawditt undertook to see if the two Professors would agree to such a meeting.

The Secretary and Registrar wrote to me on the 24th June to inform me that amongst other things that my activities and writings were a challenge to the present and proper organisation of the University and not consistent with my duties in teaching and research. I was also informed that I must be loyal to my employer.

I think it worth noting that the duties of the Secretary and Registrar, under the Statutes are:

The Council shall appoint a Registrar of the University with such functions, at such remuneration and upon such terms and conditions as it may think fit.

.. to be responsible for providing secretarial services for the Court, the Council, the Senate and any Committees or Joint Committees of these bodies.

It appears that Council permitted the Secretary and Registrar to hear the complaints of two Professors against a member of academic staff and to act on its behalf, with the support of the University Solicitor and Personnel Officer. The order of the University permitted this group to judge the research, writing and teaching of an academic without any representation from the academic members of the University. The questions which I feel I should pursue are: if faced with the above evidence, of actions taken on their behalf, would members of Council accept the order established by such actions as a 'good order'?; faced with such evidence would the Academic Assembly of the University accept that my activities and writing were not consistent with the duties which the University wish me to pursue in relation to my research and teaching?

****

As I have said this experience focused my attention on the significance of the politics of truth and good order for my educational development in my workplace. The paper on creating a living educational theory, which follows in Chapter Seven, was written in 1988 and published in 1989. It shows that I am still primarily concerned with the production of an educational theory for professional practice as if the knowledge being produced were independent of its social context. However, what I now begin to do is to integrate an understanding of the politics of truth and of a good order within accounts of my educational development. I presented such an account in 1990, to the first World Congress on Action Learning, Action Research and Process Management. This follows the 1989 paper and it was published in 1991 in the proceedings of the Congress. I explain my educational development in terms of an attempt to overcome the experience of the violation of integrity, freedom and justice within the workplace as well as attempting to contribute to the creation of a new form of educational theory.

Chapter Seven: 1989

Creating a Living Educational Theory From Questions of the Kind, 'How do I Improve My Practice?'

This paper first appeared in the *Cambridge Journal of Education* Vol.19., No 1, 1989.

Summary

This paper argues that a living educational theory of professional practice can be constructed from practitioner's enquiries of the kind, 'How do I improve my practice?'. The significance of 'I' existing as a living contradiction in such enquiries is considered and other epistemological issues related to values, validity and generalisability are discussed from the living perspective. The process of gaining academic legitimation for a living form of theory is examined in terms of the politics of truth within our Institutions of Higher Education.

Introduction

Have you ever made a claim to know your own educational development and subjected the claim to public criticism? If you have, what does such a claim to educational knowledge look like?

I'm assuming that all readers of this Journal will at some time have asked themselves questions of the kind, 'How do I improve my practice?', and will have endeavoured to improve some aspect of their practice. I believe that a systematic reflection on such a process provides insights into the nature of the descriptions and explanations which we would accept as valid accounts of our educational development. I claim that a living educational theory will be produced from such accounts.

The idea that philosophers interpret the world whilst the point is to improve it, is not a new idea. I have been urging my fellow academics for some years (Whitehead, 1982) to carry out an investigation into their own educational development as they question themselves on how they are improving their practice. I believe that academics who write about educational theory should do just that: make a claim to know their development and subject it to public criticism. In this way I believe that they will come to see that it is possible to create a living educational theory which can be related directly to practice.

Producing a Living Educational Theory

The traditional view is that a theory is a general explanatory framework which can generate descriptions and explanations for empirically observed regularities and the behaviour of individual cases. The explanations are offered in the conceptual terms of propositions which define determinate relationships between variables. Piagetian Cognitive Stage Theory is a classical example of such a theory. By their nature concepts involve grasping principles thus ensuring that theories are presented in general terms.

A commitment to the propositional form can also be seen, surprisingly, in those researchers who are committed to a reflexive approach to understanding. For example, Kilpatrick's (1951) view on the importance of dialogue in educational theory is presented in a propositional form. A more recent example in the work of Gitlin and Goldstein (1987) on a dialogical approach to understanding shows the authors presenting their case within a propositional form. Whilst I can recognise the importance of what they say about teachers forming relationships that enable school change to be based on a joint inquiry into what is really appropriate, I believe that the propositional form of presentation will prevent them getting closer to answering their final, dialogical question, *'How can we encourage the conditions necessary for teachers to enter into a dialogue aimed at understanding?'*.

Even those academics one would expect to understand the need to create an alternative to the propositional form of theory remain within it. For example Donald Schön (1983) points out that:

'when someone reflects-in-action, he becomes a researcher in the practice context. He is not dependent on the categories of established theory and technique, but constructs a new theory of the unique case'.

Schön is however committed to the fundamental category of established theory in holding to the propositional form:

'Theories are theories regardless of their origin: there are practical, common-sense theories as well as academic or scientific theories. A theory is not necessarily accepted, good, or true; it is only a set of interconnected propositions that have the same referent - the subject of the theory. Their interconnectedness is reflected in the logic of relationships among propositions: change in propositions at one point in the theory entails changes in propositions elsewhere in it.

Theories are vehicles for explanation and prediction. Explanatory theory explains events by setting forth propositions from which these events may be inferred. A predictive theory sets forth propositions from which inferences about future events may be made, and a theory of control describes the conditions under which events of a certain kind may be made to occur. In each case, the theory has an 'if...then....' form.' (Argyris, C. and Schön, D., 1975)

I am arguing that the propositional form is masking the living form and content of an educational theory which can generate valid descriptions and explanations for the educational development of individuals. This is not to deny the importance of propositional forms of understanding. I am arguing for a reconstruction of educational theory into a living form of question and answer which includes propositional contributions from the traditional disciplines of education.

Gadamer (1975) points out that despite Plato we are still not ready for a logic of question and answer. He says that Collingwood (1978) helped to move us forward but died before he could develop this logic in a systematic way. Collingwood points out that if the meaning of a proposition is relative to the question it answers, its truth must be relative to the same thing. I agree with his point that meaning, agreement and contradiction, truth and falsehood, do not belong to propositions in their own right; they belong only to propositions as the answers to questions.

In saying that the theory should be in a living form, I recognise that this creates a fundamental problem. The way academics think about theory is constrained by propositional logic. All academics working in the field of educational theory present the theory in terms of propositional relationships. However, the purpose of my own text is to direct your attention to the living individuals and the contexts within which a living theory is being produced (Lomax, 1986). Again I wish to stress that this is not to deny the importance of propositional forms of understanding. In a living educational theory the logic of the propositional forms, whilst existing within the explanations given by practitioners in making sense of their practice, does not characterise the explanation. Rather the explanation is characterised by the logic of question and answer used in the exploration of questions of the form, 'How do I improve my practice?'.

In developing such an approach I have had to come to terms with questions concerning an appropriate methodology for enquiries such as, 'How do I improve this process of education here?'. In looking at video-tapes of my practice I have had to confront the questions which arise on recognising the 'I' in the question as existing as a living contradiction. In the production of an explanation for my practice I have had to question how to include and present values whose meaning can only be clarified in the course of their emergence in practice. I have had to face questions related to validity and generalisability. I have also had to question the power relations which influence the academic legitimacy of a living educational theory.

In such a short article all I can do is outline the present state of my thinking in relation to these questions.

1) How do I improve my practice? - A Question of Methodology.
If we look at the locations where a living form of educational theory is being produced (Lomax, 1986; McNiff, 1992) we can trace the development of a number of teacher-researchers who have used the following form of action reflection cycle for presenting their claims to know their own educational development as they investigate questions of the form:

'How do I improve this process of education here?'
I experience problems when my educational values are negated in my practice.
I imagine ways of overcoming my problems.
I act on a chosen solution.
I evaluate the outcomes of my actions.
I modify my problems, ideas and actions in the light of my evaluations ...(and the cycle continues).

This form of enquiry falls within the tradition of action research. It can be distinguished from other approaches in the tradition through its inclusion of 'I' as a living contradiction within the presentation of a claim to educational knowledge.

2) A Question of Acknowledging one's existence as a living contradiction

My insights about the nature of educational theory have been influenced by viewing video-tapes of my classroom practice. I could see that the 'I' in the question, 'How do I improve this process of education here?', existed as a living contradiction. By this I mean that 'I' contained two mutually exclusive opposites, the experience of holding educational values and the experience of their negation.

I searched the back issues of *Educational Theory* to see if I could find details of similar experiences reported by other researchers. I began to appreciate how the crucial issues of logic and values continued to reappear in the Journal. From Cunningham's (1953) analysis of the 'Extensional Limits of Aristotelean Logic', through Mosier's (1967), 'From Enquiry Logic to Symbolic Logic', to Tostberg's (1976), 'Observations of the Logic Bases of Educational Policy', the debate about the logical basis of educational theory continues to rage in the literature.

A similar debate can be seen in the realm of values. We have 'The role of Value Theory in Education' (Butler, 1954), 'Are Values Verifiable?' (Bayles, 1960); 'Education and Some Moves Towards a Value Methodology' (Clayton, 1969); and 'Knowledge and Values' (Smith, 1976). What these articles pick out is the continuing concern of educational researchers with the fundamental problems of logic and values in the production of educational theory.

I began to understand the concrete problems experienced by adherents to dialectical and propositional logics when they try to establish a sustained dialogue. The nucleus of dialectics, contradiction, is eliminated from descriptions and explanations presented in the propositional form (Popper, 1963). Dialecticians claim that the propositional form masks the dialectical nature of reality (Marcuse, 1964). I traced the tension between these logics to differences between Plato and Aristotle. In the Phaedrus, Socrates tells us that there are two ways of coming to know. We break things down into their separate components and we hold things together under a general idea. He says that those thinkers who can hold both the one and the many together he calls dialecticians. Aristotle, on the other hand, demands, in his work on interpretation, that the questioner puts his question into a definite form and asks whether or not a person has a particular characteristic or not. Aristotle's propositional logic eliminates contradictions from 'correct' thought.

An understanding of a living form developed, in my case, from the combination of the following insight from Wittgenstein with visual records of practice.

'I' is not the name of a person, nor 'here' of a place, and 'this' is not a name. But they are connected with names. Names are explained by means of them. It is also true that it is characteristic of physics not to use these words. (Wittgenstein, 1953)

Now 'I', 'this' and 'here', are contained within questions of the form, 'How do I improve this process of education here?'. In viewing video-tapes of our own educational practices I believe that we can see our own 'I's existing as living contradictions. This revelation, through the visual record, is crucial for the reconstruction of educational theory. Yet there is a tendency to reduce the significance of 'I' as it appears on a page of text. It is so easy to see the word 'I' and think of this as simply referring to a person. The 'I' remains formal and is rarely examined for content in itself. When you view yourself on video you can see and experience your 'I' containing content in itself. By this I mean that you see yourself as a living contradiction, holding educational values whilst at the same time negating them. Is it not such tension, caused by this contradiction, which moves us to imagine alternative ways of improving our situation? By integrating such contradictions in the presentations of our claims to know our educational practice we can construct descriptions and explanations for the educational development of individuals (King, 1987). Rather than conceive educational theory as a set of propositional relations from which we generate such descriptions and explanations I am suggesting that we produce educational theory in the living form of dialogues (Larter, 1987; Jensen, 1987) which have their focus in the descriptions and explanations which practitioners are producing for their own value-laden practice.

3) How do we show our values in action?

The reason that values are fundamental to educational theory is that education is a value-laden practical activity. We cannot distinguish a process as educational without making a value-judgement. I am taking such values to be the human goals which we use to give our lives their particular form. These values, which are embodied in our practice, are often referred to in terms such as freedom, justice, democracy, (Peters, 1966) and love and productive work (Fromm, 1960). When offering an explanation for an individual's educational development these values can be used as reasons for action. For example, if a person is experiencing the negation of freedom, yet believes that she should be free, then the reason why she is acting to become free can be given in terms of freedom, i.e. I am acting in this way because I value my freedom. If someone asks why you are working to overcome anti-democractic forces in the work place then I believe that a commitment to the value of democracy would count as a reason to explain your actions. I do not believe that values are the type of qualities whose meanings can be communicated solely through a propositional form. I think values are embodied in our practice and their meaning can be communicated in the course of their emergence in practice. To understand the values which move our educational development forward, I think we should start with records of our experience of their negation (Larter, 1985,1987). I want to stress the importance of the visual records of our practice. In using such records we can both experience ourselves as living contradictions and communicate our understanding of the value-laden practical activity of education.

Through the use of video-tape the teachers can engage in dialogues with colleagues about their practice. They can show the places where their values are negated. A clear understanding of these values can be shown to emerge in practice through time and struggle (Jensen, 1987). The kind of theory I have in mind forms part of the educational practices of the individuals concerned. It is not a theory which can be constituted into a propositional form. It is a description and explanation of practice which is part of the living form of the practice itself. I have suggested that a dialogical form enables such a theory to be presented for public criticism. Within this form the action reflection cycle has been found (Lomax, 1986) to be an appropriate way of investigating questions of the kind, 'How do we improve this process of education here?'. In this cycle we can study the gradual emergence of our values through time as we struggle to overcome the experience of their negation. We can describe and explain an individual's attempts to improve his or her educational practice (Foster, 1980). This approach to educational theory is being developed in a community of educational researchers who are committed to forming and sustaining a dialogical community (Bernstein, 1983) and who are willing to offer, for public criticism, records of their practice which are integrated within their claims to know this practice (Lomax, 1986). I am suggesting that a form of question and answer can also show how to incorporate insights in the conceptual terms of the traditional forms of knowledge whilst acknowledging the existence of ourselves as living contradictions as we refer to the records of our practice.

4) How do we know that what the researcher says is true?—A Question of Validity
Questions of validity are fundamentally important in all research which is concerned with the generation and testing of theory. Researchers need to know what to use as the unit of appraisal and the standards of judgement in order to test a claim to educational knowledge. I suggest that the unit of appraisal is the individual's claim to know his or her educational development. Within this unit of appraisal I use methodological, logical, ethical and aesthetic standards to judge the validity of the claim to knowledge (Whitehead and Foster, 1984).

Whilst most researchers may find it strange to take a unit of appraisal as their claim to know their educational development I think the unit is clearly comprehensible. My commitment to this unit owes a great deal to the work of Michael Polanyi. As I read *Personal Knowledge* (Polanyi, 1958), and reflected on my positivist approach to research (Whitehead, 1972), Polanyi's work fulfilled its purpose of *'stripping away the crippling mutilations which centuries of objectivist thought have imposed on the minds of men'.*

'In grounding my epistemology in Personal Knowledge I am conscious that I have taken a decision to understand the world from my own point of view, as a person claiming originality and exercising his personal judgement responsibly with universal intent. This commitment determines the nature of the unit of appraisal in my claim to knowledge. The unit is the individual's claim to know his or her own educational development' (Whitehead, 1985).

I have given above some indication of the nature of the standards of judgement I use to test the validity of an individual's claim to know their own educational development. The questions I ask in judging the validity of the claim include:

a) *Was the enquiry carried out in a systematic way? One methodological criterion I have used is the action reflection cycle described above (Foster, 1980; Forrest, 1983).*

b) *Are the values used to distinguish the claim to knowledge as educational knowledge clearly shown and justified?*

c) *Does the claim contain evidence of a critical accommodation of propositional contributions from the traditional disciplines of education?*

d) *Are the assertions made in the claim clearly justified?*

e) *Is there evidence of an enquiring and critical approach to an educational problem?*

I characterise the application of these criteria as an approach to social validation. They are related to Habermas' view on the claims to validity I am making if I wish to participate in a process of reaching understanding with you. Habermas (1976) says that I must choose a comprehensible expression so that we can understand one another. I must have the intention of communicating a true proposition so that we can share my claim to knowledge. I must want to express my intentions truthfully so that we can believe what I say. Finally, I must choose an utterance that is right so that we can accept what I say and we can agree with one another with respect to a recognized normative background. Moreover, communicative action can continue undisturbed only as long as participants suppose that the validity claims they reciprocally raise are justified. However, such claims to knowledge may conform to acceptable standards of judgement yet still raise questions about their generalisability.

5) How can we move from the individual to the universal?—A question of generalisation

Instead of thinking of an educational theory in terms of a set of propositional relationships between linguistic concepts I am proposing a view of educational theory as a dynamic and living form whose content changes with the developing public conversations of those involved in its creation (Whitehead and Lomax, 1987). The theory is constituted by the practitioners' public descriptions and explanations of their own practice. The theory is located not solely within these accounts but in the relationship between the accounts and the practice. It is this relationship which constitutes the descriptions and explanations as a living form of theory. In being generated from the practices of individuals it has the capacity to relate directly to those practices. To the extent that the values underpinning the practices, the dialogues of question and answer and the systematic form of action-reflection cycle, are shared assumptions within this research community, then we are constructing an educational theory with some potential for generalisability. The 'general' in a living theory still refers to 'all' but instead of being represented in a linguistic concept, 'all' refers to the shared form of life between the individuals constituting the theory. Now history shows us that new ideas have often met with scepticism, rejection or hostility from those who are working within the dominant paradigm. Researchers who are trying to make original and acknowledged contributions to their subject, education, might expect powerful opposition to their ideas.

6) Which power relations influence the academic legitimacy of a living educational theory?—A question of the politics of truth

My enquiry has led me to the question of how to support those power relations which support the autonomy of practical rationality within education. As part of this enquiry I think it important to examine the power relations which are distorting, undermining and systematically blocking the development of dialogical communities.

'... In addition to the attempt to recover and reclaim the autonomy of practical rationality and show its relevance to all domains of culture, we realize that today the type of dialogical communities that are required for its flourishing are being distorted, undermined, and systematically blocked from coming into existence.... But today, when we seek for concrete exemplars of the types of dialogical communities in which practical rationality flourishes, we are at a much greater loss. Yet we can recognize how deeply rooted this frustrated aspiration is in human life.' (Bernstein, 1983).

Whilst this part of my enquiry is still embryonic I am continuing to study my own educational development as I engage with the following three problems.

A crucial issue in gaining academic legitimacy for a particular view of educational theory concerns the institutional arrangements for appointing examiners for Research Degrees in Education. For example in some institutions a student is not permitted, under any circumstances, to question the competence of an examiner once the examiner has been appointed by the Senate. Given that the academics in one such institution have committed themselves to the statement, *'A University has a moral purpose in society in the sense of upholding certain standards of truth, freedom and democracy'*, this raises a question on how the academics are upholding these values.

I wish to question the power relations which sustain the view that competence is a matter of appointment rather than of judgement, on the grounds that any academic judgement should, as a matter of principle, be open to criticism and the possibility of incompetence should be acknowledged. Could any academic keep his or her integrity and at the same time accept the truth of power which sustains the view that no questions of competence can be raised in the light of actual judgements?

I argue that, on principle, the power of truth is served by permitting such a challenge in relation to an examiner's judgement rather than seeing competence to be a procedural matter of appointment.

The second problem concerns the problem of self-identification in texts for publication. I would have had a problem in sending this work to a refereed Journal such as *Educational Theory*. The problem follows from a central point in this paper that academics and practitioners should identify themselves in their work-context and, at some point in their research, offer for public criticism a claim to know their own educational development. However, the guidelines and procedures of the staff of *Educational Theory* state:

'Manuscripts are subjected to a double-blind reviewing process (i.e. reviewers do not know the identity of authors, the authors will not learn the identity of reviewers) . . .

To preserve the advantages of blind reviewing, authors should avoid self-identification in the text as well as the footnotes of their manuscripts.'

In asking that an alternative form of presentation is considered by the readership of such Journals as *Educational Theory*, a presentation which demands self-identification, I am conscious of entering, as Walker (1985) says, long-standing and fiercely defended positions in the history and philosophy of science. I do not enter such a debate lightly. I have found it necessary to engage with such politics of educational knowledge for the sake of developing an educational theory which can be directly related to the educational development of individuals.

The third problem is one in which the power relations in the academic community support the power of truth against the truth of power. I am thinking about the problem of testing one's ideas against those of others. In supporting the power of truth against the truth of power, academics offer their ideas for public criticism in a forum where the power of rationality in better argument is paramount. Acknowledging mistakes is a fundamental part in developing our ideas.

In his paper, *Educational Theory, Practical Philosophy and Action Research*, Elliott (1987) treats Hirst (1983) rather gently and chooses a statement which does not fully acknowledge Hirst's mistake in advocating the 'disciplines approach to educational theory'. Elliott quotes:

'It is not so much that what I wrote in 1966 was mistaken as that what I omitted led to a distorting emphasis. Educational theory I still see as concerned with determining rationally defensible principles for educational practice' (Hirst, 1983).

Because our views about educational theory affect the way we see human existence I believe it imperative to acknowledge that mistakes have been made and to understand the nature of these mistakes so that we can move forward.

Paul Hirst has in fact made a most generous acknowledgement that he was mistaken in his view of educational theory.

'In many characterisations of educational theory, my own included, principles justified in this way have until recently been regarded as at best pragmatic maxims having a first crude and superficial justification in practice that in any rationally developed theory would be replaced by principles with more fundamental, theoretical, justification. That now seems to me to be a mistake' (Hirst, 1983).

I believe both Hirst and Elliott are making a mistake in their view of rationality. They both subscribe to a view of rationality which leads them to use a propositional form of discourse in their characterisations of educational theory. What I am advocating is that the propositional form of discourse in the disciplines of education should be incorporated within a living form of theory. This theory should not be seen in purely propositional terms. It should be seen to exist in the lives of practitioners as they reflect on the implications of asking themselves questions of the kind, 'How do I improve my practice?'.

What I wish to do is to push Elliott's position forward. I think Gadamer points the way, but his propositional logic does not permit him to make the creative leap to a new synthesis.

Elliott points out that in developing our understanding we have to risk our values and beliefs. As we open ourselves to the things we seek to understand they will force us to become aware of problematic pre-judgements and to criticise them in the light of new meanings.

Let us be clear about my purpose. I am attempting to make an acknowledged and scholarly contribution to knowledge of my subject, education. This purpose is part of my contract of employment as a University Academic. I have chosen the field of educational theory because I am committed to the profession of education and believe that it needs a theory which can adequately describe and explain the educational development of individuals. I am writing as a professional in education.

In saying this I want to distinguish my activities from those of a philosopher, psychologist, sociologist or historian. I value their contributions to education but I do not believe that educational theory can be adequately characterised by any of them. I believe the limits of philosophers, whose work I have benefited from, such as Elliott, Carr (for example, 1986) and Hirst, are limited by the propositional form of their discourse. As philosophers, rather than educationalists, they have not taken the leap necessary to comprehend the nature of educational theory. I am saying that educationalists, through studying their own attempts to answer questions such as, 'How do I improve my practice?', are constructing a living educational theory within which the work of Hirst, Carr, Elliott, Habermas and Gadamer, is usefully integrated (Eames, 1987, Larter 1987).

It seems to me to be crucial to ask the right questions in Collingwood's sense of moving our enquiry forward. In his work on *Educational Theory and Social Change*, Pritchard (1988) says that the questions are: *'How much do we wish to see, how much do we wish to understand? What conceptions, and alternative conceptions, of human practices do we have that will enable us to enhance and significantly enrich life and well-being?'*.

Pritchard argues that we urgently need studies within educational theory which will serve to demystify institutions and to unmask ideologies. He concludes:

'It is evident that the attempt to "raid" the disciplines of education and to use material drawn from these areas without considerable theoretical understanding and support is ill-advised and, ultimately, is based upon an incoherent conception of the theory of education.'

My worry is that Pritchard's questions are still grounded within the conceptual forms of the disciplines of education. In order to construct an educational theory for professional practice I believe we will have to face the practical and theoretical implications of asking ourselves questions of the kind, 'How do I improve **my** practice?'.

In the past I have been critical of academics who are unwilling to study their own educational development and subject their claim to know this development to social validation (Whitehead and Foster, 1984). It seems that Whitty (1986) voices a similar criticism in the context of the work of American and Australian sociologists on the politics and sociology of education:

'Yet, if the prescriptions of these writers are not to remain purely rhetorical, there is an urgent need for them to engage in an active exploration of the implications of their work among the political constituencies in whose interests it is supposedly being carried out' (Whitty 1986).

I hope to demonstrate my own engagement by investigating how relations which support the power of truth against the truth of power influence my own educational development. These influences are emerging as I engage with the politics of truth within arenas such as the Educational Research Associations and Institutions of Higher Education.

In conclusion I identify with a conversation between Giles Deleuze and Michel Foucault which considers the necessity for the practitioner of speaking on his or her own behalf:

'You were the first to teach us something absolutely fundamental: the indignity of speaking for others. We ridiculed representation and said it was finished, but we failed to draw the consequences of this theoretical conversion - to appreciate the theoretical fact that only those directly concerned can speak in a practical way on their own behalf' (Foucault, 1980).

The paper presented in Chapter Eight shows the beginning of the transformation in my understanding of my educational development from the propositional logic of my previous papers into the dialogical and dialectical forms of this text. As I said above, this transformation came out of the fury and disgust I experienced following the disciplinary hearing in 1987. I continued to think about the nature of an educational theory which could explain the educational development of an individual. My determination had been strengthened by the above violations to my academic freedom, integrity and sense of social justice. I presented the paper at the First World Congress on Action Learning, Action Research and Process Management in Brisbane in July 1990. I think you will see that I am now integrating my understanding of my existence as a living contradiction within the power relations of my workplace in the explanation for my educational development.

Chapter Eight: 1990

How do I improve my Professional Practice as an Academic and Educational Manager? A Dialectical Analysis of an Individual's Development and a basis for Socially Orientated Action Research

This paper was first published in the *Proceedings of the First World Congress on Action Learning, Action Research and Process Management,* edited by Colins, C., and Chippendale, P., published by Acorn Press, Australia. 1991.

Abstract

This paper outlines a dialectical approach to educational action research and attempts to synthesise a process of personal development with a process of social evolution. The dialectical approach is characterised as a process of question and answer in which an individual 'I' exists as a living contradiction in questions of the kind, 'How do I improve my practice?'. The potential of educational action research for social evolution is examined in terms of an individual's responses to contradictions in the workplace. These contradictions involve the loss of one's employment, the denial of one's originality, the denial of the right to ask questions, being disciplined for what one writes and **then having one's research legitimated in the M.Ed Curriculum of a University School of Education**.

Like critical action research (Carr and Kemmis, 1986) the dialectical approach will be shown to incorporate a consideration of values and power. This will be shown in two examples of action research and the processes of educational management. The first example involves my own academic development in relation to the good order and politics of truth of a University. The second involves my contribution to the educational management of a comprehensive school. From these examples it is argued that the dialectical approach can generate valid explanations for the educational development of an individual in a way which shows that the production of a living form of educational theory from such explanations can have implications for social evolution.

Introduction

The heuristic potential of action research is currently being explored in a variety of forms and fields of knowledge within this Congress. In the field of education, action research has become a major force in teachers' professional development, in educational management and educational theory. My own contribution to the field has focused on my claim to know my own educational development in the course of my enquiry, 'How do I improve the quality of my practice?'. My early methodological questions progressed into epistemological enquiries related to the values, logic, unit of appraisal and standards of judgement which could be used to test claims to know the nature and processes of education (Whitehead and Foster, 1984). I became interested in trying to create a dialectical form of educational theory for producing valid explanations for the educational development of an individual (Whitehead, 1985a). My attempts to gain academic legitimacy for this dialectical approach to educational knowledge developed into questions concerning the good order and politics of truth in a University (Whitehead, 1985b). These have led to the questions in this paper concerning educational action research and social evolution. I want to explore with you the potential of an individual's action research, for linking educational theory and the politics of educational knowledge with social evolution, in the context of academic and institutional management.

The dialectical nature of my enquiry, 'How do I improve my practice?' can be distinguished from other approaches to action research as it is an attempt to answer the question of contradiction posed by Ilyenkov *(op. cit.)*

In looking at video-tapes of my own teaching I came to appreciate that 'I' existed in my question as a living contradiction in Ilyenkov's sense that I hold two mutually exclusive opposites together in practice. I could experience myself holding certain educational values whilst at the same time denying them in my practice. For example, I could experience myself valuing my pupils' capacities to learn by enquiry whilst at the same time closing down their opportunity for doing so by the way I structured my lessons (Whitehead, 1977). I believe that the incorporation of 'I' as a living contradiction in explanations for the educational development of individuals, has distinguished an original contribution to the action research movement by researchers associated with the School of Education of the University of Bath (Elliott, 1989; Lomax, 1989; McNiff, 1992; Whitehead, 1989). The characteristic action research methodology which incorporates 'I' and which has developed from this work has the form: I experience problems or concerns when some of my values are denied in my practice; I imagine ways of improving my practice and choose a course of action; I act and gather evidence which will enable me to make a judgement on the effectiveness of my actions; I evaluate the outcomes of my actions; I modify my concerns, ideas and actions in the light of my evaluation.

In analysing this claim to know my own educational development I took the unit of appraisal to be the individual's claim to know her or his own educational development. The standards of judgement I used to characterise my claim to knowledge as 'educational' included the form of the action research cycle above, Ilyenkov's criteria for characterising dialectical logic, the values defined by Peters (1966) and the aesthetic/spiritual values in Buber's characterisation of the I-You relationship (Whitehead, 1985a).

I then examined the possibility of moving from such a dialectical base into a living form of educational theory. By a 'living' theory I mean that the explanations generated by the theory to explain the educational development of individuals contain an evaluation of past practice and evidence of present practice which includes the 'I's' intention (a human goal) to produce something valued which is not yet in existence. I now claim that it is possible to construct such a theory from the explanations which individuals produce for their own educational development (Whitehead, 1989b).

My enquiry moved into the politics of truth as I encountered the power relations which legitimated the judgements on two Ph.D. submissions to the University of Bath. These judgements stated that I had not shown an ability to conduct original investigations or to test my own ideas or those of others and that my work did not contain matter worthy of publication. These power relations also legitimated the instruction that under no circumstances could I question the competence of my examiners. In understanding these power relations I have used Foucault's insights into the conflict between the truth of power and the power of truth in an analysis of the procedures and rules which surround the legitimation of a dialectical claim to educational knowledge in a University.

I accept Foucault's (1977) distinction between the 'specific intellectual' as opposed to the 'universal intellectual'. He says that for a long period the 'left' intellectual was acknowledged as a champion of truth and justice. The specific intellectual was a spokesperson of the universal in the sense of moral, theoretical and political choices. In opposition to the universal intellectual, he describes the specific intellectual in terms of an engagement in a struggle at the precise points where their own conditions of life or work situate them. Foucault takes care to emphasise that by 'truth' he does not mean *'the ensemble of truths which are to be discovered and accepted.'* By 'truth', he means the ensemble of rules according to which the true and the false are separated and specific effects of power attached to the true. The struggles 'around truth' are not 'on behalf' of the truth, but about the status of truth and the economic and political role it plays.

I am offering the following account of my struggle to support the good order and the power of truth of a University as part of my enquiry into the relationship between action research, educational theory, the politics of truth and social evolution. I see this enquiry as developing from my earlier analysis of an individual's educational development which has provided the basis for personally orientated action research (Whitehead, 1985b). I am now attempting to produce a basis for socially orientated action research which will incorporate my earlier ideas.

Extending the Educational Enquiry from a personal into a social orientation—Social concerns grounded in contradictions

I wish to characterise this extension into a socially orientated action research by a dialogical form of presentation. This choice was influenced by Kilpatrick's (1951) point that educational theory is a form of dialogue which has profound implications for the future of humanity. I will begin to extend this social orientation by acknowledging my identification with the meanings in the following conversation between David Bohm (1988) George Wikman and others in which Bohm is affirming the value of originality in the perception of new meanings and relating this perception to social change:

'David Bohm: ... What actually has value would be to have a constantly creative culture. Now I suggest that such creativity is related to a constant discovery of new meanings. Generally speaking we start from old meanings and commonly make small changes in them. Sometimes we may, however, perceive a big change of meaning. An idea changes in a fundamental way although, of course some old features are still carried along, no matter how big the change is.

George Wikman: But what is it that really happens when you perceive a new meaning?

David Bohm: That's the creative step. If I say that meaning is being and something new is perceived in a meaning, something has changed in being. For example, all the perceptions that took place in science changed the meaning of the world for us and this changed the world. It first changed in the sense that we saw it differently: but science also changed the physical, the somatic level. The entire earth has been changed and it could have changed a lot more, for the better or for the worse. Therefore, at least in my own experience, being and meaning are there together.

And I'm proposing this more generally. So if somebody sees a different meaning to society or to life, that will change society. Every revolution has come from somebody seeing a different meaning in human society. For example, the meaning that some people saw was that of a very static society, where everybody was in his place and the top was overlooking the bottom. Then other people saw a different meaning, according to which people should be equal. That different meaning was the power that generated the change...' (Pylkannen, 1989).

The new meaning I am seeking to share is in showing what it means for individual researchers to speak on their own behalf as they attempt to transcend the truth of power through the power of truth in their workplace. This meaning is extended in the second enquiry as I explore the nature of educative relationships within the power of truth. I argue that 'educational' researchers who are making claims to educational and professional knowledge should be showing how they are enabling the professionals and their pupils and students to speak on their own behalf. It is the idea that researchers should be showing what it means for themselves to be living more fully their values in their workplace and showing how they are enabling the 'researched' to speak on their own behalf which I am offering as a basis for socially-orientated, educational action research.

As a dialectician who is interested in moving understanding forward through a process of question and answer I accept the category of contradiction as the nucleus of dialectics. I also believe that social change and transformation can be understood in terms of the attempts by human beings to resolve their consciously lived contradictions. Because of these assumptions I will begin with the five experiences of contradiction which have moved me into the present phase of my enquiry. I am hoping that you will identify with these contradictions and my responses in the sense that they raise fundamental questions about human existence. I am thinking of questions concerning the appropriate response to: being sacked; having one's originality and the right to ask questions denied; being told that one's research and teaching were inconsistent with one's duties to an employer; being asked to teach a curriculum based upon one's own research and writings which were at the focus of the earlier disputes and contradictions.

Whilst these contradictions are socially and historically located within a particular time and culture I am interested in exploring the potential significance of the ensuing actions for social evolution. What I have in mind is the possibility that you will identify with the experience of the truth of power which denies the individual the right to practise his or her vocation; which denies the individual the right to ask questions; which refuses to acknowledge the individual's contribution to knowledge; which mobilises other power relations to try to prevent the individual teaching and researching a chosen area. I think you will identify with these experiences in the historical sense that many other individuals have been subjected to such power relations and that the course of social evolution can partly be understood in terms of the responses which individuals and groups have made to these experiences of oppression. In my own case I am hoping that you will identify with my responses to the following contradictions in the sense that you will feel moved by them to help to generate a living form of educational theory which has implications for social evolution through its goal of human betterment.

Holding Together an Academic Vocation and Having One's Employment Terminated
The first major contradiction I had to come to terms with involved both my economic well being and my sense of vocation to make a contribution to the reconstruction of educational theory through my work in the University. Being informed that my employment was terminated meant that I experienced the contradiction of holding my sense of vocation together with the denial of my sense of vocation in the grounds given below to sack me. The grounds given for terminating my employment were:

The Academic Staff Committee's grounds for recommending that a new appointment should not be offered are as follows:-

1. *That you have not given satisfaction in the teaching of prescribed courses assigned to you.*

2. *That there is an absence of evidence to suggest that you have pursued research of sufficient quality for the assessors to be assured of your ability to perform adequately the duties of a University Lecturer; the objectives being to make acknowledged scholarly contributions to the advancement of your subject as well as to perform proper teaching and other administrative tasks.*

3. *That you have exhibited forms of behaviour which have harmed the good order and morale of the School of Education.*

The power behind these judgements was reinforced by their acceptance by the University Senate. Given the force of the judgements I think you will appreciate how much energy and commitment were required to overthrow them. I owe my existence as a tenured academic of the University to the commitment, values, actions and political and legal understandings of other individuals both within and outside the University (Whitehead, 1985b). I simply wish to share this insight with you as an acknowledgement that my past and future contributions to education, in the University, are grounded in those individuals who refused to accept the above judgements on my work. Because they engaged in the necessary political activities they overcame the power relations which were attempting to sustain these judgements. In recognition of their ethical and political commitments I could not in future jeopardise this tenure in the quest for promotion in the University of Bath. In the University, promotion is now accompanied by a loss of tenure.

Holding Together Originality and the Right to Ask Questions with their Denial
The second and third contradictions are focused on my failure to gain academic legitimacy for two Ph.D. theses I submitted to the University in 1980 and 1982 entitled, 'Educational Practice and its Theory' and 'A Dialectical Approach to

Education'. The second contradiction is grounded in the denial of my originality by the University's examiners and Board of Studies for Education. I am thinking of my claim to originality in my decision to ground my understanding of the world within personal knowledge (Polanyi, 1958). The ability to make original contributions to one's subject is traditionally respected in academic life. These original contributions are often submitted for Ph.D. examination in which examiners are asked to judge the originality of the text. When my examiners were asked the question as to whether I had demonstrated an ability to conduct original investigations, to test my own ideas and those of others, they claimed that I had not shown such an ability. These judgements were accepted by the Board of Studies for Education and my appeal against these judgements was rejected by the Board of Studies in November 1980. My approach to overcoming this contradiction has been a public one. I have great faith in the truth-seeking capacities of human beings. That is why I believe I must subject my claims of originality to public test in contexts such as this World Congress. Just as I have faith in our truth-seeking capacities I have faith that our creativity and originality together with our critical abilities will move our ideas forward. In time you will be able to judge whether I have shown an ability to conduct original investigations, to test my own ideas and those of others or whether my examiners were correct in denying that I had shown these abilities. Whether you make your own judgements public is up to you.

The third contradiction was grounded in a judgement on the University Regulations that once examiners had been appointed by the Senate under no circumstances could their competence be questioned. Given that I wished to question the competence of my examiners on the grounds of political bias, prejudice and inadequate assessment I had to hold such questioning together with the force of an instruction from the University that under no circumstances could I question their competence.

I overcame this contradiction on 1st June 1990 with a presentation to a research seminar at the Centre for the Study of Management Learning at the University of Lancaster on 1st June 1990 (Whitehead, 1990). I outlined my arguments for demanding the right to question the competence of my examiners on the grounds of bias, prejudice and inadequate assessment. In presenting the evidence which I believe would convince any rational individual that there is a case to answer I felt protected by the law which guarantees my academic freedom to ask questions.

Holding Together the Power of Truth and the Truth of Power

I experienced my fourth contradiction on May 1st 1987 when I attended a meeting held under the authority of the University Council to hear complaints about my activities and writings which had been made to the University by two Professors of Education. I was in no doubt that my activities and writings were being viewed as incompatible with the duties the University wished me to pursue in teaching and research. I was thus faced with holding together my support for the power of truth in researching the politics of truth within my University together with the truth of power within the University which was attempting to block this research.

Holding Together the Acceptance of my Research in the School's Curriculum with the Above Contradictions

I experienced my fifth contradiction at the Board of Studies of Education on May 9th 1990 when the Board agreed to send to Senate a recommendation to add two Action Research Modules to the M.Ed. programme - the highest level of taught course in the School of Education. The upsurge of interest in action research approaches to professional development has convinced the majority of staff in the School of Education that we should offer taught courses on action research. These modules, whilst drawing on the work of other academics, clearly reference my research and writings over my seventeen years in the University. Hence I was faced with the experience of contradiction of holding together the experience of the Board of Studies legitimating my research and writings in the taught M.Ed. programme with the experience of the University's and Board of Studies' denial of the legitimacy of this knowledge in previous judgements on my research. So I am in the position of being asked to teach a curriculum which includes references to the activities, writings, teaching and research whose legitimacy has been denied in judgements which are still in force.

Moving the Enquiry Forward

The fourth and fifth contradictions are related and I will now outline the action cycle I am using to resolve these contradictions by moving my enquiry forward into the good order and politics of truth within the University. What I mean by good order is related to the values of the Academic Assembly of the University:

> 'High sounding phrases like "values of freedom, truth and democracy," rational debate", "integrity", have been used. It is easy to be cynical about these and to dismiss them as hopelessly idealistic, but without ideals and a certain agreement about shared values a community cannot be sustained, and will degenerate. These are the phrases in which members of Academic Assembly have chosen to convey their concept of this community.' (The Idea of a University. Academic Assembly, University of Bath, 1988).

The Statutes of the University enable Academic Assembly to remain a democratic forum to discuss any matter of concern to the University and to pass resolutions to Senate. It is this capacity to support the power of truth against the truth of power through dialogue and democratic decision making which has focused my attention on the value of Academic Assembly in sustaining and promoting the good order of the University. Given this context my next question is, 'Can I relate action research to social evolution through an analysis of an individual's educational development?' I think Foucault (1980) points the way to answer this question through his idea that as a university academic I occupy a specific position in the economy which is linked to the politics of truth within our society. If I use this idea to show how I am changing power relations which are related to that regime of truth which is essential to the structure and functioning of our society and our world, have I not established the practical principle that this individual's actions can be related to social evolution?

My question is related to Bohm's earlier point about a constantly creative culture. I am trying to show what it means for an academic to try to constitute a 'good' order in his workplace through giving a new meaning to the relationship between the power of truth and the truth of power - a meaning which is part of the process of transcending the truth of power through the power of truth. I think my proposals for a socially-orientated educational action research rests on the extent to which you identify these contradictions as intrinsic to the power relations in your own societies and forms of life.

I claim that these contradictions can be understood in terms of a conflict between the power of truth and the truth of power. At one pole of the contradictions in my workplace is the power of truth in the values embodied by the Academic Assembly. At the other pole of the contradiction are the negations of these values in judgements which have been upheld by the truth of power of the University Council, Senate and a Board of Studies. I thus see my educational development in the good order and politics of truth in the University as an examination of what it takes to move the power of truth into an ascendancy over the truth of power. I propose to try to achieve this through public debate and dialogue within the above bodies and in contexts such as this, outside the University.

I want to make a distinction between action research and educational action research in terms of values. If action research is characterised by a particular form of systematic enquiry then there is no necessity to justify the value base of the enquiry in defining the research as 'action research'. Action research could, in these terms, be used to increase the efficiency of activities which could be morally unacceptable. In claiming that my research is 'educational' I am committing myself to upholding the values of good order. I am not willing to accept the term 'educational' to describe activities which are undermining these values.

In undertaking educational action research I accept the responsibility of making public the values which I use to characterise my activities as 'educational'. In showing what it means for an individual's educational development to try to live by the values which are embodied in the Academic Assembly's notion of good order and in trying to ensure the ascendancy of the power of truth over the truth of power I am attempting to establish a basis for a socially orientated, educational action research.

I am not restricting my view of 'educational development' to the traditional view of educational institutions such as schools, colleges, polytechnics and universities. I see any development in which individuals are learning what it means to live more fully their values in their practice as potentially 'educational'. The generality of my account and hence its relationship to social evolution rests upon the way in which others identify their contradictions with my own and find it useful in making sense of their own lives in their own action enquiry in the workplace.

The kind of enquiry I have in mind is like the first one below in which I move from an examination of the concerns created by the experience of contradiction, to the design of an action plan, to acting, evaluating and modifying concerns, plans and actions.

I now want to present the evidence on the development of my latest action cycles. The first concerns the educational management of my own learning in the good order and politics of truth within the University of Bath. The second presents evidence from my enquiry, 'How do I improve the quality of my contribution to the educational management of a comprehensive school?'. The evidence demonstrates my support for the introduction of an action research approach to professional development with its commitment to democratic procedures within the school. I want to use the second example to illustrate a point about the nature of educative relationships which I believe will challenge the validity of the propositional writings of many 'educational' researchers, particularly those researching the professional learning of teachers. At the end of each enquiry I will briefly review how I see the present position.

Constructing an Action Plan and Acting

The experiences of the contradiction and conflicts discussed above led me to submit a paper to the Secretary of the Board of Studies of the School of Education, under an item dealing with the Good Order of the School of Education, for a meeting on 9th May 1990. I wished to raise the issues concerning the above contradictions in relation to the organisation and curriculum of the School. The Head of the School of Education sought the advice of the Secretary and Registrar who ruled that the matter was not appropriate business for the Board of Studies.

Evaluation and Modified Plan

This rejection was followed by a discussion with the Head of School. My evaluation was that, if I was to set out my reasons for believing that the item was appropriate matter under the University Statutes, for consideration by the Board of Studies, then the rationality of my case would convince him to include it on the Agenda. This led me to respond with the reasons why I believed that the matter was appropriate for the Board of Studies and why I believed the matter was related to the good order of the School of Education in relation to the University Statutes. The Head of School is responsible to the Vice-Chancellor for the good order of the School of Education and my response was based on my feeling that I had not communicated my intentions clearly enough. I am seeking to place material before the Board of Studies which will reveal fundamental contradictions in its judgements relating to the organisation of teaching, research and the curricula of the School. I am also trying to explain how such contradictions have arisen and what might be done to resolve them. At its meeting on 20th June 1990, the Board decided that it should discuss the issue and I might now submit my material to the next meeting in October 1990.

I can also locate my understanding of the value of academic freedom in relation to the politics of truth, in the context of the invitation to present a paper on my research to this Congress. Following complaints made by two Professors of Education about my activities and writings at the hearing on 1st May 1987, the University required me to submit such papers to the Head of School before publication so that I might be told if I am prejudicing the University's relationships. I have submitted this present paper to the Head of School in the context of the Educational Reform Act which states that:

'... academic staff have freedom within the law to question and test received wisdom, and to put forward new ideas and controversial or unpopular opinions, without placing themselves in jeopardy of losing their jobs or privileges they may have at their institutions.'

Criteria for Judging Effectiveness

In the design of an action plan I always encourage my students to include the details of the kind of evidence they would need to enable them to make a judgement on their effectiveness. I also encourage them to make explicit the criteria on which these judgements are based. I will make a similar demand of myself evaluating the effectiveness of my actions. I would expect to see my research papers showing a developing understanding of an individual's educational development in relation to the good order and politics of truth in a university. In making judgements with universal intent I judge my effectiveness in terms of the extent to which my ideas are useful to others in their attempts to make sense of their own educational practice. If my questioning is fundamental and we experience ourselves as existing in more creative rather than hostile cultures then I would expect others to participate in the creation of a public living educational theory which could be shown to have profound implications for the future of humanity (Kilpatrick, 1951). I believe that this will occur as we explore and share what it means for our educational development as we live more fully the values of freedom, truth, democracy, rational debate and integrity, in our workplace and world and create a living educational theory through dialogue.

In evaluating my past practice I am aware of the social relations which protected my job, when my employment was terminated in 1976, and the social relations implicit in my use of the ideas of others in making sense of my own life. For example, I owe my ability to articulate my decision to understand the world from my own point of view as a person claiming originality and exercising his judgement with universal intent to Polanyi's (1958) insights into the grounds of personal knowledge. I use this insight in defining the unit of appraisal in my claim to educational knowledge. I take the unit to be an individual's claim to know her or his own educational development. In developing my understanding of the implications of the standards of judgement I use in testing my claims to educational knowledge for social evolution I have been influenced by Habermas' views in communication and the evolution of society. I accept Habermas' (1976) point that the validity claims I am making in my attempt to communicate can be judged in terms of coherence, values, truth and authenticity (Whitehead, 1989b). When I consider the validity of my claims to educational knowledge I also draw upon MacIntyre's (1988) insight that the rival claims to truth of contending traditions of enquiry depend for their vindication upon the adequacy and the explanatory power of the histories which the resources of each of those traditions in conflict enable their adherents to write. I thus see the extension of my enquiry into questions concerning social evolution to be related to the ground of my judgements in personal knowledge in that the judgements are being made responsibly with universal intent.

In addition to these points concerning validity I am interested in developing an understanding of an appropriate concept of rigour for action research. Winter (1989) has proposed six principles for the rigorous conduct of action-research which he refers to as Reflexive and Dialectical Critique, Collaborative Resource, Risk, Plurality of Structure, and Theory, Practice, Transformation. These principles, whilst open to refinement, for example in the understanding of the values which are required to conduct a rigorous form of educational action research, are the principles which I accept as appropriate for judging the rigour of my own enquiry.

I now want to move the context of my enquiry from the educational management of my professional development as an academic researcher into the context of my contribution to the educational management of a comprehensive school. I have shown what it means for a dialectical action researcher to speak on his own behalf. I now want to show what it means to engage in a dialectical form of action research in which one's professional colleagues are being encouraged to develop democratic forms of decision making and being enabled to speak, in the research, on their own behalf.

Dialectical Action Research in the Social Context of a School

I now want to extend my action enquiry into the social base of a secondary school through answering the question, 'How do I improve my contribution to the educational management of a Comprehensive School through my activities as Chair of Governors?'

Concerns

In particular I want to focus on the values of rationality and democracy and present the evidence to show how I am trying to embody these values in my form of life. Following on from my previous analysis I want to show what it means for me to be engaged in action research in which the power of truth is in the ascendancy over the truth of power. I want to do this by showing what it means to empower a teacher to speak on his own behalf rather than for me, as a researcher, to make a claim to knowledge about the professional learning of teachers without enabling teachers to speak for themselves. In judging my efforts to improve the quality of my contribution to the educational management of a secondary school I wish to focus on the value of rationality as it is embodied in the action research cycle and the value of democractic procedures in staff selection.

I will relate my enquiry to the evidence provided by the Acting Head of the school in relation to the acceptance of an action research approach to professional development and to the first democratic election for a staff development tutor. The extracts from the school's and the Local Education Authority's (L.E.A.) policy documents below show that I have moved my contribution from a position where I was part of a management structure supporting forms of professional development which did not incorporate the above view of rationality to a position which supported the above view of rationality in the way described below.

Actions

Over the past four years Avon L.E.A. has paid the University of Bath a consultancy fee to enable me to spend some time promoting action research with teachers. In March 1990, Avon L.E.A. published a booklet on 'You and Your Professional Development', which commits the Authority to providing the majority of its INSET (In-Service Education of Teachers) support through an action-research approach to professional development.

The following extracts from a paper from the Acting Head of the School to the Senior Management Team dated 5/3/90 show clearly the integration of an action research approach into the School's policy for staff development for 1990-91.

'We have for a long time at Culverhay been very concerned about an INSET Policy which requires teachers to LEAVE their classes with a supply teacher, often with no expertise in the subject area, and for understandable reasons without the same commitment to the progress of the pupils.

The advantage to the School of teachers engaged in this form of INSET is also questionable, although we have tried to reduce the problems of 'cascading' by having a 'reporting back' form, which is then circulated to the relevant members of staff.

From the L.E.A. draft Staff Development Policy, it is clear that INSET should now be much more CLASSROOM based, and resources should be allocated to support teachers as they carry out their work. Several Culverhay Staff have been involved in such INSET/STAFF DEVELOPMENT over the last few years, and the most recent example was the STRICT initiative (Supporting Teacher Research Into Classroom Teaching).

Staff are gaining experience in 'action research' techniques, which basically follows the pattern shown below:

1. *The teacher identifies or is presented with a problem, and chooses a colleague to work with to help find a solution ...*

2. *The teacher works with the colleague both inside and outside the classroom, with the aim of devising an approach which will improve the quality of education provided ...*

3. *The lesson is taught, and information collected as the class proceeds which will highlight whether or not the approach is a successful one ...*

4. *Following the class, the lesson is assessed by the two teachers ...*

5. *The next stage requires a new improved approach to the topic to be devised, building on the experience gained from the research ...*

Thus the cycle of events can be continued, with both colleagues benefiting professionally from the experience, and the quality of the classroom teaching hopefully improving as a result'

The following extract from the Acting Head shows my own commitment to the democractic principle of staff selecting their own staff development tutor.

'We have been asked by the L.E.A. to appoint a Staff Development Tutor. This position should be assessed annually. The role/qualities of this person are outlined below:-

1. *The Staff Development Tutor (S.D.T.) will be required to help staff decide on which aspects of their classroom work they wish to develop through Action Research.*

2. *The S.D.T., to be effective, needs to be accepted by his or her colleagues as an equal partner. He or she needs to be able to work alongside teachers in an open and supportive way ..... The Chair of Governors and I are both happy to see the Staff select and appoint a S.D.T. for 1990-91.'* (School Policy document 20/4/90).

Evaluation

My claim to be improving my contribution to the educational management of Culverhay School rests upon the evidence of the integration of an action research approach to professional development in the school's policy and practices. It was grounded in my view of the rationality of action research as an approach to improving the quality of education with teachers and pupils and the support for the extension of democratic practices in the workplace. The latter was exemplified in the process of staff selection of their own Staff Development Tutor.

I want to emphasise that the evidence I have presented for my claim to be contributing to improvements in educational management of a school was provided in the writings of a teacher. These were not my words; they were his. In seeing my contribution to educational management as a form of educative relationship I think my claims to educational knowledge of such relationships rest upon the acknowledgement by others of the value they have found in my activities, research and writings.

Modified Plans

On 26th June 1990 the local authority agreed to fund a curriculum innovation on technical and vocational education in the school. The teaching and learning styles favoured by this innovation are similar to the form of action cycle described above. My plans are to support the development of a school-based action research group to help the teachers to answer questions of the kind, 'How do I improve my practice?', in relation to this innovation. I will be helping to gather evidence and to evaluate the practitioners' research reports in an attempt to see if it is possible to produce reports in which both the pupils and the teachers are speaking on their own behalf. I would like to extend this idea of 'speaking on your own behalf' into 'educational' research in general, by asking a number of questions of my professional and academic colleagues.

In submitting my ideas for your criticism I am conscious of the vulnerability which comes from an openness to change because one recognises failure and error. I want you to recognise an original contribution to educational research. I may not receive such recognition because you may rightly refuse this acknowledgement. I trust that your acknowledgements or refusals will rest upon the power of your rational criticism in support of the power of truth and that you will present your criticisms openly and in a public arena.

In presenting my ideas in the above form I am conscious that it may contain an implicit criticism of your own ideas. I am thinking of those of you who claim to belong to an educational research community and who, whilst believing that your research is 'educational', do not show what your research means for your own or others' educational practice. I am addressing the following points and questions to all those who believe that their research is 'educational research'.

Further Questions

I am assuming that we share the conviction that it was right to abandon the disciplines approach to education research (dominant in the 1960s and 1970s) because it was both mistaken (Hirst, 1983) and, by virtue of the ideological power of its proponents, because it was exercising a damaging influence on the views of teachers and academics. The power of many of your criticisms helped to create a climate in which alternative views began to emerge. My worry is that you have replaced the ideological hegemony of the disciplines approach with the hegemony of your own critical/ interpretative and thus propositional forms which are clearly identified through their organising concepts as a philosophy of education (Carr, 1989 and Carr and Kemmis, 1986; Rudduck, 1989), a sociology of education (Whitty, 1986), a history of education (Hamilton, 1989, 1990) and a psychology of education (Calderhead, 1988). I recognise these texts as having value for my educational discourse but they contain no synthesis which enables education to be viewed in a way which is holistic and dynamic. If you believe your research to be 'educational', in whose sense is it 'educational'? Can you substantiate a claim to be 'educational researchers' without an examination of your own or another's educational development? I am hoping that you will respond to my questions in a way which can help to establish a personal and social basis for educational action research and help to create a living educational theory which may indeed have 'profound implications for the future of humanity'. In asking such questions I am wondering if you experience contradictions in your workplace. Watkins (1987) in his research on the contested workplace has argued that:

> 'during work experience the contradictions of work are exposed and thus may serve to undermine the existing social relations of work by revealing both the oppositional forms and the stark "reality" of the workplace'.

As well as conducting research on students I wonder whether researchers such as Watkins have a responsibility to conduct research on themselves in their own workplace as they show what it means for their educational development to live more fully their values in their practice.

My questions concerning the potential of action research and educational theory for social evolution have emerged from my recognition of the power relations which protected my job in the University and in the legal protection given to me as an academic by the Education Reform Act of 1988. This act protects my right to question freely and to test received wisdom. It also protects the freedom of academics to put forward new ideas and controversial and unpopular opinions, without placing themselves in jeopardy of losing their jobs or privileges they may have at their institutions.

In offering a case study of an individual's educational development and questioning its relationship to social evolution I am opening myself once again to criticism. I am thinking of the charges of arrogance, of making ridiculous and unsubstantiated claims, of trying to claim a potential for action research which it does not have, or of being incomprehensible from the Deakin point of view! I may indeed be mistaken. Yet of all the criteria I have mentioned in this paper for judging its validity I wish to return to Habermas' criterion of authenticity where he says that it is only through watching a person through time, in action, that we will be able to judge that person's authenticity. I must leave you to judge freely and wisely in the hope that you will feel moved to go public on your judgements on my research. I hope that you will do this within a dialogue which shows how you are trying to live more fully your educational values in your workplace as you support the power of truth against the truth of power. In this way, as I have argued, will you not be making your own contribution to the evolution of our society through education?

Acknowledgements

In producing this paper I have benefited from the advice and criticism of colleagues in the School of Education and local teachers. In particular my thanks to James Calderhead, Mary Tasker, Cyril Selmes, Chris James, Cecilia Higman, Joan Whitehead, Moira Laidlaw, Peter Watkins and Jane Raybould.

CHAPTER NINE: 1991

THE ACTIONS OF A SENATE WORKING PARTY ON A MATTER OF ACADEMIC FREEDOM

In the Summer of 1990, after some difficulties about whether it could be considered by the Board of Studies for Education, I managed to submit the letter I had received from the Secretary and Registrar in June 1987 for consideration by the Board. As a result a Senate Working Party was established to look into a claim that there was prima facie evidence that my academic freedom had been constrained. For the fourth time I am asking you to identify with an important learning experience in the workplace. The recognition by some colleagues that the reason that my academic freedom had not been breached was because of my persistence in the face of pressure, and that a less determined individual might well have been discouraged and therefore constrained, does at least have the merit of an acknowledgement that I had been subjected to pressure!

In November 1990 a meeting of the Board of Studies of the School of Education considered a letter I received from the Secretary and Registrar in June 1987 in which it was claimed that my activities and writings were a challenge to the present and proper organisation of the University and not consistent with the duties that the University wished me to pursue in terms of teaching or research. The Board of Studies passed a motion that it was alarmed at evidence of a prima facie case of a breach of academic freedom with respect to the teaching and research activities of a member of staff. At the meeting of Senate of 5 December 1990 it was noted that the Board of Studies had passed this motion and Senate agreed that the Vice-Chancellor should establish a small independent Working Party to consider further the matter claiming a prima facie case of breach of academic freedom. The Working Party could seek as necessary fuller and further information than was available to the Board and to take evidence from any source thought appropriate to satisfy the Working Party's enquiry.

I was asked by the Working Party of Mr. Brian Meakin and Professors Collins and Burrows to provide a list of constraints on my academic freedom in my work within the University. I sent a reply listing seven constraints and saying:

I am providing this list on the assumptions that,

A) academic staff have freedom within the law to question and test received wisdom, and to put forward new ideas and controversial or unpopular opinions, without placing themselves in jeopardy of losing their jobs or privileges they may have at their institutions (Education Reform Act, 1988).

B) Academic Freedom requires that individual members of universities and polytechnics are able to voice their criticisms and not be subjected to loyalty tests (Council for Academic Freedom and Democracy, 1991).

The overall conclusion of the Report of the Working Party on a Matter of Academic Freedom of May 1991 included the statement that:

'The Working party did not find that, in any of Mr. Whitehead's seven instances, his academic freedom had actually been breached. **This was, however, because of Mr. Whitehead's persistence in the face of pressure; a less determined individual might well have been discouraged and therefore constrained** *(my emphasis). Mr. Whitehead confirmed to the Working Party that, with the exceptions of the local authority data, and the right to question formally his examiners' competence, he was not being prevented at present from publishing any paper that he wished to publish, or prevented from speaking in public as he wished. However, Mr. Whitehead undoubtedly feels intimidated by the possibility of disciplinary action, and the Working Party wished to see a safeguard built into the University's procedures, for all staff, which would reduce the risk of any breach of academic freedom.'*

I would like to acknowledge that in my three meetings with the Working Party I considered the quality of dialogue and the conditions within which it took place to embody the values which the Academic Assembly of the University have used to characterise the Idea of a University. These are quoted in my paper to the First World Congress on Action Research and Process Management. I think they bear repeating here:

'High sounding phrases like "values of freedom, truth and democracy", "rational debate", "integrity", have been used. It is easy to be cynical about these and to dismiss them as hopelessly idealistic, but without ideals and a certain agreement about shared values a community cannot be sustained, and will degenerate. These are the phrases in which members of Academic Assembly have chosen to convey their concept of this community' (The Idea of a University, Academic Assembly, University of Bath, 1988).

I presented the paper which follows in Chapter Ten to the Second World Congress on Action Learning, Action Research and Process Management in Brisbane in July 1992. It shows my direct engagement with the ideas of Ortrun

Zuber-Skerritt, an academic in the University of Queensland who is promoting action research approaches in staff development in higher education. I am relating the propositional form of her analyses to the dialogical and dialectical form of my own educational theory. I am now moving to a position of testing the validity of my ideas on educational theory and educational knowledge in an international arena. Whilst I imagine that the searing experiences I have described above will always be part of my psyche, they did not prevent me from experiencing delight on the quality of the conversation I enjoyed with Ortrun and Orlando Fals-Borda who also contributed to the discussion on the paper at the Congress. I anticipate that such conversations will form an increasing part of my educational development in higher education.

Chapter Ten: 1992

How can my philosophy of Action Research Transform and Improve my Professional Practice and produce a Good Social Order? A response to Ortrun Zuber-Skerritt

This paper was first published in *Transforming Tomorrow Today*, edited by Bruce, S. and Russell, A.L., published by Action Learning, Action Research and Process Management Association Incorporated, Brisbane, Australia,1992.

Summary
The purpose of this paper is to draw attention to a new form of educational theory for improving professional practice and producing a good social order. The recent literature on action learning and action research has focused on their appropriateness as methods to develop managerial and other professional competences. Theoretical frameworks of action research have emphasised conceptual rather than dialectical forms of knowledge. This paper questions the emphasis on method and conceptual theories and argues for a greater concentration on the creation and testing of a living and dialectical educational theory for professional practice within which one's own philosophy of education is engaged as a first person participant.

Keywords
Living Educational Theory; Dialectics; Educational Development; Educational Knowledge.

Introduction
In my paper to the First World Congress I outlined a dialectical approach to educational action research and attempted to synthesise a process of personal development with a process of social evolution. I characterised the dialectical approach as a process of question and answer in which an individual 'I' exists as a living contradiction in questions of the kind, 'How do I improve my practice?', in the workplace. I gave two examples of action research - one on my own professional development in higher education and the other on my contribution, as Chair of Governors, to the educational management of a comprehensive school. To be consistent with my philosophy of action research I am now drawing your attention to an account of my own educational development which integrates this philosophy with my attempts to improve my professional practice and to contribute to a good

social order. The account is grounded in my experience of my own 'I' existing as a living contradiction in that I hold certain values whilst at the same time experiencing their denial in practice. The inclusion of 'I' in my claim to educational knowledge establishes a non-conceptual form within the account. I will contrast the non-conceptual form of educational theory which is constituted by such an account with the theoretical, conceptual framework for action research proposed by Zuber-Skerrit (1991).

Action Research: A Method for Theory Generation and Testing?

One point I would like to explore is the possibility that action researchers have given in too easily to the temptation to reduce their research to issues of methodology and model building, rather than tackling the more fundamental issues of theory generation and testing. In educational research for example, the last decade has witnessed a crisis in that there is no discernable agreement about what constitutes educational theory. The view that educational theory was constituted by the theoretical frameworks and methods of validation of the disciplines of education, was abandoned by one of its creators (Hirst, 1983) with the suggestion that we ought to be looking to 'operationally effective practical discourse' as a basis for theory generation.

The demise of the disciplines approach to educational theory has seen a corresponding increase in the adoption of action research approaches to professional development in teaching (McNiff, 1992; McNiff, et. al. 1992), nursing and police training. In the United Kingdom, Professor John Elliott (1989) has been particularly influential in promoting action research in a variety of professional settings. Professor Pamela Lomax (1989) has also been most successful in intitutionalising programmes of action research for the professional development of teachers at Kingston University. What has yet to emerge from these initiatives is a view of educational theory with widespread academic credibility. The accounts of the action researchers are judged for validity and academic rigour in terms of their methods (Winter, 1989) rather than as contributions to the creation and testing of educational theory.

I can appreciate the importance of the methods which are used to ensure validity and rigour in a research paradigm with a well established theoretical base. Is there not a danger, however, that in a period of crisis when there is a theoretical revolution in progress, the dominant concern with method is likely to be at the expense of encouraging the expression of the creativity of researchers in discovering new forms for the descriptions and explanations for the phenomena under investigation? What I am suggesting is that action researchers should, at this time in the development of the field, stress the importance of developing new forms of explanation rather than permitting their research to be dominated by method or by traditional forms of theoretical, conceptual frameworks.

To illustrate my point I will take the contents of a case report in which I explain my professional development in the workplace of a University and compare this with the contents of the theoretical framework for professional development in higher education proposed by Zuber-Skerritt (1991). My fundamental point is that my explanation contains a non-conceptual 'I', as a living contradiction, which cannot be adequately represented within a conceptual form. Therefore the conceptual form of theoretical framework of the kind proposed by Zuber-Skerritt does not have the explanatory capacity to produce an adequate explanation for my professional development in higher education.

The text represented by bold type at the beginning of each part below, contains correspondences on the actions and judgements on my professional performance which were made with the power of the formal university structures. The text represented by italic type are articles written at the time of being subjected to these pressures and subsequently published.

[The form and content of the case study formed the basis of this book].

Case Study of My Educational Development

Contents

Ortrun Zuber-Skerrit's text on professional development in higher education offers a theoretical framework for action research. It indicates how she approaches praxis and theory in higher education and the integration of theory and practice. In the section on praxis in higher education, Zuber-Skerritt discusses technical and practical reasoning and discusses the case in relation to the theories of Kelly, Leontiev, critical educational science and her own CRASP model. Theories of knowing and learning are described as behaviourist, cognitive and holistic theories. In the section on the integration of theory and practice the list of theories includes Lewin's theory, Kolb's experiential learning theory, Dewey's model of learning, Piaget's model of learning, Kolb's definition of learning, and Boud and Pascoe's extensions of Kolb's model.

My purpose in comparing the contents of an explanation for my professional development in higher education derived from action research with the contents of *Professional development in higher education: a theoretical framework for action research* (Skerritt, 1991), is to raise questions about the validity of both accounts. In criticising Zuber-Skerritt's theoretical framework I am faced with the kind of paradox I experienced in criticising the views of Professor Richard Peters, one of my teachers whose professionalism I valued highly and who stimulated a love of philosophy. In the 1960s and 1970s Richard Peters elevated the status of educational theory in programmes of professional development. In 1971, at the height of the acceptability of the disciplines approach to educational theory, I rejected the theory on the basis of reflections on my own classroom practice with my pupils and my own professional development. My reasoning was as follows. One of the tests of validity of a theory is that it has the capacity to produce an adequate explanation for the behaviour of an individual case. One of the influences on my explanation was the video-camera I had been asked to use by an Inspector to explore its educational potential in the science department of a comprehensive school where I was Head of Science. In looking at my performance I experienced myself as a living contradiction in holding two mutually exclusive opposites together. I held certain values whilst denying them at the same time.

I reflected on the logic of Richard Peters' philosophy of education with his commitment to the Law of Contradiction. This states that two mutually exclusive statements cannot be true simultaneously. I could see that the conceptual frameworks of the theories in the disciplines of education, all excluded contradiction. I followed Popper's (1963) rejection of contradiction in theories through the application of the simple laws of inference which he used to claim that dialectical forms of knowledge were based on nothing better than a loose and woolly way of speaking and entirely useless as theory. Yet, on the ground of my own experience of myself as a living contradiction, I wanted to find an educational theory which had the capacity to produce an adequate explanation for my professional development.

I decided to explore the nature of an explanation for my own professional development in higher education as I continued my educational enquiry, 'How do I improve my practice?'. The result so far over the period 1976-91 is the form and content of the above account of my educational development.

In comparing this account with the theoretical framework for action research proposed by Ortrun Zuber-Skerrit I am drawn to a similar criticism to the one I made of the ideas of Richard Peters. I recognise the professionalism in the work. I understand its value in raising the awareness and status of action research in higher education. In claiming that the theoretical framework is too limited to produce valid explanations for the professional development of individuals in higher education I do not want to damage the growth of action research approaches in professional development. I want to see them strengthened by ensuring that a valid form of educational theory is emerging from the research. For this reason I want to put forward my own stipulative definition as an alternative to the theoretical framework above. Where Ortrun Zuber-Skerritt writes about **The Case** as if the case is independent of herself, I have taken myself to be the case and provided a case report on my own educational development between 1976 and 1991.

The alternative view I am proposing is that **educational theory is being constituted by the descriptions and explanations which individual learners are producing for their educational development   in enquiries of the kind, 'How do I improve my practice?'.**

I see my philosophy of action research in terms of first person engagement rather than from the perspective of second person participant or of a third person neutral observer. I value the traditional role of an academic in making original contributions to knowledge. I see the methodology and epistemology in my claim to know my educational development as an integral part of my educational development. I ground my justification of the values, whose meaning emerges in the course of my educational development, in the name of my own education and humanity. In attempting to live more fully my values within the context of my workplace I believe that I am helping to produce a good social order. This belief is based on the evidence of my responses in the contents of the above case report, to actions and judgements which, whilst legimated by the University's procedures existing at the time, exerted pressure which, according to a University Senate Committee, might have discouraged and therefore constrained a less determined individual than myself. I see my philosophy contributing to the production of a good social order within the form of dialogical community represented in the work of Richard Bernstein (1991) and Alastair MacIntyre (1990).

I do not believe that my paper on its own should persuade you of the validity of my claims. What it can do, however, is to draw your attention to where a living educational theory is being created and it may stimulate you sufficiently to want to test the validity of this new claim to educational knowledge. Those who are interested might also wish to see how I am developing these ideas in the context of my work as Chair of Governors of a comprehensive school (Whitehead, 1990). I think of the significance of your commitment to test the validity of my ideas in MacIntyre's (1988) terms that the rival claims to truth of contending traditions of enquiry depend for their vindication upon the adequacy and the explanatory power of the histories which the resources of each of those traditions in conflict enable their adherents to write.

I suppose the main challenge to academics in the above views is the implication that their research should include a public account of their own educational development in an enquiry of the form, 'How do I improve my practice?'. To hold oneself accountable in this way, in the name of education and one's own humanity, may deter those who prefer the safety of conceptual structures. There is risk, a creative leap and an act of faith, involved in attempting to make original contributions to educational knowledge. I am fortunate that I can share my work with students, teachers and colleagues in the conversational research community of the action research group of the School of Education of the University of Bath. I do hope that you will respond and help to test the validity of my ideas.

In Part Two I describe the Action Research and Educational Theory Case Study Collection in the School of Education of the University of Bath. The dialogical and dialectical forms of presentation of these studies do appear to offer very strong evidence to suggest that the descriptions and explanations produced by individual learners of their own educational development could be constituting a new form of educational theory. I hope that you are now in a position to understand the explanatory principles in my claim to know my own educational development. I am thinking of an explanation which shows a relationship between the form of life of someone like me as a living contradiction, and the extension of cognitive range and concern in the process of answering questions of the kind, 'How do I improve my practice?'. I claim that this is a new form of educational knowledge. It has been created by a University Academic in a research programme spanning some twenty years in an investigation of his life as an educational researcher. The new form of educational knowledge combines both dialectical and propositional knowledge within the dialogical form of presentation.

The reasons I am offering to explain my educational development include a commitment to live a productive life in education through contributing to educational knowledge. I hope that you will have understood the strength of this commitment through my persistence in the face of pressure. The other reasons I have given to explain my educational development include my commitment to exercise my academic freedom to persist in questioning and publishing my findings and my commitment to support the power of truth against the truth of power.

In Part Three I hope that you will also come to understand my educational development in terms of my care for my own integrity. I hope to communicate the strength of my commitment to this care through the educative relationships of Erica Holley, Moira Laidlaw and Peggy Kok, in which I respect their right to speak on their own behalf. Erica also demonstrates a growing awareness of her context as she analyses her relationship with one pupil, a class and a colleague in a process of appraisal.

In Part Four I am engaged directly with market forces and the political forces which are being used to enable the market to penetrate education. I have begun an examination of how these are influencing my educational development and hope to contribute this study to the Case Study Collection described below in Part Two.

PART TWO

THE UNIVERSAL POTENTIAL FOR A LIVING EDUCATIONAL THEORY

CHAPTER ELEVEN

A COLLECTION OF CASES AND LIVING EDUCATIONAL THEORIES

Much of this text was first published in *Collaborative Inquiry*, No. 10, June 1993 by Peter Reason, Centre for the Study of Organizational Change and Development, University of Bath.

THE IDEA behind the collection of case studies described below is that they are contributing to a new form of educational knowledge. I am thinking of the knowledge in individuals' claims to know their own educational development. They could also contribute to the educational theories which are constituted by the descriptions and explanations which you and I, as individual learners, can produce for our own educational development as we answer questions of the kind, 'How do I improve what I am doing?'.

Whilst I make no claim to comprehensive coverage of the fields of action research and educational theory, I think you have the right to feel confident that a high level of scholarship lies behind the collection and that it should carry you to the forefront of the field. Thus I have drawn my understanding from wide experience of action research from Europe, Australia, North America and Developing Countries. These contexts include the two World Congresses on Action Research and Process Management which were held in Australia in 1990 and 1992, the National and International Conferences of the Classroom Action Research Network, the Annual Conferences of The British Educational Research Association and Conferences of the American Educational Research Association held in San Francisco in 1992 and Atlanta, Georgia in 1993.

The idea that a new form of educational theory is being constituted by the descriptions and explanations which individual learners are producing for their own educational development from their action research, means that the practitioner-researchers must speak for themselves and make claims to know their own educational development. In every case study described below the practitioners are speaking for themselves. The majority of the studies in the collection have been accredited for Special Studies on initial teacher education programmes or for Advanced Certificate, Advanced Diploma, M.Ed. modules, M.Ed. dissertations, and M.Phil. and Ph.D. research programmes. The practitioner researchers have a range of different roles across primary and secondary schools and further and higher education. They include an educational psychologist, a headteacher, an advisor, lecturers, heads of department, teachers and student teachers of English, Mathematics, Science, Art, Design, Modern Languages, Humanities and Technology. There are also a number a studies from non-accredited action research programmes.

This review of the case studies in the collection is followed by an evaluation of the contributions from the Bath Action Research Group in its global context. It includes questions to researchers in the field in a conversational form which I am hoping will encourage you to make your own contribution to our community and may prompt an invitation from you for us to join your own.

One of my dreams on coming to the University of Bath in 1973 was to show the professional development of teachers, starting from the experiences and understandings of novice teachers, as a life-long process of learning in which it would be possible to receive the highest academic awards for researching the educational knowledge grounded in one's own professional practice. In 1993 the case studies in the collection show that teachers can indeed create their own educational knowledge grounded in their professional practice and related to the quality of their educative relationships with their pupils and students.

Because of the large number of case studies, I must be selective in what I offer you. The emphasis in my own work has been the reverse of what you might expect. In order to establish the legitimacy of a different view of educational knowledge I decided that I should focus my own practice on tutoring teacher researchers for their Ph.D. and M.Phil. research degrees and then work on action research programmes in M.Ed. degrees followed by establishing Advanced Certificate and Advanced Diplomas in professional development by action research. This focus on research and continuing or in-service teacher education left me little time for developing action research for novice teachers on initial teacher education programmes.

However, I am fortunate in working with a colleague, Moira Laidlaw. By tutoring groups of novice teachers for their special studies by action research she has ensured that the collection contains contributions from her students which examiners have commented are of astonishingly high quality (for example, Sarah Darlington's, 1993, below). Moira has produced a guide for her students on *Action Research: A guide for use on initial teacher education programmes with a final report by Justine Hocking* (Laidlaw, 1992). Some idea of the nature and quality of the educative relationships through which she has helped them to improve the quality of their learning may be understood from the analysis of Moira's relationship with a student in Part Three. Moira's comments below on seven of the case studies from her 1992/93 group give some idea of their contents:

Moira asks the question:

What is the significance of your individual contributions?

Here are the students' research questions and Moira's responses:

Nigel Brown: 'How can I help my fourth year to discover their own motives for, and hence start to enjoy the process of, writing up practical work?' (Physics) This is a most unusual piece of work, set as it is, as a court case with the State versus Brown on four charges, the most serious one of which is 'wasting valuable pupil time'. You set out the context very skilfully, delving into areas of metaphor, the validity of your approach for educational knowledge and your more personal reasons for writing as you do. Throughout the study you bear your potential audience in mind all the time and this is one of the most impressive aspects of your report. The weight of your evidence of curricular learning is strong and you begin to analyse the significance of pupils speaking for themselves in a way which you see as being meaningful in your own educational development. You conclude with a line from a poem, 'Teacher': 'Before I teach you, I must first reach you,' and show us how you have lived this out in your own teaching. You state right at the end: 'If I had more time with my fourth years, I would like to look more at their autonomy. This aspect was implicitly in my original question ... What is autonomy? A learner becomes aware of the processes involved in their learning. These processes [are] normally [...] described by some psychologist or philosopher.' You have started to enable your pupils to describe these processes for themselves!

Sarah Darlington: 'How can I help Hugh become more engaged with the Green Issues part of the Green Module?' (English) This is a complex and excellently written study of differentiation in action. We see throughout this report the way in which your understanding of what constitutes differentiation in teaching your Year Eight class affects Hugh's learning. You give us frequent and detailed examples of Hugh's writing and comments and then employ an analytical technique in order to highlight their meaning and significance for you and for him. You continually remind us through your text of the values underpinning your enquiry and concerns, and you end with a statement which really demonstrates a practitioner new to the profession who is speaking with her own voice and who knows what she knows though systematic observation, reflection and collaboration with others: 'I have a framework. I have lived out this framework of values to varying degrees...I know it to be good as far as it goes. But, in my ending - to return to my beginning, I recognise the detail of th[is] pattern is movement. Things change and develop and so, I hope, will I.'

Gail Hannaford: 'How can I motivate my Year Nine class and get them to take responsibility for their own learning?' (History) The real strength of your account, Gail, lies in the way in which you have contextualised your insights into the wider spectrum of teacher education and teacher knowledge. You show us all the factors which you believe meaningfully impinge on the classroom and then you introduce us to individual children and reveal how your own understanding comes through the highlighting of individuals' learning needs. I know the real dilemmas that some of this enquiry caused you and yet still you persevered to be able to say: 'I have identified in the process so much more than I would otherwise have achieved - about my values, about my pupils' values, and about the role of the school in that interchange. I tried hard to live out my values in so far as I tried to care about each pupil as an individual. I also tried to listen to what was going on in the unspoken subtext of the classroom.' You finish with these words: 'The creative birth of insights and understandings is exhausting - but very rewarding.'

Jennie Hick: 'How do I identify my action research question?' (French) This is an enquiry which focuses very clearly on the development of a single pupil's learning yet outlining succinctly the ways in which your understanding and educational development have been enhanced through such a focus. Another strength of your enquiry lies in the ways in which you have shown the significance of your deviation from the action enquiry cycle and have liberated your thinking from the possible restraints of a given form. This is an ambitious undertaking which you manage convincingly. Your learning about the processes of learning itself is clearly documented and in James we hear a voice which develops in clarity and tone steadily throughout the study. About educational research literature you are similarly strong-minded and have this to say: 'Many of the references I have used in this enquiry are from the "living theory" found in other action research reports. Like those action researchers, I have acquired my own standards of judgement through practice with my pupils. I feel I can stand up for my values and say, "This is where I stand. I am accountable for this".'

Philip Holden: 'How should I approach 9L4 History lessons to create the most positive working atmosphere feasible in the hope of increasing the quality of pupil learning?' (History) Phil, this is the account of someone who makes explicit how he has come to know what he knows, and how this knowledge has improved the quality of his teaching and the pupils' learning. I am impressed by the way in which you are prepared to become publicly accountable for your own development, how you have searched your professional values and when found wanting, you have set about rigorously trying to modify what you are doing. Your enquiry is, it seems to me, very much an enquiry in the name of educational improvement. You state at one point: 'I do feel that initially the research rocked my thoughts on teaching - what I wanted from it and what I expected. Now ... I .. . feel that the process as a whole has been a very positive influence on my professionalism in that it showed me its frailty ... action research has allowed me to view the standards of judgement with a startling clarity. For that I am grateful.'

Lara Gatling: 'How can I enable my sixth formers to enjoy their lessons and develop the confidence to talk about Chaucer in an enquiring manner?' (English) This is a beautifully and powerfully written study which shows very clearly your personal and professional reasons for your emerging educational values. Your sensitivity to the right of your pupils to speak for themselves shines through at every stage of the enquiry and the quality of your analysis really is impressive. You provide us with evidence of pupils' learning in both a curricular and autonomous sense and describe and explain your own educational development with crystal clarity through this process. Your use of learning logs with the pupils enabled their learning to become more self-directed, your own insights to be more educationally focused, and a reader to be able to follow the development step by step. Perhaps most impressive of all for me in your account, Lara, is the way in which you document the significance for your learning and your pupil, Alison, in her log entry: 'However, I think it would be better if I knew what we were aiming for at the end so that we have something to concentrate on and refer back to ...'. You show us then how you deal with adapting your processes to Alison's needs, which is clearly one of your aims as a teacher.

Joanne Lovatt: 'How can I get the best out of all my pupils? The story so far...' **(Chemistry).** I know something of the struggle that you went through in determining the focus of your enquiry and the result is an assured piece of work in which you have described and explained the processes you and the children went through in a classroom which was becoming increasingly committed to collaborative learning in Science. I am impressed that your sense of curricular responsibility and your sense of justice for an individual pupil who was not fulfilling his potential went hand in hand in this study, and from this interaction we begin to see your own educational development. You write movingly about how David starts to find his own sense of value in working with others and conclude with this powerful statement: *I have grown to realise the importance I place on giving every child in my classroom the opportunity to benefit from science lessons. That these lessons need a calm, purposeful atmosphere, but one that allows discussion of ideas, a co-operation, an integration, a feeling of everyone, myself included, working together to reach a common aim ...*

So, as you can see, each of you has contributed something unique and yet more generalisably valuable and comprehensible. I will finish with something which Joanne leaves her reader with, something which I find inspiring in its humility and hope:

'I do not know what I may appear to the world but to myself I seem to have been only a boy playing on the sea-shore and diverting myself now and then, finding a smoother pebble or a prettier shell than ordinary, whilst the great ocean of truth lay undiscovered before me' (Isaac Newton).

[Space does not permit Moira's reviews of the work of the rest of the group, which included Rod Beattie, Matthew Brake, Catherine Chapman, Kieran Earley, Barbara Myerson and Emma Trigg. There case studies are acknowledged in the references].

The Case Study Collection contains a wealth of material from other sources. It contains work from teachers who are working on action research programmes without submitting them for accreditation as well as examples contributed by colleagues in other institutions such as those of Tony Ghaye, Marion Hammond and Terry Hewitt.

Tony Ghaye co-ordinates the M.Ed. programme at Worcester College of Higher Education. There are two contributions from Tony in our collection from **START.** This stands for **S**haring of **T**hinking on the **A**rt of **R**esearch into **T**eaching. *'How was it for you? Passionate Stories from Beginners'* is Occasional Paper 4 and *'On the Turbulent Brink: Essential Reading For Managers'* is Occasional Paper 5.

Marion Hammond, a teacher adviser with the Somerset Education Authority has provided a copy of the Somerset Humanities Action Research Project Report 1991-1992 of *History and Geography in Action: 50 Teachers' Action Research Projects into National Curriculum History and Geography Key Stages 1, 2 and 3.*

Terry Hewitt, a teacher at Sir Bernard Lovell School in Avon, has, for the past five years, provided support for teachers undertaking action research in Avon schools. Don Foster, Liberal Democrat M.P. for Bath and the spokesperson for education helped to promote action research in Avon Schools during his period as Chair of Education of Avon Education Committee in the mid 1980s. Booklets in the collection which reflect this type of support include the reports of teachers on the Department of Education and Science course *Supporting Teachers in their Classroom Research 1985/1986* and the reports from the Avon **STRICT** initiative from 1989/1990 (**S**upporting **T**eacher **R**esearch **I**nto **C**lassroom **T**eaching).

As I said above, my tutoring has been focused on the action research programmes of teachers working towards advanced qualifications. I have chosen examples below to emphasise the idea that professional development can be a lifelong process in which it is possible to achieve academic recognition at the highest levels for creating educational knowledge grounded in professional practice. I am thinking of the following awards for Advanced Certificate, Advanced Diploma, M.Ed., M.Phil. and Ph.D. degrees. In each case the individuals show how they worked at living their values more fully in their practice and how they have produced a description and explanation for their own educational development in the workplace.

Patti Budd is a Head of Department at Swindon College. Her Advanced Certificate for her study, *How can I support change in a way which fits my belief in equality of opportunity?*, was awarded in 1993. Marguerite Corbey, Jo Fawcett, Sue Jackson and Daniela de Cet were members of a group of Wiltshire teachers supported by Pat D'Arcy during her time as English Adviser. They were awarded their Advanced Diplomas in 1991 for the following studies and this award carries an equivalence of two M.Ed. modules. Daniela de Cet: *How do I improve the quality of my pupils' writing? How can I develop my teaching of poetry to my GCSE classes?* (Secondary). Marguerite Corbey: *Thinking Through Emergent Writing* (Primary). Jo Fawcett: *Writing Journeys* (Primary). Sue Jackson: *The Nature of Action Research: How do I improve my educational management?* (Primary Head).

In addition to registering for advanced qualifications by action enquiry, teachers can work at such enquiries on a modular basis and for a dissertation for the M.Ed. degree. For example, the collection contains Simon Baskett's (1992), *How do I improve the quality of group work in the (science) classroom?* and Jacqui Stephens' (1992), *How can I improve the quality of the evidence I collect concerning the quality of the learning experience whilst carrying out an LEA monitoring and evaluation?*

Two M.Ed. dissertations which are valued highly in our community are Martin Forrest's (1983) *The Teacher as Researcher - the use of historical artefacts in primary schools,* and Peggy Kok's (1991) *The art of an educational inquirer.* Martin lectures in Education at the University of the West of England. His study remains one of the most convincing examples of the value of a validation group in helping an action researcher to answer a question of the kind, 'How do I help my students to improve the quality of their learning so that they can help their pupils to do the same?' Peggy lectures in Vocational Education and Training in Singapore. Chapter Six of her dissertation is included later in this book and shows the nature of educative conversations and reflections on the values which constitute an individual's educational development.

The highest research awards achieved by our action researchers are M.Phil. and Ph.D. Degrees. The following four M.Phil. theses are in the collection together with one Ph.D. by Mary Gurney.

Don Foster (1982): *Explanations for teachers' attempts to improve the process of education for their pupils* (M.Ed. by research now called M.Phil.).

Andy Larter (1987): *An action research approach to classroom discussion in the examination years.*

Chris Walton (1993): *An action-research enquiry into attempts to improve the quality of narrative writing in my own classroom.*

Paul Hayward (1993): *How do I improve my pupils' learning in design and technology?*

Mary Gurney (1988): *An action research enquiry into ways of developing and improving personal and social education.* In the collection you will also find the five booklets which constitute Mary's (1991) integrated personal and social education programme.

Other action research M.Phil. degrees are in the University Library. For example, there are Ron King's (1987) *An action inquiry into day release in further Education,* Margaret Jensen's (1987) *A creative approach to the teaching of English in the examination years* and Kevin Eames' *The Growth of a teacher-researcher's attempt to understand writing, redrafting, learning and autonomy in the examination years.*

Other action research Ph.Ds. in the University Library include Jean McNiff's (1989) *An explanation for an individual's educational development through the dialectic of action research.* You will also find three books by Jean McNiff in the collection. These are described below. Paul Denley (1987) also drew on insights from the action research literature in his Ph.D. on *The development of an approach to practitioner research initiated through classroom observation and of particular relevance to the evaluation of innovation in science teaching.*

In my work as a tutor I try to help my students to relate their enquiries to action research literature from around the world so that they can check their own enquiries to see if they are at the forefront of the field. I try to do this by showing how I am engaging with this literature in relation to my own research. Let me see if I can do the same for you.

CHAPTER TWELVE

ACTION RESEARCH LITERATURE FROM AROUND THE WORLD

MANY STUDENTS have an understandable desire to be able to define clearly what it is they are doing. If they enrol on an action research programme they want to know what defines the programme as action research. If you wanted to know, this is what I would say to you:

In *Becoming Critical* Wilf Carr and Stephen Kemmis have defined action research as:

'Action research is a form of self-reflective enquiry undertaken by participants (teachers, students or principals for example) in social (including educational) situations in order to improve the rationality and justice of (a) their own social or educational practices, (b) their understanding of these practices, and (c) the situations (and institutions) in which these practices are carried out (classrooms and schools, for example). It is most rationally empowering when undertaken by participants collaboratively, though it is often undertaken by individuals and sometimes in cooperation with 'outsiders'. In education, action research has been employed in school-based curriculum development, professional development, school improvement programs and systems planning and policy development (for example, in relation to policy about classroom rules, school policies about non-competitive assessment, regional project team policies about their consultancy roles)' (Carr and Kemmis, 1983).

Debates on action research can be studied in Stephen Kemmis' (1985) response to Rex Gibson's (1985) *Critical Times for Action Research*, and by following the implications of Rob Walker's (1986) report on *Breaking the grip of print in curriculum research.*

According to Kemmis, Gibson criticises *Becoming Critical* on twelve counts:

1) it is intensely uncritical (i.e. it doesn't practise what it preaches);

2) its prescriptions are likely to result in increased conformity (i.e. it would produce its own rigid orthodoxy);

3) it is naive about group processes;

4) *it prefers the group over the individual, and an in-group over the out-group;*

5) *it is bedazzled by the notion of 'science';*

6) *it rejects objectivity, yet privileges its own view of reality;*

7) *it is characterised by hubris (i.e. it lacks modesty in its claims and perceptions);*

8) *it is highly contradictory (actually, not a bad thing in the human condition, but the book doesn't recognise its own contradictions);*

9) *it has far too much respect for the authority of critical theory;*

10) *it is an elitist text masquerading as an egalitarian one;*

11) *it insufficiently acknowleges that action research at the three levels of interpersonal (e.g. classroom), institutional (e.g. school or L.E.A.), or structural (e.g. economic, political, ideological) involve different activities and levels of difficulty for would-be action researchers, and*

12) *in its seeming preference for the institutional and structural levels, it is attempting to set action research off on a course very different from its present practice* (Kemmis, S. 1985, pp.3-4).

Kemmis meets each criticism clearly and persuasively. Where I see a problem however is with the logical form of both these discourses in that they are purely propositional. Both Gibson and Kemmis appear to believe that they can communicate the nature of action research through the sole use of the propositional form. In my own view of action research, educational knowledge has a dialogical and dialectical form which is not amenable to systematic representation in a purely propositional form (Whitehead and Lomax, 1987). In this respect I am drawn to Rob Walker's (1986) desire to break the grip of print in curriculum research.

Walker attacks our use of the conventional literary forms through which we communicate our research. I support his view that curriculum research adds to the *'accretion of established structures, reinforcing attitudes, values and practices and legitimizing the existing distribution of knowledge'*. Even when the content of what we say attempts to change radically the nature of educational knowledge we are still trapped within the web of the propositional form.

I agree that there is a need to shift the ground more dramatically, *'not just to change the words, but to change the language, and to change it to something closer to the vernacular, not further away from it'* (Walker, *op. cit.*). Perhaps the contributions in the case study collected listed above are moving in this direction.

The following defining characteristics of action research were presented in 1989 to an *'International Symposium on Action Research in Higher Education, Government and Industry'*. Do have a look at the proceedings of this symposium. I have found the work of Herbert Altrichter particularly useful in understanding the roots of action research. In a joint paper with Stephen Kemmis, Robin McTaggart and Ortrun Zuber-Skerrit, Herbert works at *Defining, Confining or Refining Action Research* (1990), and says:

'If yours is a situation in which

- ❏ People reflect and improve (or develop) their own work and their own situations;
- ❏ by tightly interlinking their reflection and action;
- ❏ and also making their experience public not only to other participants but also to other persons interested in and concerned about the work and the situation, i.e. their (public) theories and practices of the work and the situation.

And if yours is a situation in which there is increasingly

- ❏ Data-gathering by participants themselves (or with the help of others) in relation to their own questions;
- ❏ Participation (in problem-posing and in answering questions) in decision-making;
- ❏ Power-sharing and the relative suspension of hierarchical ways of working towards industrial democracy;
- ❏ Collaboration among members of the group as a 'critical community';
- ❏ Self-reflection, self-evaluation and self-management by autonomous and responsible persons and groups;
- ❏ Learning progressively (and publicly) by doing and by making mistakes in a 'self-reflective spiral' of planning, acting, observing, reflecting, replanning, etc.;
- ❏ Reflection which supports the idea of the '(self-) reflective practitioner';
- ❏ open enough so that further elaboration and development seemed possible;
- ❏ allowing for an ex post facto incorporation of projects into the discussion (which had not been initiated and conducted on the basis of some elaborate understanding of action research);
- ❏ and, above all, shared with respect to the process of its formulation for a specific context;

Then yours is a situation in which ACTION RESEARCH is occurring.'
(Altrichter, *et al.* 1990)

Some recent historical work by Peter Gstettner and Herbert Altrichter (McTaggart, 1992) has shown that Moreno was the first to use the term 'action research' and that he developed the idea of co-researchers as early as 1913 in community development initiatives working with prostitutes in the Vienna suburb of Spittelberg. The significance of this discovery is that it shows that action research had its origins in community action rather than in a discipline of the social sciences.

Many action research texts suggest that Stephen Corey (1953) was the first systematically to define the characteristics of this form of research in education. Corey says that the expression 'action research' and the operations it implies come from at least two somewhat independent sources, Lewin and Collier. Lewin attempted to study human relations scientifically and to improve the quality of these relations as a consequence of the inquiries. Collier, during the period (1933-45) when he was Commissioner of Indian Affairs, used the expression 'action research' and was convinced that the administrator and the layman must participate creatively in the research, *'impelled as it is from their own area of need'*.

Corey's thesis was that teachers, supervisors, and administrators would make better decisions and engage in more effective practices if they were able and willing to conduct research as a basis for these decisions and practices. He refers to action research as the process by which practitioners attempt to study their problems scientifically in order to guide, correct, and evaluate their decisions and actions. He saw this process as a co-operative activity which would support democratic values. He believed that the failure to see the necessity for co-operation in curriculum research had marred the attempts of many communities to improve their schools. He was particularly interested in gaining the co-operation of parents.

In his comparison of traditional research in education and action research, Corey stated that they are alike in that each is difficult to do well. In 1953 a great deal had been written in an attempt to improve the procedures of traditional research. Very little had been written, in the field of education, that was particularly helpful to persons who were interested in action research. Most of the references to this kind of investigation had to do with attempts to improve human relations.

A key text in the theoretical literature is the one I mentioned above, *Becoming Critical* by Wilf Carr and Stephen Kemmis (1983). It provides an understanding of the approach to action research which has been influenced by critical theory. Carr and Kemmis point out that after enjoying a decade of growth in the 1950s, educational action research went into decline. They show how a 'Technical' Research, Development and Dissemination model of educational change became established which diverted legitimacy from the small-scale, locally organised, self-reflective approach to action research. Their central argument is that:

> *'The professional responsibility of the teacher is to offer an approach to this task: to create conditions under which the critical community can be galvanized into action in support of educational values, to model the review and improvement process, and to organize it so that colleagues, students, parents and others can become actively involved in the development of education. The participatory democratic approach of collaborative action research gives form and substance to the idea of a self-reflective critical community committed to the development of education'* (Carr and Kemmis, 1983).

Carr and Kemmis have developed the idea of action research as a critical educational science. They have drawn extensively upon the work of Jürgen Habermas at the University of Frankfurt and follow his distinction between three forms of knowledge and their associated cognitive interests: the technical, the practical and the emancipatory. John Smythe (1986), a colleague of Stephen Kemmis at Deakin University for many years (recently moved to Flinders University), has pointed out that technical reflection, by being concerned only with problem solving, serves those who label the issue as 'a problem'. He believes that practical reflection, because of its concern with the moral rightness of actions in context, serves the interests of those who see themselves as the conscience of society. He says that critical reflection, because it aims to assist people to discover the historical processes that led to their social formation as well as to discover the ideological way in which thought and action become distorted, is directed towards emancipatory interests. He also emphasises that we ought to be clear about the interests being served by each form and the extent to which we are treating the political context as problematic.

One of the great weaknesses of Habermas' work and hence of those attempting to create a critical educational science based on his work is that, as Brian Fay (1977) says, he gives no idea at all how it is that what he says at the level of individual psychology can be made appropriate for someone interested in social reform. Do have a look at Brian Fay's paper on *How people change themselves: The relationship between critical theory and its audience.* It will help you to understand the 'critical theory' approach which has characterised much of the action research work by the group at Deakin University. Colin Henry, one of the group at Deakin, has contributed to our collection John Smythe's (1987) book on *Reflection-in-Action.* This contains the paper by Brian Fay. Colin has also ensured that we have the Third Editions of The *Action Research Reader* and *The Action Research Planner* from Deakin in the collection. He has also provided evaluations of the two World Congresses on Action Learning, Action Research and Process Management in 1990 and 1992 in Brisbane. I recommend that you read the key contributions to the First World Congress in the collection. These include Reg Revans' address on *The Concept, Origin and Growth of Action Learning* and John Elliott's *Action Research, Practical Competence and Professional Knowledge.*

Patricia Weeks, a lecturer at Queensland University of Technology, visited the Action Research Group in Bath in September 1992, for a seminar to discuss the Teaching, Reflection and Collaboration Project at QUT. In the booklet on *Exploring Tertiary Teaching,* in the collection, you will see some case studies of University Lecturers undertaking action research into their own teaching. This is something which is missing from Habermas' work on communication and the evolution of society.

Habermas' critique of modern society is closely mirrored by Carr and Kemmis (1983). Their work is a critique of technical rationality which is seen to dominate the way in which society understands itself and by which the dominant interest groups legitimate their oppressive political, economic and social practices.

> *'In education, research which has a critical theory thrust aims at promoting critical consciousness, and struggles to break down the institutional structures and arrangements which reproduce oppressive ideologies and the social inequalities that are sustained and produced by these social structures and ideologies.'*

I would argue that some of the case studies in the collection at Bath show how to transcend the constraints of technical rationality in a way which integrates both the individual's values and social understanding. The integration of social understandings does need to be strengthened. For example, as I respond to the work of Erica Holley and Moira Laidlaw in Part Three, I suggest that they examine more fully the nature of the social context and the power relations within which their work was produced.

The development of action research in Britain owes a great deal to the work of the late Lawrence Stenhouse and his collaborators at the Centre of Applied Research at the University of East Anglia. For example, the work of the Ford Teaching Project, 1973-1976, directed by John Elliot and Clem Adelman involved teachers in examining their own attempts to develop inquiry/discovery approaches to learning and teaching. Following this project John Elliott established the Classroom Action Research Network based at the Cambridge Institute of Education. John is now Professor of Education at the University of East Anglia and what is now called the Collaborative Action Research Network is currently co-ordinated by Bridget Somekh at the same university. Twelve bulletins have been produced by the network. His latest book (Elliott, 1991) relates action research to such issues as the National Curriculum, Appraisal and Professional Development. Clem Adelman is now Professor of Education at the Open University and has recently called for hard, joint theorising on the relationship of values, action and consequences prior to the devising of fresh options for action.

> *'Thus the disappointment on reading teachers' action research reports as purveyed by Hustler et al. (1986), McNiff (1988) and Elliott (1985). Without attributing any blame or incompetence to the teachers involved, what these accounts reflect is the belief that an aspect of teaching can be improved if it more effectively achieves a desired outcome. What these cases lack is the hard, joint theorizing on the relationship of values, action and consequences prior to the devising of fresh options for action. An understanding of teaching as a species of practical ethic is lacking. These accounts read like the pursuit of certitude, of effectiveness or predictability and in this sense are indistinguishable from the positivistic, single-item, cause-effect research which the promulgation of teaching as a practical ethic has tried to replace .... It may be that the arguments for action research as an acceptable means of educational research*

have been won, but there is no reason for complacency, a malaise that may be encapsulated by the response, 'well you've got to let teachers start somewhere'. Action research stands or falls by its demonstrable relevance to the practical ethic of education, as well as whether it is reliable, valid and refutable as a methodology' (Adelman, 1989).

I would also add that action research stands or falls by its capacity to generate living educational theories for professional practice. The idea that a living educational theory is being created from the explanations which individual learners give for their own educational development as they engage in action enquiries of the kind, 'How do I live more fully my values in my practice?', has a different base to 'critical' action research. It is not predicated upon critical theory. It is generated on the basis of questions of the kind, 'How do I improve my practice?'. It may well be that some researchers need to adopt such a critical stance before making a creative leap into seeing that they can create a living educational theory from explanations of their own educational development.

In the South West of England we have increasing numbers of teachers engaged in such action research programmes. Support is being given by members of the Action Research Group of the School of Education at the University of Bath. In September 1985 a group of teacher researchers, registered for higher degrees at Bath University, organised a seminar at the annual conference of the British Educational Research Association on Action Research, Educational Theory and the Politics of Educational Knowledge. The papers are in the collection. Professor Pam Lomax of Kingston University was present at the seminar and published her analysis (Lomax, 1986) in the *British Journal of In-Service Education.* This marked the first public recognition of the group of action researchers in Bath.

A Department of Education and Science course at the University, 'Supporting Teachers in their Classroom Research' from April 1985 to April 1986, provided over twenty teachers with support, as they analysed their classroom practice. Their reports are in the collection. An action research perspective on curriculum review and evaluation developed in ten schools with some fifty teachers as part of the Avon TRIST initiative from March 1986-87. For the following two years, Avon continued to support action research through the STRICT initiative (Supporting Teacher Research Into Classroom Teaching) and finally in 1990 an action research approach to professional and institutional development became accepted as policy for Avon Local Education Authority. The action research programme in the Summer of 1990, which followed this policy decision, involved some 80 advisory teachers and some 400 staff development tutors. Whilst it is too early to judge the effectiveness of the support being provided by Avon Authority there is some evidence to suggest that their policies for restructuring their support for educational development could not be sustained at the level of resource required by the National Government.

The development of the basic action reflection spiral, which has been used by action researchers in the School of Education at the University of Bath, began with the local curriculum development project of a group of Wiltshire teachers (Whitehead, 1976). The booklet describing this project is in the collection and describes how the teachers attempted to improve the quality of pupils' learning in mixed ability science groups. A cycle begins with the individual's experience of educational concerns, questions or problems in action of the kind, 'How do I improve this process of education here?'. It has the form:

1) I experience problems when some of my educational values are negated in my practice.
2) I imagine a solution to my problems.
3) I act in the direction of a chosen solution.
4) I evaluate the outcomes of my actions.
5) I modify my problems, ideas and actions in the light of my evaluations ....

The inclusion of the individual 'I' experiencing problems because of the negation of values emphasises that the individual is investigating his or her own practices with the intention of improving their quality. Given this base it might be assumed that action researchers reject the contributions to educational theory of the traditional disciplines of education. Indeed this was a legitimate criticism which teacher-researchers made of their own research reports at a CARN conference in 1984 (Whitehead and Foster, 1984). Do have a look at this bulletin in the collection. It will give you some idea of the hard work put into the development of CARN by Bridget Somekh at the University of East Anglia mentioned above.

I acknowledge the danger that action researchers may not pay sufficient attention to the problems of validating their accounts of practice or to acknowledging the contributions which psychology, philosophy, sociology and history can make to the construction of educational theory. For this reason action researchers associated with the School of Education of Bath University are encouraged to submit their accounts to the critical discipline of a validation group and to keep themselves informed of developments in the traditional disciplines. Martin Forrest's (1983) dissertation on *The Teacher as Researcher* in the collection provides good evidence on the way in which a validation group can assist a teacher researcher to improve the quality of the case study. We also inform ourselves of work in other action research communities. For example, we are drawn to the analyses of 'technical rationality' offered by Schön (1983) and Carr and Kemmis (1983) .

Schön argues that the dominant epistemology of practice is that of 'technical rationality'. By this he means the view that our professional activity consists in *'instrumental problem solving made rigorous by the application of scientific theory and technique.'* I certainly see this model embedded in the institutional context of my professional life where it is part of the power relations which structure research and practice. I also see it in the normative curricula of my professional colleagues in schools. Even when I question the model of technical rationality as a practitioner, educator and researcher, I am aware that I may be colluding with an institution that perpetuates it.

In his examination of the emerging awareness of the limitations of technical rationality Schön makes the point that this rationality views professional practice as a process of problem solving. In problem solving, problems of choice or decision are solved through the selection from available means of the one best suited to established ends. But, says Schön, with this emphasis on problem solving, we ignore problem setting, the process by which we define the decision to be made, the ends to be achieved, the means which may be chosen.

In educational practice, problems do not present themselves to the practitioner as given. Ron King, during his time as a lecturer in the Mechancial Engineering Department of Bath College of Further Education, has documented (King, 1987) the way he has constructed problems from the feeling of unease he shared with colleagues about the nature of their teaching and their students' learning. This dissertation is in the University Library. The crucial insight we have learnt from this work is that recognised by Schön. Although problem setting is a necessary condition for technical problem solving, it is not itself a technical problem.

Schön asks his readers to reconsider the question of professional knowledge. He asks us to search for an epistemology of practice implicit in the artistic, intuitive processes which some practitioners do bring to situations of uncertainty, instability, uniqueness, and value-conflict:

> 'When someone reflects-in-action, he [sic] becomes a researcher in the practice context. He is not dependent on the categories of established theory and technique, but constructs a new theory of the unique case. His inquiry is not limited to a deliberation about means which depends on a prior agreement about ends. He does not keep means and ends separate, but defines them interactively as he frames a problematic situation. He does not separate thinking from doing, ratiocinating his way to a decision which he must later convert to action. Because his experimenting is a kind of action, implemenation is built into his inquiry. Thus reflection-in-action can proceed, even in situations of uncertainty or uniqueness, because it is not bound by the dichotomies of Technical Rationality.
>
> Many practitioners, locked into a view of themselves as technical experts, find nothing in the world of practice to occasion reflection. They have become too skilful at techniques of selective inattention, junk categories, and situational control, techniques which they use to preserve the constancy of their knowledge-in-practice. For them, uncertainty is a threat; its admission a sign of weakness. Others, more inclined toward and adept at reflection-in-

action, nevertheless feel profoundly uneasy because they cannot say what they know how to do, cannot justify its quality or rigor ... For these reasons the study of reflection-in-action is critically important' (Schön, 1983).

Evaluating the Contributions of the Bath Action Research Group in its Global Context

I have taken the criteria of evaluation from Colin Henry's evaluations of the two World Congresses and the introduction to the 2nd Volume of the Proceedings of the First World Congress where the editors set out case studies which are about people's experiences in working together to create a new order in our society. I think it bears repeating that Colin's criteria from the First World Congress included understanding the principles of action research, especially its participatory, democratic and egalitarian values and that in his evaluation of the Second Congress he reiterated the above points and developed his view that we should be judging the effectiveness of our research in terms of its contribution to the reduction of war, starvation, poverty and corruption in the world.

The additional criterion which I apply to the work of the Bath Action Research Group concerns our contribution to knowledge and theory. Given my acceptance of Kilpatrick's (1951) point that educational theory is a form of dialogue which has profound implications for the future of humanity, I judge our work in terms of creating valid educational theories for the future of humanity.

Jean McNiff (1992; McNiff *et. al.*, 1992) has described the form of living educational theories we have been creating in the Bath Action Research Group. In her latest book (McNiff *et. al.*, 1992), Jean stresses the dialogical nature of our contributions to action research, educational theory and the creation of a good social order. In subjecting my own work to Colin's criteria from the First World Congress I think I fulfil his criteria. I spell out the criteria I use to distinguish my own action research approach and show how the criteria are met. The more substantial work I presented to the Second Congress with the 190 page case history of my own educational development, which accompanied the summary in the Proceedings (Bruce and Russell, 1992), does not directly address the issues of war, starvation and poverty. It does, however, address the conflict between the truth of power and the power of truth in a way which shows my engagement in supporting the power of truth. I accept the implicit criticism, in applying Henry's criteria to my most recent work, that it is not addressing directly the issues of reducing war, starvation and poverty. I accept that the quality of my work should also be judged in these terms.

In judging the contributions of the Bath Action Research Group in its global context I share Arphron Chuaprapaisilp's (1991) commitment to gain insights from the past, to contemplate the present using emancipatory wisdom and to take responsibility for the future. I would say that the case studies produced by participants in the Bath Action Research Group are significant contributions to the literature already produced by the Collaborative Action Research Network in the UK, by the action researchers influenced by the action research community at Deakin University (with contributors such as Robin MacTaggart, Colin Henry, Stephen Kemmis and Ortrun Zuber-Skerrit) and the Participatory Action Research networks associated with the work of Orlando Fals-Borda.

I think there are a number of original contributions from the Bath Action Research Group: revealing the nature of educative relationships between pupils, students, teachers and lecturers through the work of Erica Holley (1991) and Moira Laidlaw (1992); creating living educational theories for the future of humanity, through the contributions of Jean McNiff and Jack Whitehead; developing the methodology and epistemology of dialogical forms of educational action research, through the contributions of Kevin Eames (1993) and Peter Mellett; and exploring the politics of truth, educational knowledge and good order in the work of Andy Larter.

Many more members of the Bath Action Research Group are making their own contributions to the field and to the development of each other's work in the way shown by Jean McNiff *et. al.* (1992). However I think we are all aware of the danger pointed out by Walker:

> '*It is important not to lose sight of the intent and purpose of the project, or to design complex and demanding research or evaluation studies that might drain energy better put to other purposes. In educational research, perhaps more than in any other area of social and human research, the context of use should never be subsumed to questions of a technical kind. The temptation is to let technical questions displace educational questions. It is a temptation that needs to be resisted.*' (Walker, 1985).

I accept Walker's emphasis on the importance of the context of use in educational research. Hence I will end this section by extending my understanding of the context of use of my educational research through the work of David Hamilton (1989, 1990) and Brian Simon (1990, 1992). In thinking about the context of use I recognise that I am in the context. The context is influencing my research and my research is influencing the context. I am not attempting to extend my understanding from the perspective of the kind of disinterested scholarly pursuit of truth implicit in Hamilton's use of a range of conceptual prisms to display some of the forms that schooling has taken over the last thousand years. I am trying to extend my understanding of my context from the perspective of a committed educational researcher whose enquiries are intended as a direct contribution to the construction of a better social order. I think this view is similar to Hamilton's (1990) conclusion that teachers and learners are, at one and the same time, both the social target of schooling and the active medium through which the target can be reached. I agree that regulation and redefinition are inseparable aspects of the same social process. Given my interest in improving practice I am more interested in redefinition than regulation whilst recognising that an understanding of regulation is important in redefinition.

Hamilton is aware that his analysis has given a disproportionate amount of attention to social regulation. He sees this as an outcome of a decision to focus upon the schooling of those who are less powerful in society. Hence the analysis emphasises schooling in terms of institutional structures and arrangements which reproduce repressive ideologies, social inequalities and hierarchical forms of control. I can integrate this historical understanding of the development of schooling within my understanding of my context because it helps to explain how schooling, as distinct from education, has become embedded so firmly within the power relations which sustain our present social structures. I turned to Hamilton's *Learning about Education,* in the hope of further enlightenment about my present context of education as distinct from schooling. In stressing the history of schooling as an eloquent testimony to the self-conscious and reactivity of human beings Hamilton shows that it was the reactivity of human beings - learners as well as teachers - that helped to turn education into schooling, and teaching into school teaching. He intentionally leaves his readers with an open-ended text in the sense that certain tensions are deliberately left unresolved in the following questions:

> *'Under what circumstances, if any, is it possible to reconcile the "needs" of the learner with the "needs" of the state? Similarly, should tax-funded institutions of teacher training focus upon the skills and competences of teaching or should they, by contrast, address a different set of practices - schoolteaching? Or can they do both?'* (Hamilton, 1990)

With these tensions unresolved in my present educational context, can Brian Simon's work enhance my understanding of how to attempt a resolution? Because my interest is focused on my present context I will concentrate on what he has to say about the last thirteen years of Conservative Government because of the dramatic influence their policies are having.

My understanding of my present context is focused on the tension identified in a discussion on what was at stake for Education in the 1992 General Election.

> *'At stake is the central element in the government's domestic policies since its 1987 victory. Temporarily eclipsed by the poll tax flare-up, obscured for the moment by the arid complexity of privatisation, education nevertheless is the decisive ground on which two visions of Britain must compete, private market and public good' (Simon, 1992).*

The 1988 Education Act established the Local Management of Schools. This was part of the process to achieve market conditions. As a Chair of Governors of a school which received its first delegated budget in April 1992 I am experiencing the tensions and challenges of responding to and attempting to create certain market conditions whilst enhancing the educational goods for pupils and teachers within a school.

New legislation is designed to accelerate the process of 'freeing' schools from their relationships with local authorities. Schools are to be placed in the market place to compete with each other. Such market conditions have already influenced my work as a tutor on action research programmes for senior managers in three local authorities. The language and practices of compulsory competitive tendering have been integrated into Local Authority policies with an increase in tension within individuals' experience of the demands of market forces and the public good. This tension is reflected in the action research reports of the senior managers with whom I work (see Part Four). These reports will be examined during the 1993/94 academic year and I hope that these will be added to the collection as examples of how action research can contribute to our understanding of the process management of education in the workplace.

Writing in the context of the National Curriculum, Simon (1992) explores the influence of the teacher researcher movement and I accept his point that it is indeed a hope for the future.

> 'It is this stance, as I understand it, that characterises the reflective teacher - one who submits his or her own practice to a consistent appraisal. To achieve this is surely no easy task, but if we are to empower our youth - to enable them to achieve rationality, to be articulate, tolerant - in short to develop as students, then the teacher's reflective role, action research, a continuous questioning must be the hallmark of success. So my question is - how far is this possible, indeed practicable, in the new dispensation now coming to being? .... I believe, this movement, concerned as it is not only with classroom processes but also those relating to the functioning of the school as a whole, has represented a nodal point of change - a hope for the future. The professionalisation of teachers in this sense must lie at the heart of the educational process as a whole' (Simon, 1992).

Such a hope has, for me, a practical implication in that it involves a commitment to support this movement. Writing months before the 1992 General Election, Simon emphasises once again the tension between market forces and public good. He says that all agree that major advances in education right across the board are necessary both to enhance the quality of life in Britain and to restore the country's economic and industrial position generally. He concludes:

> 'In place of the doctrinaire reliance on market forces to shape the future, we must substitute joint, co-operative effort by all concerned to build an educational environment directed to realising the full potentialities of all our citizens, whatever their age, gender, race or social class. Such must be the objective' (Simon, op. cit.).

I now understand better the tension I experience between the influence of market forces and my commitment to contribute to the public good through education as a defining condition of my present educational context. In setting out my action plans in Chapter Thirteen I intend to use my influence to encourage the creation of living educational theories from action research, for our pupils, our profession and our humanity. I see such theories as directly contributing to the construction of an educational environment which is moving towards a better world or a good social order. This practical commitment moves beyond the conceptual forms of understanding of the historian or traditional educational theorist. It requires a personal commitment to contribute oneself to the creation of a living educational theory in the name of education and humanity.

CHAPTER THIRTEEN

CREATING LIVING EDUCATIONAL THEORIES FOR OUR STUDENTS, OUR PROFESSION AND OUR HUMANITY

SOME RECENT contributions to action research and educational theory have been discussed by Jean McNiff (1993) and John Elliott (1989). In addition, Chapter Three of Jean's book, *Action Research: Principles and Practice* (1992), contrasts different approaches to action research and outlines the concept of a living educational theory. John edited a special issue of the *Cambridge Journal of Education* on *New Directions for Educational theory and on Educational Inquiry and the Development of Teachers' Professional Knowledge.* Pages 90-100 of this issue of the Cambridge Journal relate my ideas on creating a living educational theory to the ideas of a number of international contributors. I must emphasise that the growth of the idea of a living educational theory is not a matter of applying my ideas to your practice. The growth of the idea rests upon your decision to understand your professional practice from your own points of view as professionals who are exercising their own creative and critical powers in generating valid explanations for their own educational development in the name of their own education and humanity.

I now want to consider a number of presentations at the First and Second World Congresses on Action Research and Process Management (1990 and 1992), from Britain, Australia and Developing Countries and relate these to the creation of living educational theories.

As I mentioned above the last decade has seen a significant growth of interest in action research in schools, universities and the public services. A number of texts referred to above (McNiff, 1992; McNiff, *et. al.* 1992; Elliott, 1991; Winter, 1989; Carr and Kemmis, 1986; Carr, 1990), outline the principles of action research. What is noticeable about these texts is that, with the exception of McNiff, 1992 and 1993, and McNiff *et. al.*, 1992 no author presents an account of their own sustained educative relationships in their workplace in which their students show their own educational development. Yet as each author acknowledges, a defining characteristic of action research is a study by the researcher of his or her own practice. This omission raises a similar question to that raised by Colin Henry at the end of the First World Congress on Action Research:

'A final issue is the question of authenticity, the problem of recommending to others activities we do not engage in ourselves. If someone was to tell us: "Tennis is a great game and you should play it regularly. But I don't play tennis myself and wouldn't want to play it", we might be sceptical about the advice we were given. Similarly, how convincing is it when we recommend action research or action learning to others, but never engage, or intend to engage, in action research or action learning ourselves?' (Henry, 1991)

I have raised such a critical question elsewhere (Whitehead, 1990) in relation to the work of Jean Rudduck, another British academic who has done much to promote the teacher research movement. I want to put such criticism in the context of MacIntyre's (1990) proposals for reconceiving the University as a place of constrained disagreement for the development of moral and theological arguments. One of the ways in which dominant forms of discourse retain their position is by ignoring criticism or through the exercise of bias, prejudice and inadequate assessment. Drawing on the work of Foucault I pointed out to the First World Congress how particular regimes of 'truth' can retain their 'legitimacy' through the power of their proponents. For those concerned with truth it is a matter of concern when academics do not respond to criticism which is intended to point out mistakes and errors and to offer ways of transcending such mistakes and errors.

I wonder if this partially explains why it is that with the growing literature on action research there is no consensus on the nature of the theory produced from such research. I am suggesting that the main reason is that the most influential proponents of action research have not systematically studied their own educational development and explicated the epistemological and methodological assumptions in a claim to know this development. In asking the following questions I want to include a personal form of communication. I am doing this because I want the following individuals to feel that my questions, whilst critical, carry no destructive intent. They are asked with the intention of enhancing the already substantial contributions of those individuals to educational research. I am hoping that the dialogical form of my response to their work will serve as an invitation for you to engage in conversations and correspondence with those whose work is in the collection. Through such communications you can contribute to the educational development of others and to the growth of educational knowledge.

For example, when Jean (Rudduck, 1989), you write about teacher research in initial teacher education, I could not find any evidence in your students' own voices which showed how they experienced an educative relationship with you and in which they had learned something of value. I wonder if your own enquiries could be moved forward by answering questions about the quality of evidence which needs to be gathered to enable you to show the nature of your educative relationships in initial teacher education? Do you think that those asking such questions should be answered?

When Wilf (Carr, 1989), you write about the Quality of Teaching and your enquiries do not contain your students' voices or any evidence to show how you relate your teaching to your students' learning, using the principles you advocate, I wonder if your enquiry could be moved forward by gathering evidence to show to what extent you are living your own principles in your practice?

When John (Elliott, 1991), you write about action research, practical competence and professional knowledge, I looked for some evidence which might show a direct relationship between your practical competence and your professional knowledge in the voices of those you teach. If you can offer such evidence I wonder if your enquiry could be moved forward by relating the gathering of this evidence to the principles you outline in your text on action research and educational change?

When Richard (Winter, 1991), you write about learning from experience and the six principles for the conduct of action research, I looked for evidence of your educative relationships with your students. I wonder if your enquiry might be moved forward by gathering evidence on your own rigorously conducted case study on your own professional practice in which your use of your own principles can be seen, in your students' own voices, to have influenced their educational development as Erica Holley has done in Chapter 14?

I am hoping that you will by now have sufficient evidence to judge the validity of my idea that educational theory should be conceived as being constituted by the descriptions and explanations which individual learners are producing for their own educational development. What I have in mind is the idea that each individual who wishes to contribute consciously to the future of humanity through education should offer his/her own educational theory in the form of an explanation for his/her own educational development, for public criticism. I have given some examples above on how this can be achieved. The British academic who has done most, along with Jean McNiff, to publicise this idea and to make her own original contribution is Pamela Lomax (1989, 1991, 1992), a Professor of Educational Research at Kingston University. Pamela has been extending the action research approaches to professional development into educational management and is one of the leading academics in educational action research in the U.K..

Robin McTaggart is Associate Professor in the Faculty of Education of Deakin University. In his address (McTaggart, 1992) to the Second World Congress, he explored his concerns about Western cultural imperialism in Aboriginal Australia and located his concerns in the global contexts of the influence of aid and development in the Third World. He questioned the assumptions behind the forms of economic rationalism espoused by the IMF and World Bank:

'Nevertheless, the new "economic rationalism" is a worldwide phenomenon which "guides" not only the conduct of transnational corporations, but governments and their agencies as well. It does so with

increasing efficacy and pervasiveness. I use the term "guides" here in quotes to make a particular point. Economic rationalism is not merely a term which suggests the primacy of economic values. It expresses commitment to those values in order to serve particular sets of interests ahead of others. Furthermore, it disguises that commitment in a discourse of "economic necessity" defined by its economic models. We have moved beyond the reductionism which leads all questions to be discussed as if they were economic ones (de-valuation) to a situation which moral questions are denied completely (de-moralisation) in a cult of economic inevitability (as if greed had nothing to do with it)' (McTaggart, 1992).

Robin (McTaggart), I agree with your analysis, but could not understand how you were integrating this analysis into your own action research. Given that you are feeling the de-valuation and de-moralisation in your workplace, what has been your response to this experience? How are you continuing to struggle to live out your values in the face of the structural problems you outlined in your analysis? I identified with your views of economic rationalism because I experienced the direct influence of economics on my work at a staff meeting on 17th June 1992 in the following proposal to quantify teaching loads.

'We need an income of £1m next year to stay afloat. Allowing for bought in teaching and administrative loads, this means we ought each to be earning in the region of £ 50,000 - £55,000 over the year. This can be earned either by teaching or by buying oneself out. £50,000 approx. can be earned by recruiting and teaching 15 full time equivalent students (bearing in mind not all students are fully funded). This is roughly equivalent to 450 hours contact time (i.e. an average of 12.5 hours teaching per week over a 36 week year)' (Staff Meeting Minutes, School of Education, 1992).

My contract with the University from 1976 makes no reference to earning money for the University. I earned some £ 22,000 **from** the University for 1991/ 92. It appears that next year I am expected to earn some £50,000 - £ 55,000 **for** the University. It will be interesting to examine the economic pressures on my educational development, knowledge producing research, and teaching in the years to come.

Colin (Henry, 1991), I agreed with your evaluation of the First World Congress in which you asked action researchers to take care to understand the principles of this form of research. In my contribution to the Second World Congress I was conscious of accepting your points and I took some care to heed your advice. In your evaluation of the Second Congress you reiterated the point that it is important for those who claim to be action researchers to recognise that there are defining characteristics of this form of research which they should use in judging their claim. I appreciated the care of your first evaluation. I may be being unjust in pointing out the following omission, but your second evaluation did not contain any evidence that you had examined the published proceedings of the Second Congress to see to what extent your evaluations of the First Congress had been accepted or rejected or acted upon.

In your evaluation of the Second Congress I identified with your suggestion that we should be evaluating our effectiveness in producing a participatory form of knowledge which is more human, rational and liberating than the dominating knowledge of today. I think that I have done this in the case study presented to the Second Congress (Whitehead, 1992). Do you agree? I also acknowledge and accept your stress on the importance for action researchers of locating their work in the global context of improving the world by reducing war, starvation, poverty and corrupt government. I think my own work is failing to address the issues of starvation, war and poverty and that the development of my action research should be judged by the extent to which I am beginning to show some contribution in these areas. As I write, the civil war within the borders of the republics of the old Yugoslavia is killing, injuring and destroying. In Somalia, the horror of poverty and starvation are there for all to see.

You made a point at the Second World Congress which I accepted without question at the time. You were reticent about criticising directly the work of colleagues who appeared to be supporting action research. Given your important role in helping participants in the World Congresses to evaluate the content and process management, I invite you to criticise my own action research because I value the insights which you have already shown.

Ortrun Zuber-Skerritt has worked as a senior consultant in the Tertiary Education Institute, University of Queensland. Her publications (1990, 1991a, 1991b) include *A theoretical framework for action research in the context of professional development in higher education.* This prompted my own paper to the Congress.

The point I made to Ortrun at the Second World Congress was that the publication of the theoretical framework for action research in higher education as a separate text from the case studies could encourage a separation between theory and practice which I had tried to overcome in my holistic presentation in the case study of my own educational development. Ortrun responded by explaining that there was another text which was the story of her own development and which was due to be submitted for a further Higher Degree. It may be possible to analyse this work at the Third World Congress on Action Learning, Action Research and Process Management which is to be held at the University of Bath in 1994. I think the difference between the theoretical framework produced by Ortrun and my understanding of a living form of educational theory is symptomatic of a wider debate about the nature of educational theory and practice.

Having introduced the idea of a living educational theory in the Australian context of two World Congresses it will be interesting to see if any action researchers from this context both offer a description and explanation for their own educational development as individual learners and find it useful to relate the explanation to the development of their living educational theory for the future of humanity. It should be possible for the Third World Congress at Bath University, 6-9th July 1994, to offer a fuller response to Ortrun Zuber-Skerritt's work based on the theoretical framework, case studies and story of her own development.

My reflections on the possibility of creating living educational theories from action research in an Australian context draw on Brian Fay's advocacy of an educative model and rejection of an instrumentalist conception of theory and practice:

> 'According to the educative model, theoretical knowledge is useful to the extent that it informs people what their needs are and how a particular way of living is frustrating these needs, thereby causing them to suffer; its goal is to enlighten people about how they can change their lives so that, having arrived at a new understanding, they may reduce their suffering by creating another way of life that is more fulfilling. In the instrumentalist model, social theories increase power by providing appropriate knowledge in terms of which one can manipulate the causal mechanisms that characterize a certain social order so that a desired end state is produced; in the educative model, social theories are the means by which people can liberate themselves from the particular causal processes that victimize them precisely because they are ignorant of who they are' (Fay, 1977).

At the end of his paper Fay asks the important question, 'Can one elaborate an account of how radical social change can occur given the conceptual resources of the educative model?' He says that this question must be answered if, in the end, the viewpoint of critical theory is going to provide us with a model of how social theory can inform social practice that is distinctive, realizable, and truly liberating. He ends with the point that to his knowledge, in 1977, no such account exists.

The publication which should provide an answer to this question is the third edition of the *Action Research Reader,* edited by Stephen Kemmis and Robin McTaggart and published in 1988. Whilst it omits the idea of a living educational theory and contains no contributions from the Bath Action Research Group it is still the most impressive collection of papers available on the history of action research and it offers international perspectives from North America, The United Kingdom, Continental Europe, Australia and the Third World. Both Kemmis (1993) and McTaggart have explored the implications of the view of critical theory in the above context with impressive integrity. I think they have explored the **conceptual** possibilities of critical theory to its limits. They are, however, in my view, limiting unnecessarily their contribution to educational theory by permitting their conceptual understanding of critical theory to impose its structure on their analyses, in a way which may be preventing them from seeing the significance of producing their own case studies of their own educative relationships in the workplace. I am thinking of case studies which contain the emancipated voices of their students in stories of their own educational development.

If living educational theories from action research are to be created by the above researchers they may find it necessary to study their own educational development in the context of their own workplace as they show how they are responding to the social pressures made explicit in their critical analyses. Colin Henry (1991) appears to be moving in this direction in his work on human rights education, where he accepts a view of educational research as a practical activity concerned with the resolution of educational problems and the improvement of educational practice. He concludes his analysis of the programme with the point that it is the will and capacity of teachers to reform educational practice and to contribute to the renewal of our educational institutions which is enhanced by their participation in curriculum development, research and evaluation.

Whilst his paper contains some fascinating data from a teacher researcher and pupils, it does not show the educational development of any pupil through time. As with all the contributions, from the critical theory stance, to the action research planner, the academic analysis is focused on critical theory, rather than on making a creative contribution to educational theory. From my viewpoint as an educational researcher, the analyses lack the first person engagement of the participants in trying to live out their values more fully in their practice, trying to understand their development and trying to improve the social context in which the practice is located. I wonder if their work fails the test of applying one of Fay's criteria for testing the truth of a critical theory. That is the considered reaction by those for whom it is supposed to be emancipating. As Fay says:

> 'This is because a critical theory is one that offers an interpretation of a person's actions, feelings, and needs, and interpretations must be tested against the responses that those being interpreted make to them. When a person does not, under any condition, accept a social theorist's account as giving the meaning of his behaviour, providing an accurate description of what he feels, or revealing his "real" purpose or desires, then this is prima facie evidence against the correctness of the account' (Fay, op. cit.).

If action researchers associated with a school of critical theory fulfil Colin Henry's criteria for judging action research then we could expect to see accounts of their own educational and social development in the context of their workplace. Given the nature of critical theory the implication for the lives of these action researchers is that they would experience themselves as living contradictions within the political economy and values of their workplace. I can see no such accounts in the *Action Research Reader*. It may be that future editions may acknowledge the importance of such accounts in creating living educational theories from action research for our humanity.

Orlando Fals-Borda is an Emeritus Professor at the National University of Colombia. Some 20 years ago he left his University post, feeling dissatisfied that the knowledge in the academy did not adequately reflect the practical knowledge of ordinary people. He left to work with them on land reform and developed a participatory approach to action research. His book with Rahman (1991) on *Action and Knowledge,* contains international contributions on Participatory Action Research (PAR). This is in the collection. It contains papers from researchers working in Peru, Nicaragua, Columbia, Bangladesh, Zimbabwe, Tennessee and Sri Lanka. Fals-Borda and Rahman set out the theoretical assumptions of participatory action research and, in a section on the meaning of dialogical research, Fals-Borda explains how the reconstruction of knowledge for the purpose of furthering social progress and increasing people's self-awareness takes dialogue as its point of insertion in the social process. (This dialogical position is identical to recent work in the Bath Action Research Group and developed independently.)

> *'The generation of (scientific) knowledge does not require the method of detached observation of the positivist school. Any observation, whether it is detached or involved, is value-biased, and this is not where the scientific character of knowledge is determined. The scientific character or objectivity of knowledge rests on its social verifiability, and this depends on consensus as to the method of verification. There exist different epistemological schools (paradigms) with different respective verification systems, and all scientific knowledge in this sense is relative to the paradigm to which it belongs and, specifically, to the verification system to which it is submitted.*
>
> *In this sense the people can choose or devise their own verification system to generate scientific knowledge in their own right. An immediate objective of PAR (Participatory Action Research) is to return to the people the legitimacy of the knowledge they are capable of producing through their own verification systems, as fully scientific, and the right to use this knowledge - including any other knowledge, but not dictated by it - as a guide in their own action. This immediate objective is an integral and indispensible part of the objective of dual social transformation - in the relations of material production and in the relations of knowledge'* (Fals-Borda and Rahman, 1991).

Orlando's keynote address to the Second World Congress in July 1992 focused on the contribution of PAR to the action research movement. What I found interesting, as an omission in the above text, was any dialogue. The researchers were speaking on behalf of those they had researched with rather than allowing the voices of their co-researchers to be presented in the text. The form of presentation seemed to deny the dialogical principles espoused in the text.

Another contribution from a developing country was Arphron Chuaprapaislip's paper on Action Research in Nursing Education in Thailand. This was presented to the First World Congress and is in the collection. Arphron develops an action research spiral to illustrate the way in which the learning process was enhanced through its incorporation with Buddhist teaching. In her conclusions she says:

'This study is just the beginning of a journey forwards into the realm of lifelong learning. It is influenced by events of the past and, in itself, provides a focus for future events. By fully gaining insights from the past and by contemplating on the present (using emancipatory wisdom) and by taking responsibility for the future, we gain the force to drive forwards by drawing fully upon our experiences. This is illustrated by the Buddhist Mandala which links cause and effect that are related and leads to continuous change (Paticcasamuppada, The Dependent Origination). The result is not permanent, but will be transformed to another form. Knowledge and technological changes are related through the interaction between person (mind and body) and the environment. To borrow from Buddhist terminology, productive contemplation, supported by Virtue will ultimately lead to Wisdom. To the participants, the researcher and readers of this study, the Mandala Wheel which is based on changes in cause and effect allows us to move forwards in seeking ways to learn from experience' (Chuaprapaislip, 1991).

I was struck by the similarity between the insights in this quotation, of the relation between the past, present and future, and the inclusion of such a relationship in the creation of living educational theories. I see the creation of such theories as a process of lifelong learning. I agree that this process 'is influenced by events of the past and, in itself, provides a focus for future events. By fully gaining insights from the past and by contemplating on the present (using emancipatory wisdom) and by taking responsibility for the future, we gain the force to drive forwards by drawing fully upon our experiences'. I would add that we also have the opportunity for creating living educational theories for the future of our humanity.

If educational theory is a form of dialogue which has profound implications for the future of humanity and if such a theory is being constituted by personal educational theories I expect to hear and see evidence of dialogues and action through which individuals and groups are learning something of value in the context of the future of their humanity. I am thinking of the kind of evidence being provided by Craig (1993), Clandinin (1993) and Connelly (1993) within their Canadian context. In the contributions from developing countries, however, there were no examples of such dialogues in the World Congress. Where is the evidence from those espousing participatory action research of their dialogical principles in action?

I asked this question of a researcher who had been conducting research in the context of a developing country and who had circulated a draft paper before presenting his findings to a European audience. I asked about the omission of dialogue in his paper and about the nature of the educative conversations he had experienced in the developing country. When he described some of the problems of conducting the research I asked why these problems did not appear in the paper. He explained that if he were to be honest about the problems then the continuation of the funding would be unlikely to be forthcoming because the problems would reveal corruption in those responsible for funding. I asked about the problems of being economical with the truth. These were acknowledged but the paper was still presented to the European audience with no acknowledgement of the real problems of working in the developing country. I wish to stress that I do not believe that such problems are restricted to developing countries. If we are to take Henry's evaluations seriously such problems must be addressed, wherever they are found.

In the context of a political economy of action research I was struck by Susan Noffke's (1992) analysis at the Second World Congress. What I have tried to do is to include my experience of political economy in the story of my educational development below. This has led to real conflict in living out my educational values in the workplace. Is there not something incongruous about academics continuing to gain promotion after promotion for their analyses of political economy, often from an explicitly neo-Marxist perspective, whilst the subjects of their analyses are getting poorer and being subjected to continuing and sometimes increasing forms of oppression? In this context I asked a similar question of Michael Apple, who was advocating a strategy of refusal, in a lecture to the American Educational Research Association in San Francisco in April 1992. I asked if he had any evidence of a systematic analysis of the implications for his own educational development of such a refusal in his own workplace. He provided no evidence.

I continue to ask Geoff Whitty a similar question given his advocacy (Whitty, 1989) that American and Australian Sociologists of Education should show how their work was benefiting those in whose interests it was being put forward. My reason for feeling so critical of neo-Marxist perspectives is not that I have rejected all Marxist thinking. I continue to use Marxist dialectics as the most powerful logic for understanding human development. It is the 'Grand Narrative' of historical materialism that I reject. I am suggesting that the creation of living educational theories for the future of humanity may offer a way of integrating insights from the traditional forms of knowledge whilst at the same time showing the educational development of those whose interests the creation of living educational theories was meant to serve - that is ourselves and each other.

To show what I mean by this I now want to focus your attention on what I have learnt in my educative relationships with three teacher researchers, Erica Holley (M.Phil. programme), Moira Laidlaw (Ph.D. programme) and Peggy Kok (M.Ed. programme). It is a pleasure to return to the quality of educative conversations I was interested in researching in the 1977 paper in Part One. With Erica I am learning about the importance of retaining a focus on the educative relationships with individuals and whole classes of pupils in schools, and a caring and professional relationship in accounting for oneself with colleagues who are being appraised. Whilst there is no evidence in Erica's contribution of an educational relationship with me I want to direct your attention to her work at Greendown School in Swindon because of the way she retains a focus on the quality of relationships with both pupils and staff. From Erica I am also learning more about the nature of educative relationships which can help pupils to form their own enquiries.

From Moira I am learning a similar lesson in relation to education students in a University as she shows how she helped a group of postgraduate students to engage in their own enquiries and produce descriptions and explanations for their own development. I have already presented Moira's feedback to her students as part of the above collection (see Chapter 11). From Peggy Kok I learnt about the art of conducting an educational enquiry which included a struggle to reconcile different values. In the extract from her work I think that she provides the evidence of our educative relationship in which I can be seen to be respecting her integrity in Buber's sense that I show the humility of an educator who subordinates his or her own view of the world to the particular educational needs of the student. Finally I will present an account which breaks this feeling of harmony by acknowledging that market forces are beginning to penetrate the story of my educational development. They have done this most forcefully in my work supporting action research with a group of senior managers from Avon, Wiltshire and Gloucestershire. In order to preserve the delight and quality in the accounts which follow I think we will need to protect ourselves and education from any further penetration by these forces.

PART THREE

EDUCATIVE RELATIONSHIPS

CHAPTER FOURTEEN

WORKING WITH ERICA HOLLEY

ERICA HOLLEY is a teacher at Greendown School in Swindon. She is researching her own professional practice in an M.Phil. programme with the University of Bath. Over the past year she has produced three papers whose introductions appear below. As her supervisor I am attempting to understand her values and learn how she creates such a high quality of educative relationships with her pupils and colleagues. The focus in her papers is on educative relationships and they move from an individual pupil to a whole class and to a teacher in a monitoring and appraisal process. These movements are shown in the following extracts from three separate papers. However as Erica says,

Extract 1:

I Can Speak for Myself—July 1992

This paper looks at the work I undertook from July to December 1991 with one of my year ten students, Poppy. It shows us working in a collaborative and supportive way to improve the quality of our work. It also demonstrates how I developed my practice through reflection and why I became increasingly confident to question academics who attempt to speak for me. Recognising that my practice was worth describing was a great move forward for me and so was the recognition that academics who attempt to speak for me so often get it wrong.

I have a memory from the novel *The Adventures of Tom Sawyer* by Mark Twain. It's when Tom is lost deep underground and to find his way out he ties a kite line to a rock and carefully edges his way through many passages. He doesn't let go of the kite line until he is sure of where he is and he knows there is no need to wind it back to his safe starting place. Since starting my research I've felt a bit like Tom Sawyer holding fast to a kite line. I have edged out from my original question about improving the talk of girls in my classroom; I've cautiously tried to understand and to improve my practice but throughout I've held on to the ideas about talk in the classroom presented in academic journals and books. Researchers who are not teachers have written about what teachers should try to improve in talk and what those improvements should look like and too often I've accepted those models. I've tried to write honestly and openly about what I've done but too often I've failed to write in my real voice or about my real concerns because I've held on to that kite-line of what I think I should be concerned about and what I assume writing in an academic way should look like.

In a recent pamphlet, *Democracy and Education*, Anthony O'Hear (1991), Professor of Philosophy at Bradford University and a member of the Council for the Accreditation of Teacher Education, stated that all education is *'irretrievably authoritarian and paternalist'*. My paper shows an education which is collaborative and supportive and which denies O'Hear's assertions. While he has argued that education is a *'transaction between unequals'* which will *'result in a change in the knowledge, wisdom and values of the pupil'*, I will show that my work with a student allows parity in dialogue despite the unequal power relationship, and that the work we undertake enables **both** of us to change because of our insights and our developing understanding of our own educational development.

The pamphlet provided another focus for my work and for this paper. His view of education denies mine. As my students and I live out our experiences in the classroom we negate O'Hear's descriptions of education as *'authoritarian and paternalist'*. I cannot accept his call for an education system which is *'divisive, elitist and inegalitarian'*. My rage that an academic, remote from the classroom, could deny my experience and my values in his writing, pushed forward my work as a teacher-researcher.

O'Hear's pamphlet also enabled me to recognise that my practice is worth describing because it attempts to live out values which are important to me. That recognition has helped me to let go of the line. I now feel confident to describe my practice in a way that I was reluctant to do so before. I can no longer be silent when someone in O'Hear's position is distorting and undermining the very things I care about in education.

O'Hear denies completely what I attempt to do in my work in the classroom. As a teacher I also try to be a reflective practioner systematically researching my own practice in order to improve the quality of learning for my students and for myself. When I began this research I felt supported by the teacher research movement and people like Jean Ruddock and John Elliott who seemed to understand that a new form of educational knowledge was being created by teachers producing accounts of their work in the classroom. However, even academics like Elliott and Rudduck sometimes only pay lipservice to teachers as researchers and remind me of parents who can't let their children grow up. They say they want to encourage teachers to be reflective practioners but then devalue the use of it all to the teaching profession. In doing so they, too, deny my experience.

In her book which explores reading and culture Jane Miller (1990) uses seduction as a metaphor to show how women are excluded from literary theory. For 'women' read 'teachers' as the metaphor fits. Thus teachers are seduced by academics who simultaneously include and exclude us in their writing about teaching. Our presence is taken for granted and yet denied and we are enticed into narratives which reduce us by exalting us. They speak for us. I can speak for myself.

Recent articles on initial teacher training in the *British Educational Research Journal* by John Elliott (1991) and Jean Rudduck (1991) stress the importance of critical reflective thinking in teaching. Both criticise government plans to shift initial teacher training from Higher Education to schools because they believe that all student teachers need frameworks for thinking about what they do and that these frameworks can only be provided by people like themselves.

Elliott seems to want to protect student teachers against disillusioned competent teachers while Rudduck perceives teachers as increasingly experiencing the school day as *'an intense and unremitting series of pedagogic, pastoral and administrative demands'* with little time for reflective practice. Rudduck's call for a *'language of consciousness'* and Elliott's *'model of professionalism'* seem to court teachers and yet to spurn us. They seem to offer no way in which the reflections of competent teachers can be used to show educational development.

My account of work with Poppy thus highlights a tension between the educational theory presented by academics and my own understanding of competent practice in teaching. As I wrote this paper I became determined to judge the quality and effectiveness of my professional practice by reference to my own educational standards which I understand by reflection on what I do in the classroom. Such reflections create a new form of educational knowledge which is grounded in practice and it challenges those academics who attempt to talk for me.

Working with Poppy

Why Poppy? In July 1991 I was still interested in improving the kind of conversations I had with girls in my classroom. I interviewed a number of girls from the class I knew I was to teach for the following two years. I talked to them about their humanities work and intended to follow up work with all of them. I tried to build up a picture of them as learners and wanted to find out about what motivated them. When I talked to Poppy I began to understand that her writing was important to her because she became more enthusiastic and talked more personally about it than anything else.

The part of the discussion about her writing went like this:

Erica: *Have you got any strengths that I can build on in the humanities area?*

Poppy: *Writing.*

Erica: *Any particular form of writing?*

Poppy: *Any form. I just love it.*

Erica: *How do you go about it?*

Poppy: *Well, I just write it usually. I don't think about it. You're supposed to plan it out but I never do. I always find it goes wrong if I do that.*

Erica: *Do you draft out?*

Poppy: *No, I don't do that either.*

Erica: *I see. Right.*

Poppy: *I usually edit as I go along, which most people seem to find difficult but ...*

Erica: *You find OK?*

That conversation in July formed an unwritten agenda for me in my future work with Poppy. I intended to encourage her to think about her writing and to encourage her to draft and re-draft her work because that seemed to be a good thing to do in order to improve her writing ...

We talked in the classroom during a morning session. It took place amid a lot of activity as students were going in and out of the room to do observations, surveys and so on. Poppy and I were interrupted a number of times and there's a lot of background noise on the tape. What's difficult in transcribing this is not being able to show the body language. At times in the transcript I appear to be going on a bit but it was in response to Poppy's intense look of interest and head nodding. I felt that she was willing me to carry on so that I'd get to what she wanted to pick up on. The main reason we talked was to look at her ideas for a piece of writing. The transcript shows our mutual engagement, with ideas being teased out and respected. We started by looking at the list of ideas she might write about.

Extract from a classroom conversation - 18-10-91

Erica: *Right, show me this thing. I'm really looking forward to this.*

Poppy: *I don't know why. It's like a brainstorm of my ideas - there are so many.*

Erica: *(reads) 'Looks'.*

Poppy: *Whether you think they're good or...*

Erica: *Oh, right. 'Clothes, jokes'. What do you mean, jokes? Don't understand that.*

Poppy: *Can't remember now actually.*

Erica: *People making fun of them?*

Poppy: *Could be. Yes.*

Erica: *'Friends. Enemies.' (Reads a list) Got any more? That about sums up the human race. I'm not sure what you mean by 'taste'. Is that about anxieties about peer group, then?*

Poppy: *Yes.*

Erica: *Can I write something on this book?*

Poppy: *Yes.*

Erica: *(Writes 'Is that peer group pressure?') Physical appearance. Those things always interest me. How people feel about themselves.*

Poppy: *Yes.*

Erica: *Whether they are too fat, too thin, too ugly, too beautiful. Whether their hair is too long, too short or whatever. Which one of these ... choose, say, three things that you think you've got enough ideas about to explore a bit further.*

Poppy: *Could be any of them - except allergies or diseases. I wouldn't do that one.*

Erica: *Well, look, why don't we start off with things that you've got anxieties about?*

Poppy: *All of these, actually.*

Erica: *Things that are most, sort of, make you most anxious and then - if you're going to write ...*

Poppy: *Yes, you have to know something about them.*

Erica: *Yes. OK. Do you want to start at the bottom and go up or at the top and come down?*

Poppy: *'Guilt'- All the time!*

Erica: *OK - about what sort of things?*

Poppy: *Something you think you've done wrong. You think you've offended someone.*

Erica: *Guilt about how you treat other people or what you say? 'Work'. Not much?*

Poppy: *Not on the whole.*

Erica: *Scrub that one?*

Poppy: *Yes.*

Erica: *Ok. Sex?*

Poppy: *Frequently.*

Erica: *That's anxieties about growing up and wondering what it is?*

Poppy: *Exactly.*

Erica: *Scrub that one, then?*

Poppy: *'Secrets'. If you've got secrets you don't want anybody to know so you get worried about them.*

Erica: *Right and you can't share them. So they're ... that might be difficult for a character.*

Poppy: *It would be.*

Erica: *You're still having to draw that line between what's Poppy and what's character. And that might be for your private writing that you don't want other people to read, that you don't want me to read or an audience.*

Poppy: *You can have secrets about other things, though.*

Erica: *Like what?*

Poppy: *I don't know. Secrets I haven't got secrets about.*

Erica: *Right. So you could make them up. (Yes) Fine. 'Past.'*

Poppy: *Pretty wide that, isn't it?*

Erica: *Yes, because it links with secrets, in a sense.*

Poppy: *Yes, it links with a lot of things.*

Up until that point I felt that we'd been skirting around what was concerning Poppy. We were at ease with each other and had given each other room to talk about ideas. It wasn't my aim to get Poppy to open up her private self to me because that could leave her in a vulnerable position. I wanted her to feel confident enough to write about what was important to her. She did open up, though, in a way which showed that she trusted me to listen to her and to accept that her concerns were important. I knew after I said 'families' that Poppy wanted to explore this further. She kept nodding and affirming what I said. I talked about divorced families as a hunch. I had no knowledge of Poppy's family circumstances.

Extract 2:

Accountability: Rendering an account - November 1992

In July 1992, having described my practice with one year 10 student, Poppy, in which I showed how we had worked together in a collaborative and supportive way to improve the quality of our work, I wanted to put that practice into context by describing what I'd done with the rest of her class. Was I able to show that I could work collaboratively and supportively with other students? How had my work with Poppy and the understanding I'd come to about dialogue informed my work with the rest of her class?

My work with Poppy had taken place among her class, 10 Mh, and yet I wrote about Poppy as if we'd been in a room on our own. I'd seldom mentioned 10Mh in my paper, only once recognising they were there by writing that Poppy and I ...'talked in the classroom during a morning session. It took place amid a lot of activity as students were going in and out of the room to do observations, surveys and so on. Poppy and I were interrupted a number of times and there's a lot of noise on the tape' (Holley, 1992).

Writing about one student as if the others didn't exist is like writing about the eye of the storm: it appears calm, peaceful and intense but ignores a whole lot of other things that are going on in the classroom. There isn't just her class to consider either, as what goes on in the rest of the school affects our work too. The image of a Russian doll comes to mind as I write: a student, her class, her teacher, the school, the local education authority, the DFE and so on.

My original intention, then, was to write about my practice with 10Mh over the year September 1991 to July 1992. It seemed a logical step to take and a simple enough paper to write; but it wasn't. A lot got in my way. This year I have understood the curse 'may you live in interesting times'. These times are 'interesting' because of government policies that affect the work of all schools and the people in them.

Since writing that paper about Poppy I have read much about what teachers should be doing and how they should be doing it. The writers haven't always been academics but have often been politicians, and their missives on education and teaching have had an effect on the way my school and its curriculum is managed and has inevitably touched on my work in the classroom, with 10 Mh and other classes.

The National Curriculum is still being amended with far-reaching consequences for teachers and students. Professor Paul Black who helped devise the government's tests for students recently accused ministers of a 'monumental cock-up' (*The Guardian* 1991) over changes to the National Curriculum. He believed that changes were disruptive and teachers were beginning to think that the curriculum wasn't worth taking seriously because it was bound to keep changing. At the beginning of September 1992 when the government announced yet another 'further review' of English teaching, Melanie Phillips of *The Guardian* was moved to write that the constant changes in the curriculum indicated:

> '*a turbulence of constantly changing politicians and advisers, driven by panic and political opportunism to change their minds all the time. But there is one deeper, unpalatable reason for such neurotic behaviour. It is that the government simply does not trust its teachers to exercise their professional judgement. As a result, it feels driven not merely to lay down broad parameters but to describe in ever closer detail what they must do*' (*The Guardian* 11.9.92).

The message that *'the government simply does not trust its teachers'* seemed to me to be mirrored by the way changes were made in my school and I began to feel, as the year progressed, that the school managers didn't trust its teachers' professional judgements either.

It now seems important not simply to put my work with Poppy into context by writing about her class, but to put my work in the classroom with 10 Mh into the wider context of school and politics. Not to do that would be to distort the experience of what I did.

Extract 3:

Accounting for my Work—June 1993

Until recently my research has centred upon my concerns as a classroom teacher as I've tried to understand and improve the quality of dialogue and collaborative work that takes place between myself and my students. I've characterised the work I do with students as collaborative because *'it allows parity in dialogue despite the unequal power relationship'* and the work we undertake *'enables both of us to change because of our insights and our developing understanding of our own educational development'*(Holley, 1992). I believe that collaborative work based on dialogue is crucial to improving the quality of education in school so I now want to look at another aspect of my work in school, as head of the humanities department and as an appraiser, to see if I can live out those values when working with colleagues.

In writing this account of my practice I am attempting to show what it is to work with students and colleagues to improve our work in school. In the telling of this story I am holding up my work to public criticism because I am accountable for the work I do and my accountability links me to others, students and staff. I believe that my integrity as a teacher and head of department can only be sustained by my willingness to be open to informed criticism of my work and to be held to account in this way.

The main part of this paper will be a description of the work I did with David Ross from November to March 1993 as a part of the appraisal system. I was the appraiser, David the appraisee. All teachers in the U.K. now have to be appraised and at Greendown our appraisal policy statement says:

'All staff have a right and a duty to be part of an appraisal process. Our appraisal scheme is based on the fundamental concept that teachers are competent professionals who continually wish to improve their practice and that of their students. We have adopted a view of appraisal which is based on the concept of professional research and development where staff accept a research role which will enable them to evaluate their own performance and undertake professional development. Such evaluation must, within our appraisal system, involve a sharing of experience with other professionals, in which judgements are directed at the further development of teaching and educational management'.

By stating that teachers will *'research, evaluate and share'*, appraisal becomes a process which encourages reflective practice and dialogue with others in order to improve the quality of education within the school and is therefore something I am happy to be involved in.

But life in a school isn't always so straightforward and simple. Instead of rushing into a description of the work David and I did, I just want to pause to place our work in context. Our work took place alongside a new, formal system of monitoring staff in school; such a monitoring system wasn't intended to be collaborative or based on dialogue and such a contradiction in my working life was difficult. My educational values have never been so immediately challenged and denied by the people I work with. It's important then that you understand what was going on around us when David's appraisal was taking place.

The monitoring system

The monitoring system was introduced in September 1992 despite widespread criticism and hostility to it by the majority of teaching staff. It was to be carried out by three groups of senior managers: the head and deputies; senior teachers in charge of Key Stages in the school; and heads of department. All were required to visit classes, observe teachers and complete a check-sheet to show whether the teacher concerned had achieved the list of 'basic' and 'higher level' competencies. The governors' policy entitled *'Institutional quality assurance and the professional development of staff'* stated that the system of monitoring basic practice *'defines minimum classroom performance indicators and defines minimum professional practice through the use of performance indicators for all staff... the indicators are designed to be as objective and simple as possible although some degree of qualitative judgement is inevitable'* (November 1992).

The monitoring system was described to parents in a newsletter thus: *'Greendown has been redesigned ... one result of this has been the introduction of systems for quality control to regularly check and assess the quality of teaching... We have set up a classroom 'quality control' system where all staff are regularly observed teaching and where standards of performance of staff and students can be improved ... as part of this Senior staff undertake regular monitoring sessions ... As from this September the Head and Deputies conduct regular surveys of a whole class ... Key Stage Senior Teachers make regular inspections of the classwork and homework completed by students; Heads of Departments visit subject teachers and advise on specialist techniques, assessment and the introduction of the National Curriculum'* (Parents' Newsletter, 1992).

The management team seemed to think that monitoring and appraisal complemented each other but I couldn't see how. Monitoring to me was a system of surveillance which measured a teacher's competence against a set of criteria defined by the management team; appraisal was about reflective understanding, collaboration and dialogue between teachers. This was a terrible contradiction for me. As David's head of department I was expected to monitor and judge his teaching according to what the management said were 'hard-edged', objective criteria set out on the checklist; as David's appraiser I was expected to engage in a dialogue about his practice and support his attempts to improve it. Andy Larter described the contradiction exactly: *'You can't imply, through some checklist, that someone is incompetent and then ... at a later date, say, "Really you are competent. It's just nobody's perfect". You can't be Big Brother one week and the Good Shepherd the next.'* (Larter, 9th October, 1992).

I wasn't isolated in my concerns about monitoring; they were shared by many of the staff. A senior advisor in the County was invited into the school to talk to the first group of 'monitored' staff about the process. Their comments were noted for discussion and included the following points out of a list of sixteen:

- teachers felt that the monitoring sheet should be changed in the light of experience. They felt it operated like a checklist.
- they were concerned as to how the information was to be used. They didn't want it linked to pay policy.
- they asked who the senior management talked to as a result of monitoring.
- there is confusion between monitoring and appraisal.
- teachers were unclear about the purposes of monitoring.

Such points highlighted the confusions about the monitoring process. My department used the words *'tiresome, ineffective, insensitive, insulting and punitive'* to describe the whole business. And there I was in the middle of it, expected to appraise and to monitor.

In the next chapter, Moira Laidlaw analyses her educative relationships with her students and with me as her Ph.D. supervisor.

Chapter Fifteen

Working with Moira Laidlaw

MOIRA LAIDLAW is a part-time lecturer in the School of Education. She asked me to supervise her M.Phil. research in 1991 and successfully transferred to a Ph.D. research programme in November 1992. The following extracts are from a paper in which Moira explores the value of educational literary criticism in making sense of educative conversations. In making the selections below I am aware that I am using them in a way not intended by Moira in her original work. She is aware of this, and has suggested how best I might use them to show the nature of my educative work as a teacher/tutor through the student's own voice.

As in the work of Peggy Kok which follows, I feel in Moira's work a powerful and sustained insistence on the value of educative relationships as they are experienced in practice and revealed in educative correspondences and conversations and expressed in the art of an educational inquirer.

Since reading Martin Buber's *I and Thou* I have tried to be sensitive to '**we**' as a word which can be used to incorporate another individual into my own thoughts and commitments without having checked that 'we' do share these thoughts and commitments. Of all the words I use, I try to be most careful not to violate the others' sense of integrity, your 'you', through transforming 'you' into 'we'.

I want to find a way of sharing insights into the nature of an educative relationship without violating the insights and feelings of the other. The way I have chosen to do this is to present the following text in which Moira is speaking for herself yet is ascribing to me, as a tutor, intentions, skills and understanding. Her words carry to me the authentic meaning of my educative relationship with her. I think she is communicating what I understand as the practical wisdom of an educator.

> *To have the form without the content, the mind without the heart, the way without the spirit. To adopt the language without the fully shared meanings generated from a mutual value-base is, in a sense, to have lost the values themselves which gave rise to the whole process. In other words the method of an action enquiry process can come to represent the values behind it, and as such the outcome in terms of learning and development are fundamentally distorted from genesis to completion.* (Moira Laidlaw, January 1993)

Extract 1

Some Reflections by Moira Laidlaw on Jack as a Tutor
February 1993

Socrates: 'The excellence of a thing depends upon its having a certain ordered beauty which is the result of arrangement.'(Plato - Georgias)

From here, then, I will now start to involve you in my practice by illuminating it as it unfolds.........

On the 14th January 1993, I had a conversation with Jack Whitehead (my Ph.D. supervisor) and Chris Cloke (Director of Studies for the PGCE course here at Bath). I present here an edited version of the conversation and attempt to highlight its inner meanings for my work using the technique I have described to you. (I am aware as I write this that it would be easy for a reader to receive the impression that by editing this conversation I am already changing the meanings which it is possible to elicit from the conversation. I realise this, and of course through changing the text I do alter its inner coherence. The editing was done in order to make more concise this section of the thesis. As the aim of the conversation was to discuss the programme for the PGCE students regarding the writing of the Special Study, I have included all those parts of the transcript. I have cut out some of the vagaries and the blind alleys of dialogue relating to other issues.)

C.C: What I would quite like to do would be to encourage as many students as possible to have some kind of action enquiry for their Special Study, because I feel that it would fit within the scope of what we're doing, their professional development. There are all kinds of reasons... Jack wishes to say something?

J.W: It's just when you said, 'for all sorts of reasons'.

C.C: I think that we had decided that the second one should emanate from them, whereas the S.B.E., the School-Based Enquiry, which was focused much more on what derives from a school, and that would be ideal.

Clearly here, the vital difference between the kind of research which is generated by others and one which is self-generated, like an action enquiry, has become a point of focus in a way which has never in my hearing been expressed by someone who has responsibility for the whole of the PGCE course here. Jack had alerted me to the fact that Chris had mentioned to him about the possibility of encouraging all the students to undertake an action enquiry arising out of their second teaching practice.

M.L: Their concern was given, rather than actually being their own concern.

C.C: An action enquiry is actually something which they decide on. It would give them an opportunity to focus on an aspect of their practice which would be a strength. I think that also from a practical point of view it's the kind of enquiry and study that we would want to engage in about the practice itself. Because once they come off teaching practice there is a practical problem and ... it arises from the fact that they have to hand it in straight away ... That's going to be maybe a constraint in the way that you want to function.

One of the strengths of an action enquiry is its self-determining nature, and the way in which it encourages personal responsibility and the making of meanings within educational settings. In my transfer paper (Laidlaw, 1991) for this Ph.D. I wrote the following:

'Whitehead (1985) places emphasis on the individual's right to determine the nature and course of her/his enquiry, given the necessary parameters of collaboration and the growth towards consensus at the points of change, evaluation and accountability. Greater individual autonomy and responsibility both for action and claims to knowledge are exemplified by Whitehead's work' (p.7).

I believe that such personally oriented enquiries are supremely educationally valid, in their ability to highlight the significance and potential of an individual's actions and intentions to the person conducting educational research. As long as, of course, it is understood that to comprehend one's own educational reality more fully, an individual collaborates with others at pertinent moments ...

I needed to state my misgivings about the possible consequences of taking on the supervision of so many students in an activity which I have experienced as requiring a great deal of intervention and face-to-face contact with individual students.

M.L: My misgiving that came out of that is what I said before. I know how much the face to face bit, what difference that makes in terms of the quality of what they write. Which is really what my whole research is about .... It might actually defeat its own purpose if we're not going to engage with them in that kind of individual way. I don't know personally how we can do that. ... My experience of helping students to do that, is exactly on that individual basis. So out of two years' work, I have got about fifteen to twenty case-studies.

J.W: It may be that you continue to work in the way that you're used to.

M.L: Yes.

J.W: It may be that you could get two or three sessions during the teaching practice where you continue to work in the way you do, but we might be able to run some sessions which provide the necessary support for more students who wish to undertake that sort of enquiry.

M.L: What do you mean, Jack, what sort of support? This is where I'm having some problems.

J.W: Where I think we differ is in the way in fact we would use groups. We could do some of the reading and the group work on each other's drafts. So where I think I would set them up in literally groups of about three or four students and provide the guidance which will enable them to ask the directed question to their work. The very high quality work which you get is largely due to those conversations that you are having in the face to face contacts. So I think there is a way in which you might continue to work with students who freely choose to come to you in that way, but that we could also do something of great value with the other students, some of whom might wish to meet two or three times...

C.C: There are two ... Actually in a sense with the Course Tutorial and the lecture you're going to give, there is a session there which is actually going to put them on the road. The other possibility is that provided that we clarify what it is we want staff to do, other staff might be willing and interested to hold meetings with small groups of students...

Again I am impressed with the quality of the listening that we are according each other in a search for ways forward. The advice is both practical and expressed in ways which show the value of that listening to the listener. Let me be more explicit. At one point Jack says:

J.W: It may be that you continue to work in the way that you're used to.

This ensures that I do not feel undervalued or that my past work is being criticised, simply that in the present circumstances my way of working may not be appropriate for the kind of extension that we are looking towards. Jack goes on to say, in a way which emphasises his belief in the value of my way of working, but within a practical present context:

J.W: The very high quality work which you get is largely due to those conversations that you are having in the face to face contacts, but that we could also do something of great value with the other students, some of whom might wish to meet two or three times.

I also find particularly significant here Jack's ability to demonstrate in his supervisory role a talent which Yamamoto (1991) writes about:

'in mentoring this need to see on one's own has to be carefully, if subtly preserved and enhanced so as not to deprive the individual, who is momentarily under guidance, of motivation and dignity. There must be in both the guide and the guided, a delicate interweaving of a sense of seeing and being seen. One complements the other, and the two together help each person retain and develop his or her own idea of self as a unique, competent, and worthy person' (Yamamoto, 1991, p.184/5).

Look how he starts speaking by affirming the value of my work:

'the very high quality work which you get'...

before proceeding to develop the practical action by talking about the fact that:

*'we could **also** do something of value.'*

Jack has exhibited this ability before in this conversation, and this was at the beginning when he said:

'It may be that you continue to work in the way you're used to,'

which has now resolved itself into a certainty, showing how carefully Jack has listened and helped to create and respond to the dynamics both of the personalities and the context. He has even used some of my own language, mirroring it back to me to enable me to feel even more secure in the fact that my parameters are being taken seriously and will help to create the parameters of the others. Before the above quotation, I had said the following:

M.L: I know how much the face-to-face bit, what difference it makes in terms of the quality of what they write. Which is really what my whole role is about. So I do have misgivings that it might defeat its own purpose if we're not going to engage with them in that kind of individual way. My experience of helping students is exactly on that individual basis. So out of two years' work I have got about fifteen to twenty case-studies.

Note how insistent I am on **my** experience, **my** knowledge and **my** research. I am not necessarily inferring anything negative in the way I argued here, for I believe in the value of what I am doing, but a sensitive listener would be alerted to the importance which I place upon that experience and developing understanding. Jack immediately responds with:

'It may be that you continue to work in the way you are used to'.

This is not yet definite, as the conversation is still new, but it affirms me, yet still leaving room for a development which might occur later in the conversation. Only then is he able to say with greater authority:

'It may be that you could get two or three sessions during the teaching practice where you continue to work in the way that you do, but we might be able to run some sessions which provide the necessary support for more students who wish to undertake some sort of enquiry.'

This opens the door for me to ask questions which carry my own enquiry further, still secure in the knowledge that my own way of working is perceived as having merit, although not necessarily free of all tensions. I say:

'What do you mean, Jack? What sort of support? This is where I'm having some problems'.

Jack then replies in a way which not only answers my voiced concerns but allays my unspoken needs. If you look closely at the syntax of my above concerns, you see the mainly monosyllabic, stilted sentences, and the repetition of the word 'what'. These combined elements suggest a slight anxiety, and such I was experiencing at the time. The questions are spoken rapidly on the tape, suggesting tension. The more flowing metre of the final sentence hints at a greater self-control. In a way, the admission of ignorance is a step forward here for me, and such is Jack's sensitivity to the tenor of this conversation (by which I mean not simply the words, but how they are spoken and the way the sentences are constructed) that his reply can serve both functions of practical advice and the abatement of tension. He says:

'Where I think we differ is in the way... we would use groups. We could do some of the reading and the group work on each other's drafts. I would set them up in literally groups of about three or four students and provide the guidance which will enable them to ask the directed question to their work'.

His opening comment is to make a comparison which leaves no sting in the tail. There is a great deal of nuance between a comparison which makes me (in this case) the odd one out, the one who is deviant (from the norm), and a simple concession to the truth of the variety of our ways of acting in which there is no normalised way of being. He also qualifies this 'differing' by saying the tentatively respectful, *'I think.'* In addition I am struck by how much meaning is revealed by an analysis of the metre of the words Jack speaks. There is a self-assuredness in the flowing nature of the sentences, particularly the final one, in which he uses the 'I' and states very clearly a plan of action for the good of the students, a point we allude to as of the greatest importance in this conversation, and in our work here. He places his own action firmly in the future action of the students, a tenet adhered to by many emancipatory and educational action researchers (McNiff, 1992) . One of my own explicit aims since beginning this research, and one that I was dimly aware of in my practice beforehand, is the desire to enable students to speak for themselves, taking responsibility, therefore, for their own development and meanings, and that the value of my work could in fact be judged in part by how much I was successful in this aspiration. In my Transfer Paper I quoted (Laidlaw, 1991) the following:

'This year I wanted to facilitate one student in speaking with her own voice and I believed that action research could become the path along which students could tread in order to find their way through their own educative landscapes and as a result explain it to others.'

Jack has shown something of this desire in his tying in of the value of his work with those of his students, and of locating his practice with those of his students. These abilities which are here manifested by Jack seem to me crucial aspects of an educative conversation, in which there is mutual respect, a valuing of the other and an educative intention to future action.

Many action researchers based here at Bath, either students or staff, have adopted Whitehead's (1989b) notion that living educational theories will be constituted by the descriptions and explanations of individuals' own practice. Indeed we are struggling so to do, and thus, to find within a conversation that process beginning, is a powerfully emotive one.

In Literary Criticism there are many schools of thought about the applicability of explaining the artist through his or her art. I have never subscribed to that philosophy, and my reasons are quite clear. First, I believe that there is a reductionism operating when we apply Freud's notion of pathography in such a way. If we simply ascribe cause and effect to the art we witness, then we take away from it all the numinous, which contains the experience of the aesthetic: the aesthetic partly resides in that very area of human experience which defies typography. Second, a work of art can, I believe, be judged partly on its inner coherence. Has it an inner consistency? Does its form mirror the content? Here, of course, I come up against a problem, for what I am looking at here is not yet finished, this particular work of art. It is ongoing. There will be consequences of it. It will continue to act upon us. In that sense, then, I cannot draw final conclusions, but I can posit possibilities at this stage which I can then test out on others.

It is at this point, then, if I am to find evidence from the text itself, that I turn to our constant uses of the words 'we' and 'I' in this conversation, a habit which Jack alerted me to. The use of the word 'we' has three possible connotations. First these pronouns could be a profound affirmation of our collaborative or individual responsibility and intentionality here in this project; second, they could be a sense of a fear or embracing of personal responsibility, perhaps due to a developing recognition of the enormity of Chris' original design; third, they could be an attempt to show each other a willingness to share the ideas with others who have differing degrees of experience in this kind of facilitation. As I have said before, it will not be possible for me at this stage to tender certainties for the motives behind the words, but I can, even with this abstracted analysis, show the difference in the ways in which pronouns are used. In addition, the use of 'I' or 'we' is an intentional and ontological one in action research. Whitehead's notion of the centrality of the 'I' as the manifestation of a living contradiction in our reactions to the dialectical reality which renders significant context, self and values, is relevant here. He and I have explicitly discussed this issue, and therefore the connotations which it has for us cannot be assumed for others.

In my work with Jack and also with Jean McNiff (1992, 1993 and McNiff, *et. al.* 1992) I have been struck over the years how sometimes we start to talk and write using similar syntax, metre, and even vocabulary. For example, it is almost endemic now that we use the type of phraseology: '**how we enable practitioners to understand what is happening as they attempt to improve their practice.**' This kind of subordinate clause has never been one of my own speech or writing patterns as far as I am aware, until recently, and yet I have been with both Jack and Jean and heard it being used. An extract from my diary:

13.12.92. I am wondering now how I can understand this process of the evolving educative relationship as I try to help the students understand their own educative values. For to be true to the process of education as a living art form, I must facilitate the process by facilitating my own. I believe that therein lies the artistry, the beauty and the inner coherence of the process.

What has become clear is that the use of the word 'as' here, is actually a very pertinent and crucial one to the whole nature of what happens when we conduct action enquiries. It is a concurrent process, this attempt to understand and the facilitation of others, whether an action enquiry is conducted by a Higher Education academic with her students, or a student teacher in the classroom who is investigating her/his own practice whilst trying to improve the quality of learning for the pupils.

This process of the adoption of linguistic patterns means on one level that we are simply responding to the influences we encounter. I believe that the weight of influence is heavier from Jack to the rest of us, for he is the dominant force behind the ethos of the action enquiries that we engage in here, (and I was just about to write, 'as we go about the process of improving our practice!'). I think that there is more than a simple influence occurring here. I believe that we begin to take on each other's meanings as we take on the language or we show our concurrence by the adoption of the language. This takes time and careful listening. We have ways, Jack, Jean and I, and also the other action researchers based here in Bath, of communicating using our language at times almost as a code, an elaborate code, but a code nevertheless. We are, I believe, careful not to become careless, but whereas our understandings about certain ways of relating to the meanings we wish to convey, are shared through our extensive conversations, this can (if this principle of shared meaning operates at times when the meanings and significances have not been negotiated), I would imagine engender a hiatus between ourselves and others.

I am aware as I write this that I have now a tentative understanding of why a process such as action research can be technologised. I have heard Jack talk about this before but now I am realising how the language we use has the potential to become a genuine method of sharing meanings, of keeping others from the reality behind the words, or even taking over the meanings. Either of the latter alternatives have the potential to corrupt, change or amend meanings. I also realise as well why I care so much about using words from one context to cover meanings in another context, such instances as applying managerial terms to processes of leadership in school, for example, or competence applied to processes which can transcend skills and methods, when talent, insight, intuition and values operate, as in teaching. The corruptive power of words is, I believe, being enacted upon us in education all the time (Kleinstück, 1966). To extend this idea, I am saying that processes which are inaugurated through language that has not been fully explored, understood, integrated within the ways of being of the person adopting the language, will inevitably render the process vulnerable to corruption. **To have the form without the content, the mind without the heart, the way without the spirit; to adopt the language without the fully shared meanings generated from a mutual value-base is, in a sense, to have lost the values themselves which gave rise to the whole process. In other words the method of an action enquiry process can come to represent the values behind it, and as such the outcome in terms of learning and development are fundamentally distorted from genesis to completion.** (My emphasis: J.W.)

I think of values as human goals which are used to explain an individual's form of life. As I said in my introduction I will be pointing to my values, as they are embodied in my form of life, through the use of value-words and value-judgements. The meaning of these values, as explanatory principles in the explanation of my educational development, has I hope been revealed in the course of their emergence in practice through time and interaction with others in my social context. One of the values which I have sustained throughout my life in the University is the importance of enquiry. I have tried to support the engagement of teacher researchers and student teachers in questions of the kind, 'How do I help my pupils to improve the quality of their learning?'. In the following extract from a second paper, Moira explains how she helped one of her students, Sarah Darlington, to feel engaged and to answer a similar question. I have included the abstract so that you can understand the context of the whole paper.

Extract 2

**The democratising potential of dialogical focus
in an action enquiry: June 1993**

Abstract
This paper is concerned with showing how I as a University tutor have held onto my democratic principles in working with one student in an action enquiry as she has tried to answer the question, 'How can I improve the quality of learning for the benefit of my own professional development and the pupils in my care?'. Through a conversation with the student, Sarah, I show how I facilitate in the formulation of her action research question. Her concern is on improving her understanding and action with her pupils for the benefit of their learning. My emphasis is in setting a democratic framework within which she can realise her deepest educational values. This paper also seeks to make the point that it is in focusing on what constitutes an improvement in the quality of learning, and to what end that educational knowledge is formed and developed. This paper makes a claim that it is the dialectical nature of attempting to act on democratic ideals in the search for educational improvement that can create an epistemology for educational practice.

Introducing Sarah.
'When I started my second teaching practice, I had already decided I wanted to do an action enquiry. I felt then as I do now, that I tend to be naturally introspective and that evaluation, in one sense, comes easily to me. Whenever student teachers get together, we always end up discussing how we did it, how we could do better, how someone else did it. The case study provides a much more detailed and analytical one than most conversations could offer' (Darlington, 1993, p.1).

This comment from the beginning of her write-up shows the level of her self-insights, and rationale for adopting an action research approach to professional development. We had already talked about data collection, and the importance of the emergence through the accounts and in practice of the learners' own voices. By this I mean a form of expression which reveals an autonomous commitment to a line of learner-initiated enquiry, which may indeed take the form of questioning the teacher/ tutor or suggesting lines which the teacher might follow in order to enhance the learning experience. Sarah wrote to me with a focus for our first one-to-one meeting, and said:

'I want to talk to you about data collection which is worrying me. I've already thought about my own diary, pupils' learning logs, questionnaires, and National Curriculum levels. I'm not sure if video and tape-recorders in the classroom are appropriate. (14.3.93)

I was concerned that in her letter to me her question, 'How can I make the National Curriculum more accessible, enjoyable and challenging to my Year Eight class?' was unmanageable in scope for a ten week teaching practice.

How can I enable Sarah to focus educationally in order to improve the quality of learning?

This was the question which I asked myself at the beginning of our conversation on 18th January 1993. It was clear to me that she had already begun the process of reflection linked to some form of practicable action. For the sake of length I have edited some of the conversation, but have attempted to keep the central meanings intact.

This is how our conversation started:

SD: When I wrote to you at the 'imagining the solution' stage, a question I had in my mind, was, what does differentiation mean in English as opposed to any other subject? How do you implement differentiation in English? And it seemed to me from my limited experience that the area where it really comes into play is when the kids start writing.

ML: What makes you say that?

SD: I say that because everyone can respond to literature at some level.

ML: That's very clear. I don't necessarily have to agree or disagree. It's your enquiry. But I wouldn't say that I had noticed that it necessarily manifests itself in the writing more than in other areas... I think there are subtleties which manifest themselves just as meaningfully in the way they say things. The way they listen... My question would be, what is it in the processes that you are engaged in, Sarah, that have actually moved a child from point (a) to point (b)?

Sarah's comments reveal how much she has reflected upon her need to understand the way in which her pupils learn. She takes control of the conversation right from the beginning, and my opening comment is designed to enable her to expand on what she understands as a way of coming to understand better. I also stress her ownership of what she's doing, but am prepared to challenge her from an English-teaching point of view. From this point she goes on to give examples of why it is the writing that she wants to focus on. About her question (on which she had written to me prior to our meeting) she says:

SD: It's too huge. I cannot do that in four weeks.

She is quite adamant about that so I am able to seize the initiative, because it appears that she is ready to start formulating her question, something which in my own Guide (Laidlaw, 1992) I stress as being of paramount importance in terms of both setting out and having a benchmark from which the enquirer can measure subsequent insights.

ML: So how can you phrase a question that shows that your own educational development has helped in the learning of at least one pupil in your care?

SD: In connection with writing, do you think?

ML: What do you think? That's the point. That's what you've come up with, so I suggest we look at that.

My initial question is clear and focused. Sarah's response shows some insecurity (*'do you think?'*) and my reply indicates my belief in both her responsibility and my respect for her. I think at this stage there is a real sense of enquiry beginning. I go on to say:

ML: And maybe now we need to phrase that into an action enquiry question.

The 'maybe' is gentle and Sarah from here goes on to talk about something she has done with her 'target' group. She is clearly not quite ready yet to begin to phrase the question. She talks about her concern to give the children worksheets as a single way of differentiating, and about her concern to give children tasks at which they can succeed in order to fuel their motivation and self-esteem. Our conversation then continues:

ML: I think for this study you are going to have to concentrate on a very few children.

SD: I think you're right. I've written down here, 'target just one?' There's this lad, Hugh, and he's very low ability. I could work with him, but there's a child at the other end of the spectrum, the brightest, very lazy. It would be a real challenge trying to support one end and at the same time stretch the other end. One or the other?

ML: If you're moved to make a choice, then I suggest you make a choice.

It seems to me that in this part of the conversation, Sarah is showing again her capacity to understand the educational and administrative implications deeply (*target just one?*) yet at the same time wondering how this can be put into practice. My reply confirms her ownership of what she does (and her responsibility for making decisions), acknowledges her right to come to her own conclusions, and yet offers a way forward. She then responds:

SD: And now I think I do have to concentrate on just one pupil, a weak learner. I see. Yes.

So again I come back to my agenda in this conversation which is about how I can enable Sarah to focus educationally. The formulation of an action research question is part of a generative process (see McNiff, 1992 and McNiff *et. al.* 1992) and thus needs to be handled with real care, for the wording, the coming to understand what the question entails, seems to me in my experience as a facilitator of action enquiry, to gain epistemological and ontological significance. By this I mean a significance which reaches further than mere semantics and delves into not only what can be understood through the processes which are inaugurated in its name, but also the nature and validity of the conclusions drawn from such a process. I have also found that the questions I pose about my practice determine what values I am able to live out and that they reveal much about my view of the world. Therefore forming the question is not simply a pathway to practice, but to knowledge, living out one's values and coming to understand what is valid and significant about that knowledge.

ML: So let's talk about your question, then. I think now the time is better. With words that are going to release your creativity rather than restrict it. How can you form this question that is going to take into account all the elements that you are concerned about?

By phrasing my question in this way, I can enable Sarah to focus on any aspects that seem to her to be important. And this she does:

SD: We've got writing. We've got one end or the other and I'm moved to Hugh. I think I need to go away and think about that. It's going to be either supporting or stretching, don't you think? Does that seem right? I think there is something about making the curriculum available.

ML: Making the curriculum available, that is an important point. After all you are an English teacher. And your report will be required to show evidence of learning about English.

Sarah lists what she thinks are the key points at this stage in her developmental thinking. My repetition of her point about the curriculum is crucial, and as I say to her later, *'in our case-study collection (1991-93) we have none which reveal evidence of both curricular and personal learning'*. As a student teacher and future full-time teacher, Sarah is going to be accountable for the quality of her English pedagogical skills. She is on a teacher education course as well as conducting an action enquiry: indeed the two processes share a great degree of confluence. I go on to stress:

ML: It isn't just about a pupil taking responsibility for her or his learning, it's also learning about what? And that's why I think that your emphasis on the NC attainment targets is very relevant here. It's one way you can measure success.

SD: So are you saying that I should have a question of the kind, 'How can I help so and so?', or 'How can I help a person's learning in this Green issues module?'

ML: The way you phrase and focus that will determine not only the data you can collect, but also your own educational development and the way you can take this forward, this knowledge and understanding, into your future career.

SD: So I think I have to make a decision now about which child.

ML: Yes.

Sarah shows a high level of sophistication in her response to my comments. She recognises that the validity and meaningfulness of what can be developed begins to become apparent from this early stage if it is seen as significant on many levels. Indeed she confirms this insight in her final write-up:

'Action Research is a bit like throwing a stone into a pool. Even a small stone can produce wide-reaching ripples. For me, the small stone of my question has developed my thinking about the way I see myself in the classroom and about how I relate to the many individuals in my classroom' (Darlington, 1993, p.13).

And in the conversation:

*SD: **Depending on the child I choose, will also determine the kinds of statements and knowledge I can have.** Supporting. I keep saying supporting. This is about getting them to the next stage. They are learning. You could perhaps have a question like, 'How can I help so and so develop his learning in this module, or this aspect of work?' I suppose that would do. That is quite tight, isn't it?*

ML: Yes, except 'learning' is huge.

There is a sense here in which Sarah is thinking out loud. On the tape her voice seems slightly excited for she certainly appears to be finding her own learning direction. If she has the confidence to think out loud, then her earlier seeming insecurity *(don't you think? What do you think?)* is being overcome. My own experience (Laidlaw 1991, 1992) and some of my reading: Brown (1993), Claxton (1991), Hick (1993), Hocking (1992), Holden (1993), Neill (1937), Norwood (1992), McNiff (1993), Rogers (1984) and Watkins (1991), suggest that consequential learning which helps teachers to improve the quality of learning for the pupils in their educational institutions often occurs within a challenging but supportive framework. Sarah takes my point about the hugeness of the 'learning' notion and laughs for the first time in the discussion. We go on then to talk about whether she should concentrate on writing in her question. In her final report she writes:

'I am glad that the action research question I finally chose did not restrict me to looking at writing only' (Darlington, 1993, p.12).

A few moments later she says (taking control by summing up so far):

SD: We have been talking about the behaviour viewpoint, and with the writing, in one piece he might be able to achieve level three, but in the next level four. Although that looks like an improvement, I don't think that's necessarily so. It's not enough. Yes, and I think that perhaps I am tending to think not about the evidence of what they are learning [but] how I am differentiating. Do you see what I mean?

ML: Yes, I do.

SD: That's why some of the things I am thinking about might not be appropriate. It's about me, not the pupils.

*ML: But it's about both. Action research is about professional development **and** pupil learning.*

Her astuteness that apparent improvement may not be so easily articulated enables me then to reassure her categorically that what she is about is twofold. She writes about the importance to her of this reassurance:

'It was quite a surprise when it dawned on me that my development was relevant to the research too. Moira talked about [this].'

I could then challenge her further:

*ML: This is something that I am going to bring up in the Validation meeting, but I think I will say it here. Don't worry about it when you hear it. It's quite a question. **'In an account of your professional development, what evidence do you have that your pupils are learning anything of value and that they are taking some responsibility for their learning?'***

This was something that Jack Whitehead (in his capacity as my Ph.D. supervisor) and I had formed the day before. Our discussion had shown me potently how crucial it is to evolve a generative question with my students, but that their own response to a wide-reaching formulation could also help them to focus within carefully constructed parameters. I think the above question is an opening up to the students of the perceived values of democracy in action, to the assumption that ownership of learning promotes an improvement in that learning, and that their professional development is framed by their response to those factors. Sarah's reply is prompt.

SD: Read it again!

ML: (Reads it again.) I am going to challenge you with it, because I think that's where our professional development should be tending. Towards a greater understanding of pupil learning. Therefore the quality of your pupils' learning is probably going to be heightened if they are taking some responsibility for it. Does that make sense?

She is now able to say the following:

*SD: I think it is one of the jobs of an educator: to try and develop more autonomy amongst children. If you give them that, this responsibility, then ... it will carry on into adult life and you're teaching them so much more than just English. Also you're teaching them something about the **value** of the curriculum, the **value** they're getting out of it.*

Sarah writes in her final report:

'I feel that I have demonstrated fully in the preceding pages that Hugh did take responsibility for his own learning. But did he learn anything of value? First I needed to ask, 'whose value?' (Darlington, 1993, p.33)

Hugh had written (which Sarah cites):

'I have done my research very well when they [sic] was not enough information but I wrote a letter to esso house [sic] asking them for some info on cars and pollution and they sent me some.' (11.4.93)

I am not suggesting that the reason Sarah saw the value of understanding personal responsibility in learning was just because of our conversation, or that Hugh could thus write such an evaluation, but I am claiming that Sarah was given the space as well as the direction to develop her notions of educative 'value' and 'responsibility' in our conversation. I would claim this therefore as an educative process.

She goes on to say at this point:

SD: So, back to the question. We can either have, 'how can I help so and so to develop an understanding'...and then I've written down, 'and thereby moderating his behaviour?'

Again she is taking control in her learning process. She emphasises that we are trying to find a question. We talk a little about whether she is trying to enable a child to learn and thereby improve his behaviour, or whether his behaviour can be modified thus improving his learning. Then she says this:

SD: How can I help so and so engage with the Green Module, thereby moderating his behaviour?

ML: Isn't it, 'How can I moderate his behaviour in order to enable him to engage with the Green Module?'

SD: You see, I think the interest comes before the behaviour.

ML: Right, I see. I understand. Do it from that, then.

SD: Should I include that bit about behaviour?

ML: Try it without.

SD: How can I help X become engaged with this Module?

ML: The thing is, if he doesn't improve his behaviour, then I haven't got anywhere.

I recognise the degree to which at this point I am pushing Sarah. My sentences are controlled and relatively short, my language directive and succinct. This stage of a dialogue is always difficult for me. It is the point at which the dialectic I experience between living out my respect for the ideas and the selfhood of others against foreseeing possibilities which might be at variance with the other person's intentions and insights, becomes problematic. It is, for me, a precarious balance. My experience tells me that an educator must try hard to tread this narrow path successfully for the sake of the learning experience and the well-being of the student: I do not wish to disempower. I realise that as Sarah's tutor I have greater institutional authority. She has come expecting to be guided by my experience to a certain extent. I am conscious that a question which is formed with the onus on improving behaviour rather than on **learning something of value** will not be able to get at the kind of knowledge which Sarah is seeking. It will become, in the long-run, a psychological rather than an educational study. However, Sarah is an education student, and **I see the process of education as constituting the promotion of learning something of value.**

At the end of her study, she reveals her standards of judgement which she wishes to take forward into her career. The last one of these runs thus:

> *I recognise that first and foremost I am an educator; it is my responsibility to develop the learning of individuals. I am not a counsellor or a child-minder! Moira said (12.3.93), 'I know you are trying to encourage, but you also have to educate them. The question is, how can you encourage pupils lacking in self-confidence whilst at the same time challenging them educationally?'* (Darlington, 1993, p.37)

We talk about this shift from care to education for a while and then Sarah says:

SD: It's interesting, isn't it, how we've moved from the National Curriculum question to this one. It's so complex.

ML: But it shows the interrelatedness of everything in teaching, from motivation to achievement, process, outcome, expectations, everything. So look how far you've come in terms of your own understanding of what you're doing and what you know.

SD: I think it's slow.

ML: It's not slow at all.

SD: I write things down and it takes time, but I suppose I am learning what I know and what I need to know. I feel sort of reassured because I thought I wasn't getting anywhere with this thing.

This part of the conversation seems to be the lull after the potential storm. That I have been quite directive turns here into Sarah again taking stock. This habit of hers to stop and think in order to consolidate is a powerful mechanism by which she communicates her learning and enables me to respond in a most positive and supportive manner. She then goes on to say:

SD: I think they [the students] should have the right to challenge. It's about responsibility for their own learning. We've established a question. Now it's about getting the appropriate data. Things like learning logs, National Curriculum levels, other teachers' observations. Can you think of any other data that I should be getting at this stage?

And now she is coming back to her original concern which she highlighted in her letter to me. This seems to me to be someone who understands and who feels confidence. Because Sarah has taken the lead again, I can then reply to her question thus:

ML: The only other one, which might not be practical, would be, in some way to have a conversation with Hugh going, which actually, if you can do it in the right way, might give him enormous encouragement about how important he is, about how much you value his opinion.

SD: Yes, I had put that down: 'how about a discussion with the 'target' one?'

ML: That's part of the differentiation process as well, isn't it?

SD: Yes, because whilst I am sorting out who to target, I am learning as well about who learns what and how. And if we have a discussion about this, this should help him develop his learning.

I interweave her opening remarks about differentiation into the present concerns and in her last utterance, Sarah consolidates that in her own way. I think my question is the right one both pedagogically and in terms of the value of democratic practice underpinning it. Sarah's anticipation of this idea reveals her own understanding, her own values as well, and a sense of how it will turn out in practice.

SD ...Yes, it's getting a lot of shape now. This morning I thought it was too huge. Yes and now it seems manageable. I can see my way forward now. Great! Good! The other thing is, how do we see success?

Again she takes stock. Again she takes initiative, yet includes both of us in the process (*we*). Several times in the conversation she has said 'we' and 'you' rather than 'I', and now the time has come to enable her to see the significance of taking full ownership over what she is doing. After all, an action research question depends upon the centrality of the 'I' as a causal agent for change. Therefore I use her form of wording and reflect it back to her as an educational challenge. I then say:

*ML: How do **you** see success?*

And then even more pertinently:

*ML: How would Hugh see success?.. That is a vital point. It's just come to me. I've never asked that question before. I have always said to a student, 'How will **you** measure success?' But of course, if we're talking here about how is your account of your professional development going to reflect the learning of your pupils, then in some guise or other, in some way that's right for you both, you are going to have to square that with Hugh's ideas.*

SD: Yes! And that's about him having responsibility for his own learning. Wow! That's really neat. That puts him in that strong position. It's not being imposed; it is his choice. It's the key, isn't it? Choice. So that's honestly it.

For the rest of the conversation (a few minutes) we discuss the ethics of concentrating on one child for a research enquiry, and how she can approach Hugh in ways which will develop his learning and simultaneously through her research, aid her understanding of his learning.

Conclusion

Reflective practice seems all the rage at the moment. In our School of Education we talk to our students about reflective practice. It is written in to our course and tutorial handbooks for example, but nowhere within the main stream of the course is the vital nature of focusing on coming to understand the complexity of the educational practice through dialogue, sufficiently emphasised to my mind. However, the work of Jack Whitehead has formed a network through which much research, Higher Degrees, in-service training are conducted; and in which dialogue is seen as the cornerstone of good practice, 'good' being characterised partly through its ability to promote democratic learning processes. Writers like Donald Schön (1983,1987) describe and propose many ways in which educators reflect and formulate their rationale for practice. He does not specifically advocate a dialogical approach. Indeed he writes almost entirely using conceptual models and nowhere do we see how his concepts achieve a practicable reality. In enabling such spaces with my students I believe I help to realise democratic processes within the learning, and thus enhance the learning itself.

In my conversation with Sarah I am claiming not only that she was given the space to discover and develop those aspects of her educational values which would lead to improving the learning of herself and Hugh but there is, within this, the scope to leading a better life for them both: through her new understanding she is beginning by the end of the dialogue to realise that her encouragement of Hugh, her valuing of him as an individual learner, is more than simply a functional procedure, and perceives instead its potential to shape the epistemology of her practice within which he is empowered to give voice to his own concerns in his own way. To evolve such a democratic epistemology enables (in my terms and, I believe, Sarah's too) all those actively and positively associated with it to lead better lives. Through negotiating our meanings we come closer to realising what is of generalisable value in human existence, and how, by extension we might realise that practically. In Dewey's terms, we:

'make the ties which bind persons together more perceptible' (Dewey, 1966, p.316).

Nigel, a Physics PGCE student this year, also undertook an action enquiry. He set his final write-up as a court case in which he was being tried by the state for wasting valuable pupil-time! When I showed him a draft of this paper, he said:

*NB: I've been thinking about metaphor again. Stories, fiction, fables with a moral, someone tells you those. The moral is someone else's. Dialogue, well, that's a way of moving forward. It's about negotiation. You can't **tell** it like it is, we have to make it up together. It's a step in the right direction anyway.* 11.6.93.

In the following chapter, Peggy Kok reveals, through conversation and reflection, a tension and resolution between our educational values.

Chapter Sixteen

Working with Peggy Kok

DURING THE 1990/91 academic year I tutored Peggy Kok for two action research modules and her M.Ed.. dissertation. Peggy was on study leave from the Singapore Technical and Vocational Training Board. In the following chapter from her M.Ed. dissertation, *The Art of an Educational Enquirer*, Peggy analyses four educative conversations in which she is experiencing a tension between her commitment to the values of excellence and the social order in Singapore and to the values of freedom, justice and democracy within a different form of social order.

Peggy's chapter is presented in full below. I do not want to edit it as it reflects a struggle for meaning whose authenticity I witnessed. Yet I do want to engage with her text at the points where I think it is revealing something significant about my own educational values and competencies. You will see my responses in this typeface. I do hope that these are not experienced as violations of Peggy's text.

Chapter 6 of *The Art of an Educational Enquirer*

In Chapter 1, I had likened the writing of this dissertation to Dewey's (1934) notion of building a cathedral:

'Probably the aesthetic quality of medieval cathedrals is due in some measure to the fact that their constructions were not so much controlled by plans and specifications made in advance as is now the case. Plans grew as the building grew... Every work of art follows the plan of, and pattern of, a complete experience, rendering it more intensely and concentratedly felt.'

I had made many changes to the original outline of my dissertation in the course of writing but the overall objective of the dissertation has always been kept in sight. Each change had followed reflection upon what I had written and consultation with my supervisor. The writing of the previous chapters was pure labour of thoughts. However, I feel that it somehow lacked the aesthetic quality that Dewey was talking about. It did not possess the intensity of a 'complete experience'. It was a technically competent piece of work so far - the cathedral is merely structurally sound.

This last chapter is part of the dissertation where art enters it. Art as defined by Dewey (1934) is not an object to be put on a pedestal and admired by the privileged few. Instead art should be seen in the light of the experience of the artist in the creation of an object.

'With respect to the physical materials that enter into the formation of a work of art, everyone knows that they must undergo change. Marble must be chipped; pigments must be laid on canvas; words must be put together. It is not so generally recognized that a similar transformation takes place on the "inner" materials, images, observations, memories and emotions. They are also progressively re-formed; they, too, must be administered. This modification is the building up of a truly expressive act. The impulsion that seethes as a commotion demanding utterance must undergo as much and as careful management in order to receive eloquent manifestations as marble or pigment, as colours and sounds' (Dewey, *op. cit.*).

In this chapter, you will be able to see how the commotion of emotions arose within me, how they were managed and directed towards manifestation as a work of art. I will show that the writing of this chapter has been an experience that follows the order below:

'Life itself consists of phases in which the organism falls out of step with the march of surrounding things and then recovers unison with it - either through effort or by some happy chance. And, in a growing life, the recovery is never mere return to a prior state, for it is enriched by the state of disparity and resistance through which it has successfully passed. Life grows when a temporary falling out is a transition to a more extensive balance of the energies of the organism with those of the conditions under which it lives' (Dewey, *op.cit.*).

It is the story of how I had passed through the turmoils experienced when I discovered that my values were in conflict with those advocated in the living educational approach to action research and how I resolved those conflicts, finding a balance between my 'energies' and the conditions under which I live in my country and in so doing I have fashioned a work of art out of the rigid structure of the earlier chapters. The content of this chapter is made up of real-life experience. A large part of it was derived from the tape-recording of the third and fourth conversations I had with Jack Whitehead and an interview with Jim Harvey, Director of Studies (Transcripts 3, 4 and 5).

Dances with Action Research

I was courting action research for the six months that I had been on the two action research modules. There were times when I had wanted to call off the relationship and there were times when I considered marriage. At the end of my assignment for the second module I saw myself very much like the hero in the film *'Dances with Wolves'* and summed up my feelings for action research in the following way:

'I see the present stage of my development in action research as being at the point where the soldier, out of loneliness at his post, built a fire and did a Red Indian Dance round it. He was able to forget his inhibitions and the fact that he was white and for the duration of the dance he was just communicating with his friends through dance unaware that they were watching him. He was called Dances with Wolves because a wolf was near him when he was dancing. Perhaps I may be called at this stage of my educational development - Dances with Action Research. Perhaps I am shedding my inhibitions more and more, now that my understanding of action research has deepened through the two inquiries I carried out in this assignment' (Kok, 1991).

As a result of my intense involvement with action research over a period of six months, I had decided to probe deeper into this unorthodox way of doing educational research through a dissertation which I knew would take me to the core of action research based on the living educational theory approach. As can be seen from the previous chapters in this dissertation, I had positive feelings about action research as the sensible alternative to the traditional method of doing educational research. I had demonstrated my understanding of the form and content of the living educational theory in the preceding chapters. From there, I could have proceeded according to my original plan of applying the set of criteria I came up with to some action research case-studies and finish up the dissertation with whether I thought action research was capable of standing up to criticisms that it lacked rigour and validity. This plan was not followed through because after the first two interviews with Jack Whitehead in which the purpose was to get real-life knowledge about his theory, it suddenly dawned on me that there were ideas that I could not agree with and that there existed fundamental differences between Whitehead's and my concept of what 'values' should be.

Experience of Disharmony

It all began when I discovered that the values that permeated the action research inquiries of both Whitehead and those who practise his living educational theory approach to action research, were values which I could not advocate to be the dynamic force behind the action research which I would do in the Vocational and Industrial Training Board. It was not so much the discovery of the difference in values between us but the realisation that in order to do action research and be true to the living educational theory of Jack Whitehead, I would have to actively promote the values that form the basis of his theory. Because of the realisation that there was no way in which I could take action research back to my place of work with the values held by Whitehead that a sense of alienation overcame me. Although I have adopted the form of the living educational theory approach to action research, I was not prepared to retain the values that were central to this approach:

Peggy: I notice that the values that you hold are very strong in the areas of democracy, justice and freedom and when I looked through the case studies, these values were also reflected there in the work of Erica, Kevin Eames and Moira. These are the values you hold and which others working with you are also holding. That's why you aim for change, not just in the teachers but also in the students for a better society, am I right?

Jack: Yes, you are right. Go on.

Peggy: I was confused all over again. I read Dewey's (1966) *Democracy and Education*, the chapter on *'Vocational Aspects of Education'*. I read it some time ago but did not find that I could use any of it, didn't really get much from it. Yesterday, I read the chapter again, took down some notes and found myself disagreeing with the whole lot of it. That's (what Dewey had written) the ideal. Where I come from and you know it, it's the total opposite of what Dewey is advocating for education and vocational training. What he disagrees with, I agree with because that's my society and then I began to ask myself, 'Can I have these values of freedom, democracy and justice?' Well, as an individual, as a person, probably. I don't know. But being where I am, in that kind of set-up, I cannot hold these values because if I do, it will be in total opposition to my place of work and even my country. I can't go back and ask the trainers to train their students to be more democratic, to question, because we are in training and it is very complicated. The students who come to us are not academically inclined. They come to us for a skill and all we teach them is skills and our better society is that they get a job, everybody gets a home and we have progress in our way - mechanistic, materialistic but that is our way of life.

What then are the values that I hold which are contrary to those held by Whitehead?

'If I go back, what are my values and if I intend to do action research there, I must have values because it (action research) is meaningless without the values. I would say that based on who I am, what I have been through, the situation I am in, who I work for, my country, I think that my values would be in line with those of the government, and that is 'excellence' in whatever you do and I will hold this value when I train my students and they will do likewise when they train their students.'

Whitehead made his view regarding educational values very clear when he said:

'Now this is something that you and I have talked about, about the way which in educational research, it is the values which characterise whether what you are doing is educational or not. And you know within my own culture, I have selected values which I think have universal potential, they may not have, but I think they have and those are the ones you've picked out - democracy, freedom and justice.' (All extracts above are from Transcript 3)

The following extracts from the transcript of the fourth conversation we had provide further clarification of Whitehead's position:

Peggy: We were talking about values and how your set of values of democracy, freedom and justice are fine for your culture and in a way you are going for social revolution. Jim had said, 'Jack is for revolution, I'm for evolution.' (Transcript 5). What do you have to say?

Jack: I think that if we take the positive view of revolution which is Kuhn's idea and the debates he had with Popper about changing a way of thinking, changing the way we act in the world then yes, I feel I am a revolutionary in that sense. Now, I take that to be a positive view - revolution - where you get paradigm changes. Kuhn talked about the structure of scientific revolution in a very positive way. It was a way of taking ideas forward. But if he used it in a way which tended to have negative connotation, which had to do with the revolutions in places like the Soviet Union because of commitment to a particular ideology so that it became a class struggle between capital and labour, then in that sense of a revolution, then I am not a revolutionary. My own belief is that if you work from what I call the ideological base, if you work trying to transform the way people think, the values they subscribe to, the form of action that they take, then you will lead to social improvement, you will lead to the transformation of the world to greater democracy, to greater freedom and greater justice. Now that is where I place my faith for social change and social improvement rather than in mobilising on a class-based struggle, the power relations between power and labour.

Can you see in the section Peggy has italicised above that I am seeking to communicate to a student the values which have characterised my educational development throughout my research programme? I am expressing a commitment to transform the way in which people think, the values they hold and the actions they take in a way which leads to greater freedom, greater justice and greater democracy. Back to Peggy.

Why was there a conflict and why couldn't the conflict of values be resolved? My difficulty in fully accepting Whitehead's values as the basis for the action research that I would be prepared to do lies in the explanation below:

'I really appreciate that I have come into a culture where I am exposed to these values, like you say they are universal values. But also I have to fight against what I am, what I have been brought up as, the country I grew up in, the set-up that I work with. So I find that on the one hand these are human values (democracy, freedom and justice) that I should as a human being hold. On the other hand, I am in a country where I see progress, I don't see people starving, I don't see beggars and for everything the government takes from us - the taxes - we get it all back. People have homes so I think it is not bad too and what Dewey says about vocational training, that it should not be slotting people, putting people into specific occupations and then they are stuck for life, well, I don't agree with that. To a certain extent it is true, people who are streamed or channelled find themselves in vocational training and they will be technicians, they work in factories but it is not true to the extent that the government makes sure of progression for people in their lines of work. There are classes, funds for training, you can study, you can move, you are not stuck in a rut, you are not forever a production worker. I don't agree with Dewey's view but of course he is in another culture that is different from mine. He has not been in my culture to see that done in a way which he thinks is wrong. Things work and people are happy.'

I agree that the values of freedom, democracy and justice are universal in that they do promote peace and make the world a better place for every one in it. I respect people who hold these values and believe that the world should be transformed through education towards those ends. I experience a great tension in trying to sort out two sets of values (a) the values of freedom, democracy and justice which I can see are noble and agree that people should hold these values for a quality of life that goes beyond material and economic successes and (b) the value of excellence in whatever we strive towards be it at a personal, group, work or national level. I believe that the first set of values is good but I happen to place more importance on the second set of values and both sets are directly opposing in nature but at the end of the day, it's the second set of values that won. As Jack said:

'You've dealt with something which is really fundamental in terms of the economic and material base of people's existence which is a value which doesn't come into democracy, justice and freedom that we do need: that value that the vast majority of us place on economic survival and you have actually put that as a central value. That is where there is a conflict between various values. Very different balance. But I think you've got on tape here the nature of the values that you hold.' (Transcript 3)

Towards the end of the third interview, I still had not found a way to resolve the tension that was tormenting me:

Jack: What you have got on tape here is very important about tensions you have experienced and are experiencing.

Peggy: I am in training, not education. For twelve years I have been in vocational training and I can't suddenly change and say that just because certain values are embraced in the West, this is progressive thinking and I should go back and advocate change for society through education.

Jack: I suppose the difference is this: my work is in education, the degree you are going to get is a Master of Education. I think that we have actually fulfilled what I understand by the criteria of education. I've seen you thinking, developing. So from my point of view, the process of education I have seen working within you...

Peggy: I have been educated. I wasn't educated in schools, I was taught. I wasn't even educated in the university. But I think I truly had an education here.

Jack: This is what my father told me about the university. He said that in his whole working life he had very little time to think because of the nature of his job and once you get into full-time employment you will find very little time to think about education. Now hopefully this year, you've been able to - and I've seen you working extremely hard but with the time to think, so even if you now go back into a context that - like my father was describing, the vast majority of his life - is going to be training - is going to become better and more efficient and excellent in training, the fact that you've had twelve months...

I have had twelve months to think and I felt very privileged to have had this time to develop my mind but I was not contented with having had the time to think. I wanted something concrete, something usable, something that I could do in the future that would draw on all the thoughts and experience I had accumulated here in the University of Bath and which would enhance my practice although I am aware that the quality of thoughts manifested in practice cannot be measured in tangible terms. I should have been happy to finish this dissertation with what Whitehead had proposed in the third interview:

'What you could do is simply leave the ending of your dissertation where you are at the moment, that is, the recognition that there are different value positions within your own commitments and in the commitments of this group here, couldn't you? I mean that is true.'

I was conscious at the moment of saying this that I was holding to Buber's view of the educative relation in which the educator subordinates his or her own structured view of the world to the particular being of the student. At this moment I had accepted Peggy's right not to embrace my educational values and to hold firm in her own. I think this ability is one of the great achievements of an educator. It seems to me that this ability prevents the abuse of power in an educative relationship. Peggy was free of any intentional constraints on my part that she should conform to my educational values. I had accepted Peggy's right to be different. However Peggy moves on ...

That was true - right to the very end of the third interview, that was the position I held. I left the interview feeling that an ending like that to the dissertation and to the one year of work in action research would have been education for education's sake. My feelings were exactly those described below by Dewey (1934):

'The rhythm of loss of integration with environment and recovery of union not only persists in man but becomes conscious with him; its conditions are material out of which he forms purposes. Emotion is the conscious sign of a break, actual or impending. The discord is the occasion that induces reflection. Desire for restoration

of the union converts mere emotion into interest in objects as conditions of realization of harmony. With the realization, material of reflection is incorporated into objects as their meaning. Since the artist cares in a particular way for the phase of experience in which union is achieved, he does not shun moments of resistance and tension. He rather cultivates them, not for their own sake but because of their potentialities, bringing to living consciousness an experience that is unified and total.'

I had wanted to write this dissertation the way an artist creates a work of art. I wanted to be able to step back when this dissertation is finished and be able to see a synthesis of all that I have thought about and experienced in the form of a harmonious whole. I needed to carry on, to move forward with what I had learnt. The stumbling block was my inability to take back with me the set of values of freedom, democracy and justice which was the motivating force behind the living educational approach to action research. I could import the method of doing action research and leave the values behind but that would be like telling people to how to do something without telling them why and without them wanting to change their own practice themselves. I was still plagued by the tension of seeing two sets of values which I could not reconcile and which I believe are equally good. To choose one over the other would mean annihilation of half of what I believe in and leave me with a sense of incompleteness. I was out of rhythm with life but I did not give up hope that my tensions could be resolved. If one can break one's back doing manual work then my brain almost suffered the same fate. Fortunately, by the fourth interview the next day, I had found the synthesis I had been looking for.

Resolution

It was sheer agony trying to overcome this tension within me and to finally decide for myself what I should do. Peters (1973) was right when he wrote:

'Independence of thought is not a natural unfolding; it is a laborious achievement.'

I had spent all my waking hours reflecting on the conversation with Whitehead in the third interview. I had to see things in perspective. I went home and read once more Corey's (1953) *Action Research To Improve Schools* the first book written on action research in education. I read again Rudduck and Hopkins (1985) *Research as a basis for teaching: Readings from the work of Lawrence Stenhouse* and R.S. Peters' (1959) *Authority, Responsibility and Education*. I then came to the following conclusion [as I wrote in my journal]:

'Yesterday when I went home I was thinking of what Jim had said - I was listening to the tape of the interview with him on the bus - the first question he asked was, 'What's the difference between action research and what Jack is doing?' I asked him what he thought action research was and he said that action research was just problem-solving. You don't have to put the 'I' in it. Values don't have to come into it. I thought perhaps that's another view of action research. I have been exposed to most of the time just your brand of it and I thought maybe it will be quite interesting to see if he's right. I went back and read Corey and I find that this is nearer to Jim's definition of action research - problem-solving. But it is one step ahead of Jim's definition because Corey says that it is the practitioner who should do action research and he says that it has to be very scientifically done so he says you have to set up a hypothesis, test the hypothesis, not quite in the way that you do it but for example I may have this hypothesis that in this situation, if I applied this method the kids would do better. Then the teachers would either alone or collaboratively go into this action research. They could collect data, they could go into quantitative analysis, come to a

decision, apply it and decide whether they have improved. So I find that this is still one step away from what Stenhouse is advocating. Stenhouse moves away from the quantitative but focuses more on the meaning generated by the teacher, what the teacher is capable of doing herself, because she has experience and knowledge, tacit knowledge - that kind of thing. Then I find that what Stenhouse is advocating is still one step away from what you are doing. It appears to me that you take Stenhouse's idea of the teacher as researcher but you put the "I" inside, the values. At the end of it I put it down in a hierarchy like this and said, "Let's look at Jim's version, then go into Corey's - because he was the first person to write about it - and then into Stenhouse and then into your theory. I find that of the four, maybe because I have spent so much time on your theory - but having looked at the overview in a way, I think that your theory is more powerful than all the rest because I've been through it and if you put the "I" in it, change will come because when you put the 'I' in it, it is the teacher who says, 'I want to change because I see the need to change' Whereas in the other cases it is, "Here's the problem, how do you solve it?' Stenhouse is of course better than the other two because he says, "Look at the teacher, I believe that the teacher has the judgement to know what's right and wrong and how to improve her practice." But in your case you put the values in.'

Having now put things in their proper perspective, I was able to resolve the tension of the past few days in the following way:

'When it comes to values of democracy, freedom and justice, I've thought about it. I said yesterday that I couldn't bring those values back and use them as the base for the education of the trainees the way it is done here. You are actually educating your young to be more critical so that you move towards a society which is more questioning and not take things handed down by authority; and the whole idea is you work towards a better society in that way, human rights and things like that. I thought about it. I can't bring it back and have the trainees embrace these values. I can't preach these values to the trainees in the VITB. But as I read R.S. Peters' 'Authority, Responsibility and Education' the chapter on 'Education and seeing what is there' - there is this part where he said:

"Individual inventiveness is always to be understood against a background of a public inheritance. And though good teachers always encourage individuals to develop their own point of view, they also provide them with the necessary equipment to have one."

And it is education which provides this equipment, which transforms the wild wishes and intuitions of the individual into an informed understanding and inventiveness. For we have to be trained to see things as they are - and to see what no one else has seen. That's what you are doing. You provide the teachers with the equipment i.e. through action research to be more critical, to be more open to ideas, to develop themselves and they in turn use this process to develop their students in that way. So you can do it this way. I thought about it. I like what R.S Peters said about providing teachers with the necessary equipment to develop their own point of view. I am a teacher trainer, or educator whatever, well, my business is to train teachers to be effective in their job. If I can't reach the students (trainees), I don't think I want to because of my values, I could reach the teachers and say that if you want to improve your job then one way is to be more reflective, to be more critical and to work more democratically and collaboratively, to have part of these values (freedom, democracy and justice) so that they can improve their job, and the consequence would be that the trainees will benefit because of their improvement. Just as I have come here and have *gone through this process and I think educationally I have improved. I have read things which I have never read, I have been exposed to your theory, I have had these conversations with you to develop intellectually in this way. So I hope that when I go back and do action research it would be towards this end, that I would equip my trainers with whatever is necessary to develop their own points of view - to question me if I were to tell them that 'This method is good', not to just take it but to question and to develop, to think what is good for them in their practice. That's all I can do. I can't go for social change.'*

I found harmony at last in coming to a compromise between the values of freedom, democracy and justice and the values I held regarding excellence in doing a job. The action research that I take back with me to my place of work will be based on the values of excellence which I will promote in using action research in teacher training just as Whitehead promotes the values of freedom, democracy and justice in his action research activities in the United Kingdom. I have to make very clear that it is the value of excellence that powers the action research that I would be prepared to do back in my place of work:

Jack: *So I think you have got a way of working in terms of how you described it with your teachers that will enable you to live out your values.*

Peggy: *Yes, but **the ultimate aim in that is still they have to be excellent in what they do, they have to be effective**. It is very instrumental in achieving this very objective kind of end, but I want to see results, I want to see that their practice is improved, that they should be better than they were - like me. I know that I am intellectually better than when I first came. My capacity has been stretched and improved. So that is how I'll see the goal for these teachers I train. They should always believe in excellence and they should live it out and they should have proof that they have improved. And the way I go through with it is to use your process of action research because I think that is the most powerful of all because the teacher herself examines her values and of course these values will be towards excellence and here she wants to improve, that is the important thing.*

Whitehead sums up exactly my position at this point of the conversation when he said:

'I think when you hear this tape, you will hear the kind of resolution to the kind of tension that you expressed the other day and I think you've really worked through to a position which enables you to resolve some of the tension you have. So I think you now see a way forward when you go back to relate to the teachers that you are working with in a way that enables you to bring in some of the educational values you hold whilst at the same time enhancing their skills in the direction that you believe to be enhanced. So that's what I feel in terms of that conversation.'

Personally I feel that the ability to resolve the tension I was experiencing for the past few days is expressed most clearly in the following excerpt from the fourth interview:

'I am not in education. I am not a teacher in the Ministry of Education. And in the Vocational and Industrial Training Board, neither am I a member of the training staff - I don't train students in acquiring skills - I am in a strange position where I could, I should educate people, I am dealing with trainers who would train another group of people. So I suppose having come this far, I've had the opportunity to think about it,

my role. The way I have seen my role as a teacher trainer, has been very narrow, because I see my role as a trainer in skills. I impart teaching skills to the trainers who then impart trade skills to the trainees. So may be this is what R.S Peters talks about as the "tunnel vision" that you just see things from a framework. For twelve years I have seen my role within a framework of skill training. I think this experience here, having had the opportunity to think about what education is, I am able to see, I can see that there is a wider world, there is a world outside of this framework that I work in. It's not just training because if you just train people to teach and they just apply the skills that they learn from you, it is mechanistic, you are after all dealing with human beings. So maybe I see my role should not be merely to train people mechanistically as we have been doing but also to educate them...to train them to be more independent in their thinking. See I use the word 'train' again. or rather to provide them with the facility to think for themselves and questioning of me, not of authority, but of me, to dare to come and discuss in the open, not to be defensive, if they are challenged in turn. But really I think this kind of education should also come into the preparation of teachers who are vocational trainers. I think I see that now. The teachers would be poorer if they just went away with a set of skills. They would be much enriched if the way they have been prepared for teaching trains them to develop educationally and individually and as human beings. I think I see this other side now.'

I had found the solution at last in being able to incorporate the two conflicting sets of values into a way of doing action research that I can accept and carry out. Because action research is in essence participatory and collaborative, involving critical reflection and judgement, people have to work closely and harmoniously. If freedom, democracy and justice are values which people can be encouraged to hold in the process of inquiring into ways to improve their practice, then the process of action research will proceed more smoothly. In other words, the values of freedom, democracy and justice will, for me, become part of the process of action research and not the basis of action research.

I had said explicitly that the value that underpins the form of the action research that I would take back with me would be the value of excellence in performance. It is at this point that I moved away in spirit from the living educational theory because as I had told Whitehead:

'the values that I bring back - not your values, but the values I have come to on my own.' (Transcript 4)

I am now able to step back and enjoy my art.

This Chapter of Peggy's dissertation had a profound influence on me of the same quality as the one I experienced in 1971 on reading the work of Michael Polanyi. The reason I would say our relationship was an educative one was because both tutor and student learned something significant. Peggy learned how to hold together values she initially believed to be opposed. I learned to refocus my attention on to the educative power of conversations and correspondences.

I now want to move on to consider my work with a group of senior managers from Wiltshire, Avon and Gloucestershire, who are undertaking action research programmes for their Advanced Diplomas in Professional Development. This work (1991-1993) has focused my attention on the extent of the penetration of market forces into the working lives of local authority managers. It is raising my concerns about the increasing penetration of these forces into my educational context and hence my educational development. This tension has stimulating the action plans which conclude this account of my educational development. As you might expect they contain the intentions and values which I hope to use in judging the quality and effectiveness of my contribution to education, in theory and practice.

PART FOUR

INTO THE MARKET PLACE

CHAPTER SEVENTEEN

WORKING WITH LOCAL AUTHORITY MANAGERS 1991-1993

Between 1991 and 1993 I have worked as a tutor on a two year action research programme with senior managers from Wiltshire, Avon and Gloucestershire. Whilst my primary interest is in enhancing the professionalism of teaching and education within our schools and universities I also want to see education fully integrated as a life-long activity within all workplaces. Because of the sustained commitment of Conservative Governments since 1979 to ensure that market forces can directly influence all aspects of our lives as citizens and workers I think you will identify with the local government managers below, Bob Elsey, Ashley Wirdnam and John Hodge, who are learning what it means to try to improve the quality of their practice whilst having to respond to the influence of market forces. Their experiences have highlighted the need for urgent action to protect education from a similar penetration by market forces. Hence in my final section I will be suggesting the need to work together to create An Education Council, to enhance the professionalism of educators and teachers and to sustain the values of education in the face of the pressures described below.

Bob Elsey is a manager working in Wiltshire and responsible for providing a purchasing and distribution service for other local authorities. The Government's legislation involves radical change in the way local authorities manage their services and has meant a rapid change in the nature of Bob's work. The enormity of the legislative changes facing local government meant that he had to face the challenge of finding a new sense of order out of the confusion created by such a major transformation. He has expressed his concern and problem in a way which includes 'I' as a living contradiction holding together both order and chaos. He writes:

> *Since October 1992 my work and to some considerable extent much of my life has been dominated by the rapid and voluminous changes imposed on the Local Government by the National Government. The scope and extent of my responsibility in providing a purchasing and distribution service to some ninety local authorities has meant that the effects of the changes have been extremely complex to assimilate and 'manage'.*
>
> *The problem is that over the last few months the developments, changes and work issues of significance have occurred at such a pace that I am having considerable difficulty in focusing on a real concern and in getting the randomly recorded thoughts in order or at least in such a state that they will help to resolve some of the problems I face.*

Bob moved on to develop an action plan of analysing the implications of the major pieces of legislation for his work in order to make an appropriate response. This included analysing the implications of the new Education Act which continues the move to increase the direct influence of market forces on local authorities and schools. This move has been felt rather too keenly by many workers in Gloucestershire.

Ashley Wirdnam works for Gloucestershire. Over the past two years he has directly experienced the influence of government policy in moving public services into the market to experience competition between business units. Ashley's resilience in the face of these policies as colleagues have faced redundancy is a source of inspiration. I would like to share this with you through the action plan that appears below.

Action planning is a fundamental part of action research. The action planner used at Bath contains 'I' as a living contradiction and in the plan below Ashley follows a pattern of questioning I think you will recognise as a common sense, yet disciplined approach to improving practice. I think you will also recognise the value of an individual's creativity in responding to a social context increasingly dominated by market forces. The planner has the form:

What do I want to improve? What are the reasons for my concerns? What might I do to improve my practice? How will I know that my practice has improved? What kind of evidence will I need to gather to make a valid judgement on the quality of my management practice and process? What will I try to produce for our next meeting?

Here is Ashley Wirdnam's action plan:

ACTION PLANNING FOR SURVIVAL AND IMPROVEMENT

1. What do I want to improve?

I am in the process of merging my training unit with the teacher training unit located in the Education Department, to form a single training business unit. This conforms with current County policy to establish a range of business units in the professions identified in the 1992 Local Government Act in anticipation of their being exposed to compulsory competitive tendering (CCT). The new unit will be formed on the 1st January, 1993 as the Professional Development Consultancy (PDC), with its head (Director) being the current head of the teacher training unit, with myself as deputy.

I am concerned to establish the PDC as a viable business unit which could survive commercially when it is exposed to CCT. This must be my main concern but within it there are many others that inter-relate closely with it. For example:

a. *In the new structure I will be the No. 2, whereas at present I am the 'boss' and have enjoyed a fair degree of autonomy for several years. How will the new structure work in practice, and how will I come to terms with it?*

b. *How will my relationship with my new boss develop, particularly as we shall be working in buildings 4 miles apart, with the inevitable potential for communications problems that that generates?*

c. *How will I and my staff react to the growing emphasis on commercialism and the need to analyse what we do in terms of what it will pay rather than what the client(s) need(s)?*

d.   How will I develop my role as a contractor, working with an ex-colleague from the Personnel Department Management Team, who is now taking over my previous duties as the Client Training Manager for the County?

e.   What will be the main focus of my work when the business unit is fully established? My client manager role will have gone and I will inevitably be required to take on a more active training role than in recent years. Should I begin to specialise as a trainer and develop expertise in certain specific areas which complement those of my existing staff, or should I use my experience as a general trainer to 'cover' the work of my staff and concentrate on developing new business opportunities?

f.   As far as managing my part of the business is concerned, should my emphasis be on improving the way the unit operates, in order to make it more efficient and responsive, thus making it more cost effective, or should I concentrate on developing the product (e.g. range of training programmes) in order to have a stronger base from which to market the unit's skills and services?

2. What are the reasons for my concerns?

The future is full of uncertainty and change. Many issues are beyond my power to influence (e.g. Local Government Reorganisation) and at the end of the day I need to continue to work in order to maintain my standard of living. Staying in employment is therefore a primary consideration and hence making a success of the new business unit must be at the top of my priorities. I also want to maintain the jobs of my staff. In my new contractor role I shall have much less influence on the County's training policy than in the past but believe that a strong commitment to training is going to be vital if the County is to survive the challenges of the next decade.

3. What might I do to improve my practice?

The list is almost endless, but what emerges as the focus of my new job will dictate what I need to do to improve my practice. This will become clearer in the next few weeks as a business plan is developed and agreed with my Director and staff. I expect this to highlight those areas within the business needing priority attention, and the process should also help to clarify my new role and key tasks.

4a. How will I know that my practice has improved?

The ultimate test will be commercial viability of the business unit, inside or outside the County Council, with the continuance of the jobs of my staff and myself being an obvious indicator of that viability.

4b. How am I going to find out?

In the short run the business unit will be protected from direct competition but this is not expected to last more than two years. After that the signs of success or failure will be obvious, but before then our ability to satisfy our clients and our real costs in doing so should provide some satisfactory evidence of our likely viability.

4c. What kind of evidence will I need to gather to make a valid judgement on the quality of my management practice and process?

The evolution of the business against the business plan should provide the basic evidence necessary in the short term, irrespective of how good the business plan actually is. In the longer term the evidence of viability and survivability should be pretty clear to everyone.

5. What will I try to produce for our next meeting?

The obvious thing is an agreed business plan but whilst this exists in draft form already, it is unlikely to be completed until the new year as there are several details of our cost base still to be resolved with the County. Progress with it and final agreement by Members to endorse our plans (expected late November) is more realistic.

Ashley has continued to modify his planning in the light of new developments and has produced a description and explanation of his own learning and educational development as a local authority manager.

John Hodge works for Avon in the county solicitor and deputy clerk's department. He has worked there since Avon's inception in 1974. In July 1993 he is facing the probability that Avon will cease to exist in April 1995. His job, until recently, appeared more secure than many colleagues' in other departments because of the way in which it was funded. John's action enquiry has focused on improving the quality of his management through the introduction of a process of appraisal. John asked the question:

> **How will the introduction of appraisal into the general administration division of the county solicitor and deputy clerk's department improve my own management practice and that of the staff reporting to me?**
>
> *My Concern*
>   *I have decided to concentrate on the introduction of an Employment and Personal Development Review Scheme for all Section Heads who Report to me.*
>
> **What evidence will I be able to produce?**
>
> *Details of interviews I have conducted.*
> *Notes of review meeting.*
>
> **How will I know if I have been successful?**
>
> *I will still be here and have coped with an increasing workload with diminishing staff and finance.*

John's full report on his learning as he answered the question is too long to include here. It is focused on the introduction of an Employment and Personal Development Review (EPDR) scheme by Avon County Council. The Council states that the scheme is being introduced to support its overall objective of providing the best possible service to the public: *'The scheme recognises that the Council's staff are its most important asset and that its aims are best served by helping staff in achieving job satisfaction and developing their full potential to succeed in providing quality services in response to their needs'.*

John continues:

> The scheme stresses 'discussion' rather than 'appraisal' to make it clear that the postholders are asked to take an equal part in the event, not merely to receive a plan of action devised on their behalf. This is helped by excluding disciplinary, grievance and pay issues from the scheme. The purpose of the discussion is to establish agreement between the postholders and the Reporting Office on an Action Plan which will identify the postholders' main task priorities and responsibilities for the coming year and to help develop the postholders and their job skills.
>
> The postholders are asked to prepare their thoughts in a systematic way before the discussion in the following way:
>
> i)   Outline what you believe to be your most important tasks and responsibilities (by reference to your job description if you wish).
>
> ii)   Analyse your performance in relation to these. Could it be improved? If so, how?
>
> iii)   Are there any 'constraints/barriers' which hamper your performance? If so, please list them together with the effect they have.
>
> iv)   How does your Reporting Officer's managerial style affect your performance?
>
> v)   Do you feel that you have any special abilities which are not fully used? To what sort of work do you consider you are best suited?
>
> vi)   What action needs to be taken by (a) you, and (b) your Reporting Officer in respect of your performance and development in the period between this and the next discussion?
>
> vii)   Do you have any views on your next career step?
>
> viii)   In your discussion you will need to ensure that all issues relevant to your role and relationship with your Reporting Officer are raised. List these if they are not covered above.

Up to this point the EPDR scheme can be understood as a similar form of action planning to that used in the action research programme. However, the action research approach to professional development is more extensive than a process of action planning. It also includes a postholder's account of their management learning which has been submitted to a form of public validation. In producing an account, which contains a description and explanation for his own self-managed learning and submitting it for validation to a group of participating colleagues, John Hodge has shown how such a scheme can be extended to include criteria and evidence for judging the quality and effectiveness of his management practices and process.

In offering an account of his own self-managed learning as a local authority officer John Hodge has not only provided evidence on his competent practice, but also demonstrated the qualities of an educated citizen.

This can be seen in John's full participation in the action research programme. He has not only submitted his account for validation, but has also responded to the accounts of others. The criteria used below by participants to test the validity and enhance the rigour of the accounts are taken from one of John's responses to a colleague in a neighbouring authority. I cannot overemphasise the importance of these 'validation' groups in which colleagues would provide evaluative feedback on the quality of each other's case study. Here are John's comments on the criteria he uses together with some extracts from his judgements:

Criteria

I have read your account and considered it against the following criteria:
i)   *evidence of background reading;*
ii)   *accurate recording of events;*
iii)   *rigorous collection and interpretation of data;*
iv)   *demonstration of the relationship between the data and the local problem;*
v)   *is the story told in a way which captivates my imagination?;*
vi)   *is the story presented in a clear and comprehensible form?;*
vii)   *are the claims being made backed up sufficiently with evidence?;*
viii) *does the report contain an explanation in the sense of giving reasons why things have happened as they have, as well as looking to see if it contains a description of your management learning?*

Judgements

There is not much evidence of background reading but I think, like me, you were caught out and did not really concentrate on this aspect of the study until the last session. In the penultimate paragraph you refer to personal contact. If you are looking for another book reference, Tom Peters and Nancy Austin make reference to managing by walking about, in their book 'A Passion for Excellence; The Leadership Difference'.

In the paragraph entitled 'Ask The Questions' I think it would be useful to offer an explanation of what you mean by 'success' in the second line, and perhaps bring in something there about how should you train your staff so that in the 'Establish Proof' section you could offer evidence of how that training is worked. Under 'Document' you have probably outlined the actions, the consequences of the actions, as well as the results. Under 'Investigations' I would suggest that you test your theories in the validation group.

****

In conclusion I will leave you with my action plans with their statements of concern, imagined ways forward, and the kinds of evidence I intend to gather to enable me to make a judgement on the quality and effectiveness of my actions. I am asking you to do more than engage with these plans and to suggest improvements. Because of the enormity of the political and economic forces which are restructuring our society on market principles, I recognise that collaborative action is needed to arrest these forces and to insist on the strengthening of democratic procedures to protect the educational values celebrated in this text. I am asking you to suggest ways in which I could increase the collaborative power of my actions. You may have noticed that I have not used 'we' a great deal in this text. Yet I fear that unless 'we' begin to share a sense of common purpose, and work politically to achieve our purpose then many of the values expressed above will be suppressed without much of a collaborative struggle.

CHAPTER EIGHTEEN

ACTION PLANNING FOR MY FUTURE, JULY 1993 - AUGUST 2009

A) Concern - How do I improve the quality of my eduational politics?

As I reflect on my relationships with the senior local authority managers from Avon, Wiltshire and Gloucestershire, I am struck by the dramatic changes over the last two years from a concern with improving the quality of a social service to survival in the market place. The tension I feel is different from the above experiences of contradiction which have formed my educational development. The tension is due to a conflict between educational and academic values and the values of the market place. I am not one of those who sees no place for market values. I value the industrial and commercial world which helps to sustain my sense of material well-being. I share the concern of many environmentalists and industrialists that it makes good sense to protect our environment. I also see the necessity of sustaining democratic procedures to protect the values of our civilized society in our health and education services against being undermined through the direct influence of market forces.

When I talk of market forces I mean those forces which are dominated by the search for profitable return on investment and where free competition rules the market place. It is because these conditions spawn the Maxwells of the world that I insist that we need democratic forms of accountability to ensure that the interests of ourselves as citizens are being met.

My concern for education is that the Conservative Government legislation is removing democractic constraints on the free competition of the market place. Local education authorities will no longer be able to protect educational values. Their control over schools is being removed and their services are becoming business units as described above. Teacher education in University departments of education is under serious threat as competition is being stimulated by enabling schools to take on the role of initial teacher education. The qualities of professionalism in the Postgraduate Certificate of Education may not be required by new teachers entering schools. The tension I feel is because I see the government undermining the professionalism I have been seeking to enhance. I share the concerns and analysis of Pamela Lomax and Cynthia Jones (1993):

'The current political climate is one in which the values underpinning much of our education are being attacked, at a time when the basis of teachers' professional authority is being dismantled for political and economic reasons. Within this scenario of political mismanagement there are teachers who are working creatively within the system to develop educationally worthwhile outcomes. We believe that it is this creative force of teacher action research that can maintain teacher autonomy and professionalism in the face of current de-skilling changes'. (p11)

Intended actions

Thus I need to find a way of acting which will resist the de-professionalisation. The strongest protection could be The General Teaching Council (England and Wales). John Sayer's great achievement has been to bring together some 40 Unions and other bodies in a Forum of Associations with a common mission statement. On the other hand its weakness from a professional point of view is that it does not have a policy on an integrated programme of teachers' professional development. The body which does have such a policy but without the potential political power of the GTC is The Education Council supported by Tyrrell Burgess.

My own action plan is to support the development of The Education Council with its commitment to build on the sense of professionalism of individual teachers. I intend to do this in the local and regional context of the University of Bath by linking the action research approach to professional development to building the membership of The Education Council. The way I intend to contribute to this development is through my memberships of The Education Council, The Steering Committee of the Collaborative Action Research Network, and the Council of the British Educational Research Association (BERA) and as a BERA observer on the Forum of Associations for the General Teaching Council (England and Wales). I will attempt to develop a coherent policy which develops a theme of my 1988 Presidential Address to the British Educational Research Association on the development of a Research-based Professionalism in Education. Can you think of any other actions I should take to achieve my purpose?

Evidence to make a judgement on actions

Evidence could take the form of: the submission of discussion and policy papers to the above organisations which focus on strengthening collaborative action in creating The Education Council; evidence from publicity on seminars and workshops designed to enhance the status of the Council. Please let me know what further evidence would enable you to make a judgement on the effectiveness of my actions.

B) Concern - How do I contribute to the development of an integrated programme of teacher education?

i) Government policies on teacher professionalism do not contain an integrated approach to professional development. I believe that a profession should have a sense of a process of life-long learning which can enhance professional self-esteem and improve the quality of professional practice.

ii) Tom Russell (1993) has explained why questions of the kind, 'How do I help my pupils to improve the quality of their learning?', should form of the basis of initial teacher education programmes. Given the view of educational theory and educational knowledge presented in this book I think you will understand my concern that programmes of initial teacher education should be constructed on the basis of a research-based approach to answering such questions. The Action Research and Educational Theory Case Study Collection contains examples of what can be achieved by novice teachers who use this approach. The new postgraduate education programme at Bath has what is known as a Subject Didactics component and an Educational and Professional Studies component. In the past students have expressed some difficulty in integrating the different components of our PGCE programme. I hope to show the students and teacher mentors I work with, that the form of educational theory outlined in this text offers a way of integrating the different components of a novice teacher programme, in a way which can contribute to the construction of living educational theories.

Intended actions

I intend to work at the creation of an integrated programme of teacher education from working with novice teachers on a postgraduate certificate programme through Advanced Certificate, Advanced Diploma, M.Ed., M.Phil., and Ph.D. degrees at Wootton Bassett School in the kind of partnership with the School of Education at the University of Bath described by Kevin Eames (1993a, 1993b). The School is committed to developing an action reseach approach to professional development. Eight members of staff have expressed interest in registering for an advanced courses module on questions of the kind, 'How do I improve my practice?'. I intend to tutor this group of teachers from September 1993. I will also be responsible, together with school-based mentors and a senior tutor, for ten novice teachers on the new postgraduate education programme. This will involve teaching an educational and professional development programme at the University and liaising with novice teachers and teachers in the school. I intend to explore and evaluate the quality of my tutoring on this programme in relation to the quality of my students' educational development. Can you think of anything else I should be doing to achieve my purpose?

Evidence to make a judgement on actions

I intend to produce evaluation reports from students, pupils, teachers and myself on the development of an integrated programme of teacher education in relation to the educational development of individual students and teachers.

C) Concern - Does the idea of living educational theories have any validity in national and international contexts as a form of dialogue which enables individuals to contribute to the future of humanity?

I have suggested that educational theory is a form of dialogue which has profound implications for the future of humanity. I have offered a way of thinking about the constitution of educational theory which can include any individual who will produce a description and explanation for his or her own educational development as s/he answers questions of the kind, 'How do I improve my practice?.

Intended actions

The Annual Conference of the British Educational Research Association (BERA) is a forum for communicating and testing the validity of ideas from research. My proposal to present a paper to BERA 1993 at Liverpool University on reconceptualising in-service teacher education has been accepted. I will be proposing the development of an integrated programme of teacher education based on the above ideas.

I am also joint convenor, along with Pamela Lomax, Professor of Educational Research at Kingston University, of the third World Congress on Action Learning, Action Research and Process Management to be held at the Unversity of Bath on 6th - 9th July 1994. The theme of the Conference is taken from Erica Holley's work, 'Accounting for Ourselves', and should offer the opportunity to test the validity of the above ideas in an international context. Together with Jean McNiff and Pam Lomax I have agreed to edit a series of texts on practitioners' professional learning.

I am seeing the value of electronic communications in sustaining my relationships with researchers in Canada and America. Tom Russell, at Queen's University, Kingston, Canada, Mary-Lynn Hamilton at the University of Kansas, and Stefinee Pinnegar at Brigham Young University have introduced me to the American Educational Research Association (AERA). The formation of a Special Interest Group on the Self-Study of Teacher Educators is a forum in which I intend to submit my ideas for validation. I have submitted proposals for the April 1994 Conference in New Orleans.

Evidence to make a judgement on actions

I need to produce evidence in the publications of those attending the Congress and the American Educational Research Association Conference and of those they influence, that the above ideas have influenced their thinking and their educative relationships with their students. I am thinking of examples such as Tom Russell's (1993) paper to the Canadian Society for Research in Education in which he integrates the three original ideas from my research, along with those from other researchers, in a paper on the authority of experience.

D) Concern - How can I improve my collaboration with colleagues?

I am concerned to share ideas with my colleagues, to test the validity of their ideas and my own and to learn about the ideas of others through collaborative enquiry. I recognise a weakness in my approach to some of my immediate colleagues in the School of Education. I need to improve my relationships with reference to my values of care, trust and respect. I need to overcome my perception of their acceptance of the power and authority of those individuals who mobilised the University's power against me in one or more of the above experiences. There are also colleagues outside the School of Education with whom I would like to work.

Intended action

Three of these colleagues, Judi Marshall, David Sims and Peter Reason from the University's School of Management, wish to work with me to create a Centre for Action Research for Professional Practice in which we will offer an action research programme for graduate students. We asked Judi to write a statement about what she saw as our shared intentions. I agree with her view that:

> 'We see this programme as an opportunity both to share our experience, thinking and practice with participants, and to create a collaborative learning community in which we can work together on these themes. We realise that this will involve struggles as well as harmonious engagement. We four bring our differences to this endeavour as well as our similarities. Whilst we are all passionately committed to the core principles of action research, we have our individual interpretations and priorities, our own particular constituencies. Also we shall be challenging ourselves and each other to live up to our aspirations, to develop our own practice - this will sometimes be delightful and sometimes uncomfortable or painful. Our meetings so far have had these multiple qualities. We are excited by our collaboration and with the prospect of extending it to others'.

Evidence to make a judgement on actions

Judi continues:

'All four of us see our work with people registered for postgraduate degrees as central to our roles in the University, as activities to which we bring our whole lives. Through this work we are seeking to live in action our fundamental values, and to influence the social and organizational worlds with which we connect. To do this we are continually open to learning alongside our students and colleagues, seeking to improve our practice'.

What kind of evidence would you suggest I gather to enable a judgement to be made on the quality and effectiveness of my actions? Can you give good reasons why I should not devote my energy to working collaboratively with my colleagues on the creation of a Centre for Action Research for Professional Practice?

****

I wonder how you are feeling. Has my story retained your interest? Have I persuaded you that a new form of educational knowledge can be created from the descriptions and explanations which individual learners can produce for their own educational development? Have I shown you clearly the values which constitute the explanation for my educational development? Did I move you with me in my exploration of how to live as fully as I could the values of freedom, justice, truth, and goodness in my educational development? Did you experience these values as explanatory principles in my account? Did I demonstrate sufficient learning about the ideas of others for you to be convinced of my capacity to test my own ideas and those of others? Have I shown the capacity to conduct an original investigation into the nature of educational theory and educational knowledge? Does the story of my educational development and the values and understandings embodied within it have any potential for contributing to the creation of a better social order?

I wonder if you will feel engaged enough to seek out our educative communities and help to strengthen our capacity to support each other within a growing sense of care and community. One of the most delightful texts which I think might persuade you to make contact with our educative community is *The Role of Self in Action Research* (Ghaye and Wakefield, 1993), a publication from the Collaborative Action Research Network and Hyde Publications. Tony Ghaye writes in the foreword:

'The basic form is a conversation between action researchers. It is a conversation about the issues and concerns that arise from their work and their understanding of it. The conversational form allows two people to express a personal point of view and to respond to each other and to the action research being presented. Action research presented in a conversational form is educational, professional and legitimate. These

conversations represent something of the identities of those engaged in them. They convey a sense of self, a sense of relationship with another, and a sense of commitment to understand self, others, and the context in which the professional practice takes place'.

I am offering the above account of my educational development as a contribution to such ongoing educative conversations. In the moments of drawing this book to a close I read the fourth of Edward Said's (1993) Reith Lectures:

Is there such a thing as an independent, autonomously functioning intellectual?.

'An amateur is what today the intellectual ought to be, someone who considers that to be a thinking and concerned member of a society one is entitled to raise moral issues at the heart of even the most technical and professionalised acitivity as it involves one's country, its power, its mode of interacting with its citizens as well as other societies. In addition, the intellectual's spirit as an amateur can enter and transorm the merely professional routine most of us go through into something much more lively and radical; instead of doing what one is supposed to do one can ask why one does it, who benefits from it, how can it reconnect with a personal project and original thought. There is no getting around authority and power, and no getting around the intellectual's relationship to them. How does the intellectual address authority: as a professional supplicant, or as its unrewarded, amateurish conscience?'

Reading Said's words brought back memories of a letter I received in 1968 from Ken Merton, the deputy head of my first school, when I posted on the staff room notice board an extract from the 1968 Reith Lectures. This was a month after the Big Kamara incident. The extract also contained references to authority. Here is the letter which continues to entertain and infuriate me.

11th December 1968
Dear Mr. Whitehead,

Although you personally may not have posted in the Staff Room the excerpt from a Reith Lecture, I regard you as the leader of the group responsible and I accordingly address this letter to you.

This is the second notice exhibited in the Staff Room to offend certain of our colleagues. I agree that the letter is deliberately provocative. I am sending a copy of this letter to all Main Building Staff on whom I wish to impress the following instructions:-

Any non-official criticisms, (implied or stated), posted for public exhibition, should be torn down.

Yours sincerely,
K. Merton.

This serves to emphasise Said's point that there is no way of getting around power and authority. My life in education, as a teacher and intellectual, can be understood as an attempt to reconstruct educational theory and educational knowledge in the context of power and authority. I have examined this development in relation to groups of individuals who are aligned with my institution and who derived power and authority from their institutional positions and knowledge and use of its procedures. I have also shown some determination in educative relationships with my research students not to violate their sense of integrity. Whilst I have tried to resist speaking on behalf of my students, I will end by embracing the words of Sarah Darlington (1993), an education student from a group tutored by Moira Laidlaw for her action research special study. Extracts from their work together have already appeared in Part Three.

I find writing hard. T.S. Eliot said:

> *'Words strain,*
> *Crack and sometimes break, under the burden,*
> *Under the tension, slip slide, perish,*
> *Decay with imprecision, will not stay in place,*
> *will not stay still'.*

And that has been my experience. I am offering a cracked, flawed and faulty reflection on my experiences, but here it is, such as it is.

(Darlington, 1993)

Sarah was praised by examiners for the astonishingly high quality of her work. I do hope that Sarah and other teachers like her who are the future of the profession find my work authentic, useful, hopeful and entertaining in their lives in education. If you feel directly addressed do please respond. If you feel I could do more or I could direct my activities in more beneficial ways for education, do let me know.

I have tried to establish a new form of educational knowledge which could be useful in enhancing the knowledge-base of the profession. I know that there is more to do. My own commitment will be to sustaining a position in the University until August 2009 which enables me to provide support for teachers like Moira Laidlaw, Erica Holley and Peggy Kok as they enhance the profession through research which shows how they are embodying the values which constitute educative relationships with their pupils. I am thinking of the values of care, integrity, freedom, justice and knowledge not only in the context of their educative relationships with their pupils. I am thinking that you and I should support these values as educated citizens who embody them in the constant attention which is needed to ensure that the power of truth holds sway over the truth of power in constituting improvements in our society and communities. In my experience, market forces if unconstrained by such principles as democratic accountability support the truth of power. As my colleagues David Packham and Mary Tasker (1993) have pointed out, the purposes of a University are intrinsically different to the purposes of a market. Whilst I do not want to sell my integrity, freedom and sense of justice in the market place I think I should answer the question of what do get paid to do. I get paid to make scholarly and acknowledged contributions to knowledge of my subject, education, and for teaching.

I have presented a case study of my own educational development as a new form of educational knowledge. It is a form which every individual who is asking questions of the kind, 'How do I improve my practice?' or 'How do I live my values more fully in my practice?', could use to contribute to the creation of living educational theory. As I have said I believe that educational theory is a form of dialogue which has profound implications for the future of humanity. I think your description and explanation of your learning as you explore the implications of trying to live your values as fully as you can does have a contribution to make to a good social order. I think our contributions are likely to be greater if we can find ways of sharing our accounts with the same qualities of sensitive, human understanding and insight being shown by Erica and Moira in their educative relationships with their pupils and students. When Peggy left the University to return to Singapore she gave me her dissertation, 'as a gift'. It is a gift I treasure because I can see within the text that I am living my own educational values as I am helping Peggy to develop her own.

I have produced this work with you in mind. I hope that you have felt addressed directly and that it makes a contribution to enhancing the quality of your lives in whatever context you are trying to improve.

BIBLIOGRAPHY

Abdullah, M. (1982), *Educational Theory: A Koranic Persepective;* Saudi Arabia, Umm AL-Qura University.

Adelman, C, (1989), 'The Practical Ethic Takes Priority over Methodology', in Carr, W. (ed), *Quality in Teaching - Arguments for a Reflective Profession;* Falmer Press.

Allen, R.T. (1978), 'The Philosophy of Michael Polanyi' in *Journal of Philosophy of Education,* Vol. 112, 78.

Altrichter, H. *et. al.* (1990), 'Defining, Confining or Refining Action Research' in Zuber-Skerritt, O. (Ed.), *Action Research for Change and Development;* Griffith University Press, Brisbane.

Argyris, C, and Schön, D, (1975), *Theory in Practice: Increasing Professional Effectiveness;* Jossey Bass, London.

Avon Local Education Authority (1990), '*You and Your Professional Development;* Avon Local Education Authority, England.

Ball, S. (1990), 'Management as Moral Technology: A Luddite Analysis' in Ball, S. (Ed.), *Foucault and Education: Disciplines and Knowledge;* Routledge, London.

Bayles, E.E. (1961), 'Are Values Verifiable?' in *Educational Theory,* 20 pp. 71-78.

Bernstein, R.J. (1983), *Beyond Objectivism and Relativism;* Basil Blackwell, Oxford.

Bernstein, R.J. (1991), *The New Constellation;* Polity Press, Cambridge.

Black, P. (1992), Speech reported in *The Guardian;* Guardian Newspapers.

Bohm, D. and Peat, D. (1989), *Science, Order and Creativity;* Routledge, London.

Bower, T. (1991), *Maxwell: The Outsider;* Reed/Mandarin.

Briggs, J. and McCluskey, F. (1989), 'Ultimate Questioners; The Search for Omnivalent Meaning' in Pylkkanen, P. (Ed.), *op.cit.*

Brown, M. (1993), 'How can I help my fourth year to dicover their own motives for, and hence start to enjoy the process of, writing up practical work?'; Action Research Group, School of Education, University of Bath.

Buber, M (1923), *I and Thou;* T. & T. Clark.

Burgess, T. and Adams, B. (Eds.) (1980), *The Outcomes of Education;* Macmillan, see the Chapter by J. Stephenson.

Butler, D.J., (1954), 'The role of value theory in educational theory' in *Educational Theory,* 4, pp. 69-77.

Calderhead, J. (1988), *The Professional Learning of Teachers;* Falmer, London.

Carr, W. (1986), 'Theories of Theory and Practice' in *Journal of Philosophy of Education,* 20, pp. 177-186.

Chapman, C. (1992), 'How can I make French fun for my Year Nine group and make them want to learn?'; Action Research Group, School of Education, University of Bath.

Chuaprapaisilp, A. (1991), 'Improving Learning from Experience' in Colins, C. and Chippendale, P. (1991), *Proceedings of the First World Congress on Action Research and Process Management,* Vol. 2; Acorn Press, Australia.

Clandinin, D.J. and Connelly, F.M. (Eds.) (forthcoming), *The Professional Knowledge Landscape;* New York; Teachers' College Press.

Clark, C. (1976), 'Education is not an Academic Discipline; A reply to Professor Peters' in *Educational Studies,* Vol. 2, No. 1

Clayton, A.S. (1969), 'Education and some moves towards a value methodology' in *Educational Theory,* 19, pp. 198-200.

Claxton, G. (1990), *Teaching to Learn;* Cassell, London.

Collingwood, R.G. (1978), *An Autobiography,* Chapter 5, 'Question and Answer'; Oxford, Oxford University Press.

Corey, S. (1953), *Action Research to Improve School Practices;* Teachers' College, Columbia, New York.

Craig, C.T., 'Coming to know sacred stories in the field of education' in Clandinin, D.J. and Connelly, F.M. (Eds.) (forthcoming), *The Professional Knowledge Landscape;* Teachers' College Press, New York.

Cunningham, E.C. (1953), 'Extensional Limits of Aristotelean Logic' in *Educational Theory,* 3, pp. 92-107.

Darlington, S. (1993), 'How can I help Hugh become more engaged with the Green Issues part of the Green Module?'; Action Research Group, School of Education, University of Bath.

Day, C. (1993), 'Reflection; a necessary but not sufficient condition for professional development' in *British Educational Research Journal,* Vol. 19, No. 1, pp. 83-94.

DFE (1992), *Choice and Diversity; A New Framework for Schools;* London, HMSO.

DFE: OFSTED (1992), *Framework for the Inspection of Schools.*

Dunlop, F. (1977), 'What Sort of Theory Should We Have?' in *Journal of Further and Higher Education,* 77 (1), Spring.

Eames, K. (1987), *The Growth of a Teacher-Researcher's Attempt to Understand Writing, Redrafting, Learning and Autonomy in the Examination Years;* MPhil, University of Bath.

Eames, K. (1988), 'Evaluating a Teacher-Researcher's Choice of Action Research' in *Assessment and Evaluation in Higher Education,* Vol. 13, No. 3, pp. 212-218.

Eames, K. (1993a), 'Action research in schools: Into practice' in *British Journal of Curriculum and Assessment,* Vol 3, no. 3, pp. 29-33.

Eames, K. (1993b) 'A Dialectical Form of Action Research-based Educational Knowledge: A Teacher-Researcher's View' in Ghaye, T. and Wakefield, P. (Eds.) (1993), *C.A.R.N. Critical Conversations: A Trilogy, Book One, The Role of Self in Action Research;* Hyde Publications, Poole, Dorset.

Earley, K. (1993), 'Mistah Earley - he dead! How can I ensure that in teaching *The Importance of Being Earnest,* I am not too teacher-centred?; Action Research Group, School of Education, University of Bath.

Elliott, J. (1987), 'Educational Theory, Practical Philosophy and Action Research' in *British Journal of Educational Studies*, Vol. 35, No. 2, pp. 149-169.

Elliott, J. (1989), 'The Professional Learning of Teachers' in *Cambridge Journal of Education*, 19, pp. 81-101.

Elliott, J. (1991), 'A Model of Professionalism and its Implications for Teacher Education' in *British Educational Research Journal*, Vol. 17, No. 4, pp. 309-318.

Fals-Borda, O and Rahman, M.A. (1991), *Action and Knowledge;* Apex Books, New York.

Fals-Borda, O. (1992), 'Convergencies in Theory and Action for Research, Learning and Management' in Bruce, C.S. and Russell, A. (1992), *Transforming Tomorrow Today;* Action Learning, Action Research and Process Management Association Incorporated, Brisbane, Australia.

Fay, B. (1977), 'How people change themselves: the relationship between critical theory and its audience' in Smythe, W.J. (1986); *op.cit.*

Feyerabend, P. (1975), *Against Method;* London, Verso.

Forrest, M. (1983). *The Teacher as Researcher; the use of historical artefacts in primary schools;* M.Ed. Dissertation, University of Bath.

Foster, D. (1980), *Explanations for teachers' attempts to improve the process of education for their pupils;* M.Ed. Dissertation, University of Bath.

Foucault, M. (1977), 'Intellectuals and Power - A conversation between Michel Foucault and Giles Deleuze, in Bouchard, D.F. (Ed.), *Michel Foucault, Language, Counter-Memory, Practice;* Basil Blackwell, Oxford.

Foucault, M. (1980), in Gordon, C. (Ed.), *Power Knowledge;* Harvester, London.

Fromm, E. (1960), *Fear of Freedom*, p.18; Routledge and Kegan Paul.

Gadamer, H.G. (1975), *Truth and Method;* London, Sheed and Ward.

Gatling, L. (1992), 'How can I enable my sixth formers to enjoy their lessons and develop the confidence to talk about Chaucer in an enquiring manner?'; Action Research Group, School of Education, University of Bath.

Ghaye, T. and Wakefield, P. (Eds.) (1993), *C.A.R.N. Critical Conversations: A Trilogy, Book One: The Role of Self in Action Research;* Hyde Publications, Poole, Dorset.

Gibson, R. (1985), 'Critical Times for Action Research' in *Cambridge Journal of Education*, Vol. 15, No. 1, pp. 59-64.

Gipps, C. (1993), 'The Profession of Educational Research' (Presidential Address) in *British Educational Research Journal*, Vol. 19, No. 1, pp. 3-16.

Gitlin, A. and Goldstein, S. (1987), 'A Dialogical Approach to Understanding; Horizontal Evaluation' in *Educational Theory*, 37, No, 1, pp. 17-29.

Griffiths, M. and Davies, C. (1993), 'Learning to Learn; action research from an equal opportunities perspective in a junior school' in *British Educational Research Journal, Vol. 19*, No. 1. pp. 43-58.

Gurney, M. (1988), *An Action Enquiry into Ways of Developing and Improving Personal and Social Education;* Ph.D. Thesis, University of Bath.

Habermas, J. (1976), *Communication and the Evolution of Society;* Routledge, London.

Hall, S. (1991), 'And not a shot was fired' in *Marxism Today;* December 1992.

Hamilton, D. (1989), *Towards a Thory of Schooling;* Falmer, London.

Hamilton, D. (1990), *Learning About Education - An Unfinished Curriculum;* Open University Press, England.

Hayward, P. (1993), *How do I Improve my Pupils' Learning in Design and Technology?;* M.Ed. Dissertation, University of Bath.

Henry, C. (1989), 'Participatory Research in Australia; Action Research in Human Rights Education'; a Paper presented to the Participatory Research Conference 'A Celebration of People's Knowledge', Calgary, Alberta, Canada, July 12-15.

Henry, C. (1991), ' Reflections at the End of the Congress; If Action Research were Tennis' in Zuber-Skerritt, O. (Ed.), *Action Learning for Improved Performance;* Aebis Publishing, Australia.

Hick, J. (1993), 'How do I identify my action research question?'; Action Research Group, School of Education, University of Bath.

Hirst, P. and Peters, R.S. (1970), *The Logic of Education;* London, Routledge and Kegan Paul.

Hirst, P. H. (Ed.) (1983), *Educational Theory and its Foundation Disciplines;* London, Routledge.

Holbrook, D. (1980), *What It Means To Be Human;* unpublished manuscript, Cambridge, King's College.

Holden, P. (1993), 'How should I approach 9L4 History lessons to create the most positive working atmosphere feasible in the hope of increasing the quality of pupil learning?', Action Research Group, School of Education, University of Bath.

Holley, E. (1991), 'I Can Speak For Myself' in Whitehead, J. (ed.), *A Tutorial Guide for Action Research;* Action Research Group, School of Education, University of Bath.

Hume, D. (1738), *Treatise on Human Nature;* Oxford, Oxford University Press.

Ilyenkov, E. (1977), *Dialectical Logic;* Progress Publishers, Moscow.

Ilyenkov, E (1982), *The Dialectic of the Abstract and the Concrete in Marx's Capital;* Progress Publishers, Moscow.

Jensen, M. (1987), *A Creative Approach to the Teaching of English in the Examination Years;* M.Phil., University of Bath.

Kemmis, S. (1986), 'Of tambourines and tumbrils; a response to Rex Gibson's "Critical Times for Action Research"' in *Cambridge Journal of Education,* Vol. 16, No. 1, pp. 50-52.

Kemmis, S, (1993), 'Foucault, Habermas and Evaluation' in *Curriculum Studies,* Vol. 1, No. 1, pp. 35-54.

Kemmis S, and McTaggart, R. (Eds.) (1988), *The Action Research Reader;* Deakin University Press.

Kilpatrick, W. (1951), 'Crucial Issues in Current Educational Theory' in *Educational Theory,* 1 No. 1, pp. 1-8.

King, R. (1987), *An Action Inquiry into Day Release in Further Education;* M.Phil. University of Bath.

Kosok, M. (1976), 'The systematization of dialectical logic for the study of development and change' in *Human Development,* 19, pp. 325-350.

Laidlaw, M. (1992), *Action Research; A Guide for Use on Initial Teacher Education Programmes;* Action Research Group, School of Education, University of Bath.

Larter, A. (1985), 'What ought I to have done? An examination of events surrounding a racist poem': a Paper to the symposium *'Action Research, Educational Theory and the Politics of Educational Knowledge'* at the Annual Conference of the British Educational Research Association.

Larter, A, (1988), *An Action Research Approach to Classroom Discussion in the Examination Years;* M.Phil., University of Bath.

Lomax, P. (1986), 'Action Researchers' Action Research; A Symposium' in *British Journal of In-Service Education,* 13, No. 1, pp. 42-50.

Lomax, P. (Ed.) (1989), *The Management of Change, BERA Dialogues No. 1;* Multilingual Matters, Clevedon, England.

Lomax, P. (Ed.) (1990), *Managing Staff Development in Schools; an action research approach, BERA Dialogues No. 3;* Multilingual Matters, Clevedon, England.

Lomax, P. (Ed.) (1991), *Managing Better Schools and Colleges; the action research way, BERA Dialogues No. 5;* Multilingual Matters, Clevedon, England.

Lomax, P. and Jones, C. (Eds.) (1993), *Developing Primary Schools Through Action Research - Teachers' Reflections on Assessment at Key Stage 1;* Hyde Publications, Poole, Dorset.

Lovatt, J. (1993), 'How can I get the best out of all my pupils? The story so far ...'; Action Research Group, School of Education, University of Bath.

MacIntyre, A. (1988), *Whose Justice? Which Rationality?;* Duckworth, London.

MacIntyre, A, (1990), *Three Rival Versions of Moral Enquiry;* Duckworth, London.

Marcuse, H. (1964), *One Dimensional Man;* London, Routledge and Kegan Paul.

McNiff, J. (1989), *An Explanation for an Individual's Educational Development Through the Dialectic of Action Research;* Ph.D. Thesis, University of Bath.

McNiff, J. (1992), *Action Research: Principles and Practice;* Routledge, London and New York.

McNiff, J. (1993), *Teaching as Learning: an action research approach;* Routledge, London and New York.

McNiff, J., Whitehead, J. and Laidlaw, M. (1992), *Creating a Good Social Order Through Action Research;* Hyde Publications, Poole, Dorset.

McTaggart, R. (1992), 'Reductionism and Action Research; Technology versus convivial forms of life' in Bruce, S. and Russell, A.L. (Eds.), *Transforming Tomorrow Today;* Action Learning, Action Research and Process Management Incorporated, Brisbane, Australia.

Miller, J. (1990), *Seductions; Studies in Reading and Culture*; Virago,

Mitroff, I. and Kilman, R. (1978), *Methodological Approaches to Social Science;* San Francisco, Jossey-Bass.

Morrell, D, Speech in *The Times Educational Supplement,* 19.12.68.

Mosier, R.D. (1967), 'From Enquiry Logic to Symbolic Logic' in *Educational Theory,* 17, pp. 32-38.

Myerson, B. (1993), 'A Report on my Development as a Teacher'; Action Research Group, School of Education, University of Bath.

Noffke, S. (1992), 'Action Research and the Politics of Knowledge Production'; a Paper to the Second World Congress on Action Research and Process Management, Brisbane, 1992.

Norwood, K. (1992), 'How can I enable my year 12 History class to take more responsibility for their learning about Chartism?'; Action Research Group, School of Education, University of Bath.

O'Hear, A. (1991), *Democracy and Education;* The Claridge Press, London.

Peters, R.S. (1966), *Ethics and Educations;* Allen and Unwin.

Peters, R.S. (1977), *Education and the Education of Teachers* (see the discussion on pp. 138-140 for the view of the logic of the disciplines approach to educational theory); Routledge and Kegan Paul.

Phillips, Melanie (1992), 'Minsters are wrong again on education' in *The Guardian* 11.9.92.

Plato, *Gorgias*; trans. Hamilton, W. (1960); Penguin Books Ltd., London.

Polanyi, M. (1958), *Personal Knowledge;* Oxford, Oxford University Press.

Polanyi, M. and Prosch, H. (1975), *Meaning;* Chicago, University of Chicago Press.

Popper, K. (1963), *Conjectures and Refutations;* Oxford, Oxford University Press.

Pritchard, M. (1988), 'Educational Theory and Social Change' in *Cambridge Journal of Education,* Vol. 18, No. 1, pp. 99-109.

Pylkkanen, P. (Ed.) (1989), *The Search for Meaning - The New Spirit in Science and Philosophy;* Crucible, England.

Reason, P. and Rowan, J. (Eds.) (1981), *Human Inquiry;* J. Wiley.

Rogers, C. (1983), *Freeedom to Learn for the Eighties;* San Francisco; Bell and Howell.

Rudduck, J. (1989), 'Practitioner Research and Programmes of Initial Teacher Education' in *Westminster Studies in Education,* 12, pp. 61-72.

Rudduck, J. (1991), 'The Language of Consciousness and the Landscape of Action; tensions in teacher education' in *British Educational Research Journal,* Vol. 17, No. 4, pp. 319-332.

Said, E. (1993), *Professionals and Amateurs; The Reith Lectures;* The Independent, p.14, 15th July, 1993.

Schön, D. (1983), *The Reflective Practitioner - How Professionals Think in Action;* Basic Books, New York.

Schön, D. (1987), *Educating the Reflective Practitioner;* New York, Harvester Press.

Simon, B. (1990), *Education and the Social Order, 1940-1990;* Lawrence and Wishart, London.

Simon, B. (1992), *What Future for Education?;* Lawrence and Wishart, London.

Smith, P.G. (1976), 'Knowledge and Values' in *Educational Theory,* 26, pp. 29-39.

Smythe, W.J. (1986), *Reflection in Action* (p.21-22); Deakin University Press.

Tostberg, R.E. (1976), 'Observations on the Logical Bases of Educational Policy' in *Educational Theory,* 26, pp. 74-82.

Trigg, E. (1993), 'How can I encourage my Year Twelve to enjoy their English lessons and take responsibility for their learning about Hardy's poetry?'; Action Research Group, School of Education, University of Bath.

Van Manen, M. (1990), *Researching Human Experience - Human Science for an Action Sensitive Pedagogy;* Althouse Press.

Walking, P.H. (1979), 'Structure of Knowledge Theory: A Refutation' in *Educational Studies,* 79, Vol. 5, No. 1.

Watkins, P. (1987), 'Student participant observation in the contested workplace: the policy dilemmas of in-school work experience' in *Journal of Education Policy,* 2, 27-42.

Watkins, Z. (1991), 'To Thine Own Self Be True'; Action Research Group, School of Education, University of Bath.

Walker, R. (1985), *Doing Research* (p.181); Methuen.

Walker, R. (1986), 'Breaking the grip of print in curriculum research' in *Journal of Curriculum Studies,* Vol. 18, No. 1, pp. 95-96.

Walton, C. (1993), *An Action Research Enquiry into Attempts to Improve the Quality of Narrative Writing in my own Classroom;* M.Ed. Dissertation, University of Bath.

Weiner, G. (1989), 'Professional Self-Knowledge versus Social Justice: a critical analysis of the teacher-researcher movement' in *British Educational Research Journal,* Vol., 15, No. 1, pp. 41-52.

Whitehead, J. (1972), *A preliminary investigation of the process through which adolescents acquire scientific understanding;* unpublished M.A. Dissertation, University of London.

Whitehead, J. (1976), *Improving Learning for 11-14 year olds in mixed ability science groups;* Wiltshire Curriculum Centre.

Whitehead, J. (1977a), 'Improving Learning in Schools - A In-Service Problem' in *British Journal of In-Service Education,* Vol. 3, No. 2, Spring.

Whitehead J. (1977), 'The Process of Improving Education Within Schools'; a Paper to the 1977 Annual Conference of the British Educational Research Association.

Whitehead, J. (1992), 'Assessing and Evaluating an Individual's Educational Development' in *Assessment and Evaluation in Higher Education,* Vol. 7, No. 1, pp. 22-47.

Whitehead, J. (1985a), 'The analysis of an individual's educational development' in Shipman, M. (Ed.), *Educational Research: Principles, Policies and Practice;* Falmer, London.

Whitehead, J. (1985b), 'The Logic of Educational Knowledge'; a paper presented at the Annual Conference of the British Educational Research Association, University of Sheffield.

Whitehead, J. (1989a), 'Creating a Living Educational Theory from Questions of the Kind, "How do I improve my Practice?"'in *Cambridge Journal of Education,* 19, pp. 41-52.

Whitehead, J. (1989b), 'How do we Improve Research-based Professionalism in Education - A Question which includes action research, educational theory and the politics of educational knowledge?' in *British Educational Research Journal,* 15, pp. 3-17.

Whitehead, J. (1990), 'How can I Improve My Contribution to Practitioner Research in Teacher Education? A response to Jean Rudduck' in *Westminster Studies in Education,* Vol. 13.

Whitehead, J. (1991), 'How do I improve my professional practice as an academic and educational manager?' in Colins and Chippendale, P. (Eds.), *Proceedings of the First World Congress on Action Learning, Action Research and Process Management,* Vol. 1; Acorn Press, Australia.

Whitehead, J. (1992), 'A response to Ortrun Zuber-Skerritt' in Bruce, S. and Russell, A.L., *Transforming Tomorrow Today;* Action Learning, Action Research and Process Management Association Incorporated, Brisbane, Australia.

Whitehead, J. and Foster, D. (1984), 'Action Research and Professional Educational Development' in *Cambridge Action Research Network, Bulletin, No. 6,* pp. 41-45.

Whitehead, J. and Lomax, P. (1987), 'Action Research and the Politics of Educational Knowledge' in *British Educational Research Journal,* Vol. 13, No. 2, pp. 175-190.

Whitty, G. (1986), 'Recent American and Australian Approaches to the Sociology and Politics of Education: Review Artricle' in *Educational Theory,* Vol. 36, No. 1, pp. 81-89.

Winter, R. (1990), *Learning from Experience;* Falmer, England.

Wittgenstein, L. (1953), *Philosophical Investigations;* Oxford, Basil Blackwell.

Yamamoto, R. (1990), *'To See Life Grow; The Meaning of Mentorship in Theory into Practice'* Vol. pp. 183-189.

Zuber-Skerritt, O. (1990), *Action Research for Change and Development;* CALT, Griffith University, Australia.

Zuber-Skerritt, O. (1991a), *Professional Development in Higher Education: A Theoretical Framework for Action Research;* Griffith University, Brisbane.

Zuber-Skerritt, O. (Ed.) (1991b), *Action Learning for Improved Performance;* Aebis Publishing, Brisbane.

Zuber-Skerritt, O. (1991c); *Action Research in Higher Education; Examples and Reflections;* Kogan Page.

INDEX

Jack Whitehead began teaching in 1967 at the age of 23, with a science degree and a commitment to help his pupils to improve their scientific understanding. He also believed that the development of his teaching and sense of professionalism would be enhanced through understanding educational theory. He moved from school science teaching to educational research in 1973 as a Lecturer in Education of the University of Bath. His move was prompted by his study and rejection of the educational theory legitimated by London University, on the Academic Diploma and M.A. courses between 1968 to 1972. His rejection was based on the failure of the theory to explain the process of improving his pupils' learning. After six years teaching he felt confident that teachers could create their own educational theory for their own professional development which could be related directly to the process of improving pupils' learning. He thus defined his task as supporting teacher researchers in the creation of educational theory for professional development.

He is politically motivated in the sense of working to ensure that the spiritual, aesthetic and ethical values of education, including equality of opportunity, freedom, democracy and social justice, are not reduced to a form of economic rationalism where the market forces of competition and profit become the dominant values of education. He fears that since 1979, the conservative legislation on education is profoundly flawed, because of the way market forces form its central principle. He believes that new educational legislation is urgently needed to embody the values of education and to enhance the quality of education and teaching as a profession. He believes that living educational theory holds the key to the creation of a good social order because it involves teachers and other citizens accounting to themselves and others in autobiographical enquiries of the kind, 'How do I help my pupils to improve the quality of their learning?', and 'How do I live my values as fully as possible, in the context of my workplace and society?'. His aim is to continue his research into educational theory, teacher professionalism, improving the quality of pupils' learning and the creation of a good social order, with teachers and other citizens at the University of Bath until his retirement in 2009.

Unpopular Culture